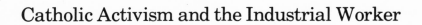
Catholic Activism and the Industrial Worker

Catholic Activism

and the Industrial Worker

Neil Betten

A Florida State University Book

UNIVERSITY PRESSES OF FLORIDA

Gainesville

Library of Congress Cataloging in Publication Data

Betten, Neil.
   Catholic activism and the industrial worker.

   "A Florida State University book."
   Bibliography: p.
   Includes index.
   1. Church and labor—United States—History.
2. Church and social problems—Catholic Church.
I. Title.
HD6338.2.U5B47   261.8'5   76-17280
ISBN 0-8130-0503-5

CONTENTS

To my parents

whose dedication to unionism
inspired my interest in
labor history

My interest in the relationship between Catholicism and labor originally grew out of my admiration for Dorothy Day. Studying Miss Day and the Catholic Worker Movement inevitably led to study of other groups such as the Association of Catholic Trade Unionists, which branched off from the movement. I soon realized that although Catholics constituted the bulk of the industrial work force, the largest religious segment of American union membership and of labor leadership, and that Catholic leadership vitally concerned itself with labor, labor historians and economists virtually ignored post World War I Catholic labor activities. With this book I hope to fill at least part of the historical vacuum.

Studying Roman Catholic activities and ideas was alien to me, both as a labor historian and as a Jew. I am indebted to many Catholic friends and colleagues who provided advice and clarified unfamiliar concepts, and to numerous others who contributed to the completion of the work. My colleague and friend, William D. Miller, read several sections of the manuscript and readily answered my numerous queries. Historians Hyman Berman, David O'Brien, and Staughton Lynd made helpful criticisms. I owe Raymond A. Mohl a special debt for providing me with a detailed stylistic critique. Of course I alone am responsible for all errors.

Librarians and archivists made my work easier, often providing me with important leads. I wish to thank the archival staffs of Wayne State University, University of Notre Dame, Marquette University, Catholic University of America, The New York Public Library, University of

Pittsburgh, Pennsylvania State University, University of Minnesota, and the St. Paul Seminary.

Financial aid from Indiana University Summer Faculty Fellowships, the Tozer Foundation, and the Council on Research in Economic History supported the work at various stages. Ms. Rosali Zak, Ms. Josiane Stampfli, and Ms. Linda Gotko typed the manuscript. I have a special debt to my wife, Edie, who suffered through the project, helping me in numerous ways.

INTRODUCTION

In the late 1960s, Catholic activists moved to the forefront of American radicalism. In disrupting draft induction centers and attacking capitalism, young students and clerics launched something seemingly very new in American Catholicism—a dynamic Catholic left. During this period of social turmoil, dissident Catholics allied themselves with secular radicals in attempting to stimulate massive change in the American social, economic, and political systems.

American Catholic radicalism, however, was not new; it had roots in the recent past. Although tactics varied vastly, the disillusionment of the 1930s sometimes resulted in responses similar to those of the late 1960s. Many of the radical institutions that proliferated during the Great Depression focused on the worker, since activists generally assumed that change would come from the laboring classes. Accordingly, various Catholic groups competed for labor's support while they also attempted to influence the individual worker. Frequently in conflict with each other and allied with non-Catholic groups of similar complexion, Catholic worker-oriented organizations took numerous ideological directions. The polarization of Catholic conservatives, reformers, and radicals, and the emergence of a significant Catholic left, mirrored the basic trends in American society during the 1930s.

Left-wing radicalism had become quite fashionable, particularly among intellectuals, while American willingness to experiment with the New Deal and communist influence in the Congress of Industrial Organizations (CIO) created an atmosphere allowing labor to explore new ideological paths. Some Catholic labor organizations theoretically intended to keep the conservative wing of the labor movement anticommunist but still responsive to necessary change. Most Catholic labor institutions encouraged noncommunist prolabor tendencies and primarily limited their anticommunism to rhetoric, at least in the 1930s. In general, Catholic leaders shifted their political stance to the left. They overwhelmingly supported the CIO in its conflict with the American Federation of Labor (AFL), accepted allies on the noncommunist left, and became directly involved with the worker through many reformist and radical Catholic labor organizations. In response to the depression Catholic leaders expanded the church's social welfare function, supported national economic reform, and in some cases advocated radical change in the capitalist system. Catholic spokesmen and activists built on Catholic reform traditions of the late nineteenth and early twentieth century; some also moved in innovative directions having little to do with past politics. Although American Catholic spokesmen had concerned themselves with the worker and the labor movement for almost a century, significant Catholic radical responses to labor and economic conditions emerged for the first time in the 1930s.

CHAPTER ONE

Catholicism and American Labor Reform—
Mid-Nineteenth and Early Twentieth Centuries

Following the Civil War, expansion of American industrial capitalism faced only insignificant opposition. Favorable government treatment of private enterprise spurred the development of national markets in such industries as steel, textiles, machinery, copper products, and transport. Government not only aided and colluded in management's exploitation of labor and capital's expropriation of natural resources, it also directly subsidized the construction of railroads and other forms of transportation. Society, nevertheless, defined laissez-faire as its official reality, the system's intellectual apologists fostered Social Darwinism, and business sponsored a Horatio Alger mythology.

Undoubtedly what a person believed about society affected his role in it. Still, myths alone could not feed and house the poor. European and Oriental immigrant workers found the streets of the "promised land" not paved with sparkling gold but rotten with uncollected refuse from the citys' slums. The worker's real wages (1892 = 100) climbed from 49 in 1886 to over 100 in 1920. This rise in income, however, did not fully reflect the common worker's life. Unskilled workers labored up to twelve hours a day, lived in squalid slums, and suffered long periods of unemployment (which resulted from economic cycles beyond their control). Depressions occurred in the 1870s and 1890s, while shorter panics and recessions caused havoc in 1884, 1903, and 1907.

Depression following the panic of 1873 exhibited in microcosm the period's social problems. One student of the period estimated unemployment at four million in 1877 with an additional 100,000 workers striking, making the largest ratio of unemployment to the total population to that time. A contemporary survey reported that approximately 25 percent of the workers in New York City could find no jobs. Even those who found work faced economic hardship. According to one study, the cost of food dropped 5 percent between 1873 and 1876, while wages fell at least 25 percent. Some estimates placed the wage drop at 50 to 60 percent. A contemporary examination of the prices of 60 products suggests that retail prices dropped 20 percent from 1873 to 1877. During the same time period incomes of the elite railroad workers and furniture carpenters dropped 30 to 40 percent, while between 1873 and 1880 the textile industry reduced wages 45 percent. Newspapers of the day, including those supporting the federal administration, printed many stories documenting the seriousness of the problem. In 1877, the *Interocean*, an organ of the administration in Washington, admitted that there "never was a time in the history of the United States when a greater amount of misery, poverty, and wretchedness existed than at the present time." The *New York Sun* suggested that masons and stonecutters go to Scotland for work. "How the unemployed . . . have got through this," the *New York Tribune* mused early in 1878, "God only knows." The *New York World* printed a survey of conditions showing that thousands "lived [on] from 70 cents to $14.00 a week; that hundreds subsisted on the refuse from the city." Prolabor newspapers such as the *Irish World* and *Labor Standard* portrayed an even more severe picture.[1]

Sometimes the unemployed quit looking for work and became vagrants. They begged food from door to door and slept in jails that allowed overnight lodging. Others camped near railyards and found temporary shelter in boxcars. The jobless and homeless migrated to warmer climates in winter, traveling on freight trains when they could. These tramps and hoboes, as the middle-class press called them, numbered about one million.

What alternatives did workers have in facing industrial reality? During the depression, labor unions collapsed; some workers turned to radical politics, even terrorist organizations; others rioted, as during the railroad riots of 1877; some sought traditional political avenues of escape while searching for work and accepting charity. In times of prosperity, however, workers found labor unions effective. The Knights of Labor hoped to unify the working class, to realistically confront concentrated capitalism with labor. It failed; but what it could not do for the many, the AFL accomplished more successfully for the few. By ignoring pleas of unskilled immigrants and organizing mainly highly skilled workers whose market advantages permitted victories over capital, the AFL added a measure of strength and dignity to the working class elite. After 1905, unskilled black and immigrant workers could join the radical Industrial Workers of the World (IWW) to battle for social and economic justice. During and after World War I, however, the combined forces of federal, state, and local government, working with employers and vigilante groups, destroyed IWW's occasional effectiveness.

The unemployed and the poor could turn to social welfare institutions. Public agencies had existed since the colonial period, but to receive their benefits the poor not only had to be destitute but also willing to relinquish remaining human dignity. Private charity was sometimes less objectionable to the poor, and the settlement house movement of the late nineteenth century did provide a more humane avenue for aid. While the expansion of settlement houses officially occurred among secular welfare institutions, it was also connected to social reform in religious circles. Protestant reaction to poverty and industrial crisis had both theological and institutional ramifications. Liberal theological Protestant spokesmen rejected the idea of the poor as depraved, and explained poverty as determined by social and economic conditions. Protestant reform, through the Social Gospel Movement, established institutional churches, settlement houses, and welfare agencies, and even engaged in politics in order to uplift the worker and bring salvation to society by reforming the existing system. Contrary to most historians' depictions, however, this movement was not totally confined to Protestantism. German Jews who had immigrated in mid-nineteenth century directed a Jewish variation of the social gospel. Appalled by the poverty and appearance of their Orthodox brethren arriving from East Europe in the latter part of the century, the German Jews established social reform and welfare institutions. Similarly, Catholic reformers organized agencies to dispense charity, find employment, and Americanize the Catholic immigrant.[2]

In the late nineteenth and early twentieth centuries American Catholic reformers joined social critics of other faiths in supporting moderate political and economic change of the status quo. Catholic reformers wanted the social and economic system to function more equitably so that the poor and the overwhelmingly Catholic urban working class would have opportunity for advancement. Therefore Catholic leaders, many with working class backgrounds, supported moderation of capitalist excesses. The Catholic reformers, however, rarely advocated scrapping the capitalist system. Not radicals, they simply sought an avenue for gradual improvement of conditions.

Catholics lacked a radical bloc that might have prodded these reformers to the left, and the influential conservative element within American Catholicism did little to foster reform objectives. While conservative bishops held any potentially radical priests in check, the reformers of the nineteenth-century clerical establishment also reinforced hesitancy and inaction. Concerned liberal bishops advocated programs to aid the worker; yet these reformers functioned as optimistic evangelists. Convinced the Catholic theological influence would engulf the Protestant majority, the liberals did not hesitate to work with Protestants or to adopt much of their outlook. In taking such a stance, the reformers had to defend themselves against charges of Protestant contamination leveled by Catholic conservatives at home and abroad. Their defense predominantly stressed the virtue and innocence of American society. Apologists for the American system because of their optimistic theological outlook, the reformers could not advocate the system's destruction because of economic inequities.[3]

Although Catholic reformers consistently pictured the essential nature of American existence as the best that could be achieved, they still supported moderate piecemeal change in order to improve living conditions of the worker; thus economic conservatives within the church accused them of being radicals. Isaac Thomas Hecker, a major Catholic figure of the mid-nineteenth century and a leading American theologian, clearly illustrated this ambiguity. Catholic conservatives attacked his support of separation of church and state, his complete acceptance of procedural democracy, and his belief that the church needed to adjust itself to contemporary conditions. When discussing the social, economic, and political systems, he preached reform but only gradual and moderate change. He was, in fact, an apologist for the "American way of life." The United States should become Catholic, he argued, to save the existing system.[4]

In the 1870s the liberal Catholic leadership considered government intervention in the economy (by limiting child labor, for example), high employer taxes, and, before the Depression of 1873, employer benevolence as ultimate cures for social problems. In contrast to accepted American industrial practices, the Catholic leadership stood with those advocating change, but only carefully limited change—a mere tinkering with the capitalist system. James Cardinal Gibbons, today eulogized as a great spokesman for labor, never saw serious flaws in American social conditions. In an article praising steel magnate Andrew Carnegie, for instance, Gibbons called on the poor to exercise Christian patience. Carnegie's ruthless suppression of labor during the homestead strike of

1892 preceded the Gibbons article. In a sermon in 1916, the year Mesabi iron miners were killed while striking to improve working conditions, Gibbons preached the inevitability of rank, station, and wealth which "result from a law of life established by an overruling Providence." Gibbons considered polygamy, political corruption, and delays in executing legal sentences the major problem of American society.[5]

Critics as well as admirers have depicted John Ireland, Archbishop of St. Paul, as a hero of Catholic reform of the late nineteenth century. He limited his liberal zeal, however, to mild reforms. Ireland opposed the workers in the Pullman strike of 1894 and generally abhorred militant labor agitation. He associated most labor activism with socialism and accepted the economic viewpoint of the Republican party. Respect for capital, he wrote, must be supreme. "I have no fear of capital. I have no fear of vast aggregations of capital in the hands of the companies." He defended the legitimacy of trusts; "so terrible in the eyes of some, [trusts] are, when looked into and analysed, only the union of many personal fortunes." While Ireland wrote apologies for monopolists, Catholic reformers such as Father John Talbot Smith and Morgan Sheedy demanded legislation to cope with corporate and industrial abuses. They advocated government intervention to end child labor, monopolies, corporation malpractices, and slum housing; they also wanted government to sponsor the building of suitable living areas for the poor, including abundant recreational facilities. Smith and Sheedy believed that the system would function more efficiently and benevolently if government adopted welfare measures and placed corporations on the defensive.[6]

Many Catholic social reformers who advocated governmental social welfare activities also sought compulsory arbitration to replace labor strikes. Only then, they argued, would the human and economic costs of industrial disputes end. After the mid-1880s, Catholic social reformers, allied with more conservative Catholic elements, supported an arbitration program. William J. Onahan, Chicago businessman and government official, emerged as the most outspoken Catholic advocate of this view. Onahan also supported unions, hated socialism, and considered poverty the result of moral deficiency. "The labor question," he stated, "is not so much a question of labor as it is of liquor, laziness, and loafing." Although the conservative *New York Catholic Review* advocated compulsory arbitration to prevent violent revolution-spawning strikes, most Catholic leaders supported arbitration because it meant de facto recognition of unions and strengthened the weak industrial worker. Thus, like the other reforms, arbitration would help the worker, make the system more benevolent, and curtail the support for more massive industrial and economic change which would threaten American capitalism.[7]

The Paulist magazine *Catholic World* provided space for a number of clerical social critics, many of whom went beyond the cautious reformism personified by Onahan. Jesuit F. W. Grafton, for example, considered capitalism a "social evil." Father Joseph McSoreley sought an ideological basis for the reconstruction of society. William J. Kerby, the founder of the National Conference of Catholic Charities and effective teacher and scholar at Catholic University, also published in *Catholic World*. He defended some socialist economic policies and advocated a society that would take over "the economic function of production." Although going further than most Catholic reformers, the *Catholic World* contributors chose the road of theoretical gradualism. Grafton considered collective bargaining the ultimate technique to reform capitalism, while McSoreley could only advocate further study of the economic system. Kerby, on the other hand, did support substantial alteration of the economic system but unrealistically hoped it would proceed from a spontaneous change in human attitudes—from an instinct of acquisitiveness to an instinct of cooperativeness. The *Catholic World* contributors did not advance specific programs and policies outlining clear radical change, but relied on reformist institutions, study, and hope.[8]

Kerby, the most outspoken and intellectually complex of the group, pioneered many of the distributist concepts later utilized by Hilaire Belloc and others. He also helped to formulate the thought of Monsignor John A. Ryan. Early twentieth-century Catholic reform centered around Father Ryan, the dominant figure of Catholic social thought for four decades. During the progressive period, Ryan argued that the economic system needed considerable readjustment, and he advocated change more comprehensive than that urged by typical middle-class reformers. He worked fervently against poverty by actively advancing a minimum wage, the eight-hour day, woman and child labor legislation, unemployment relief, and what has become known as social security. He also supported the strike and boycott, compulsory government mediation and labor arbitration in many industries, either public ownership or government control of natural monopolies, and graduated income and inheritance taxes. Ryan, believing that a wider distribution of public ownership would diffuse income, argued that the "majority of workers will gradually become owners, at least in part, of the instruments of production without ending capitalism." Although Ryan debated socialists, he considered himself a sympathetic critic and foresaw an economic order built around cooperation between labor and capital. He felt that of the competing socialist ideologies, the more conservative variety dominant in the United States "is not necessarily wrong if it can be made practicable." Ryan tolerated the economic goals of the conservative wing of the Socialist party, and felt the main tenet of its economic program did not fall "under the condemnation of . . . the moral law of the Church." In spite of being a sympathetic critic of the socialists, Ryan was neither a radical nor a Christian Socialist—as some historians have classified him. He debated against advocates of socialism, consistently condemned its moral and ethical aspects, and attacked the socioeconomic extremism, as he saw it, of the more fervent radicals. In his autobiography, Ryan stated that during this period he spoke "more frequently and more fundamentally" in opposition to socialism than in support of unionism, but he stressed that in all the addresses on socialism "I had a great deal to say about social reform." Ryan rejected a radical transformation of society, but advanced a reform program considerably to the left of most Catholic social thinkers before 1930. Thus, although no radical, Ryan seemed daring from the Catholic perspective.[9]

The major Catholic spokesmen advocating social change were reformers. It is true that some American Catholic priests and laymen considered themselves genuine radicals. This minute segment doubted the efficacy of competitive capitalism and advocated vast changes in the social and economic structure of society to be made within a short period of time. However, these individual radicals hardly represented a Catholic radical tradition in the United States.

In the mid-nineteenth century, C. Wharton Collens, known as a Catholic communist labor reformer and cofounder of the Christian Labor Union, fitted into this category of independent Catholic radicals. He called for the perfect charity of the early Christians and advocated a system similar to that of St. Thomas More's *Utopia.* Christians, according to Collens, should take vows of poverty and obedience and live in closely knit communities where they would strive for perfection and produce surplus wealth for the poor. While the views of Collens paralleled those of the radical fringe of European Catholicism, his support among American Catholics was infinitesimal. A recent student of Collens correctly concluded that he "had no discernible influence on American Catholicism. His Christian socialism, founded on his early reading in Owen and Fourier, put him completely beyond the pale of American Catholic thought . . . . He was, and remains, a sport in the history of American Catholic thinking."[10]

Many Catholics did, however, become followers of Henry George. Lack of land ownership and desire for land reform among Catholics in Ireland accounted for George's popularity with Irish-Americans. Land reform had become the main tenet of Irish Catholic social reformists in the old country. Father Edward McGlynn, the pastor of New York's St. Stephen's Church, the largest Catholic parish in New York City, was the most renowned Catholic follower of George. Although George advocated no more than a "single tax" to remove profits accrued to land that increased in value, his critics considered him and out-and-out socialist intent upon destroying all private property. The conservative Archbishop of New York, Michael A. Corrigan, warned fellow Catholics "to be zealously on guard against certain unsound principles and theories which assail the rights of property." The Archbishop removed McGlynn from St. Stephen's when the priest ignored his directive and continued single tax agitation. The Pope then excommunicated McGlynn when he refused to go to Rome to explain his opinions and conduct. Reform leaders within the church defended McGlynn, not because they sympathized with his views but rather because they believed his condemnation would turn sympathizers away from the church and sway labor toward radicalism. In 1892, responding to McGlynn's support among liberal clerics, the Pope's representative lifted the sentence of excommunication.[11]

Unlike the followers of George, whose genuine radicalism seemed questionable since the basic nature of competitive capitalism remained intact under the single tax movement, Fathers Thomas McGrady and Thomas Haggerty to a great degree belonged in the tradition of American radicalism. McGrady became a major figure in the socialist movement during the early part of the twentieth century. He lectured throughout the country in defense of socialism, arguing that socialism was not antithetical either to religion or to Catholicism. Thomas Haggerty turned from socialism to anarcho-syndicalism and became not only a member of the IWW but also one of its first major theorists. He advocated an anarchistic, industrial, communal society to be brought about through class warfare. Both priests became isolated within Catholicism and both their lives eventually separated from the church.[12]

The small group of Catholic social thinkers who challenged the nature of capitalism in the United States did not represent an American Catholic tradition. As individuals who accepted radical views, they were only incidentally Catholics and not part of a Catholic movement. Only McGlynn, a dubious radical, had a significant following among Catholics, but this seemed to rest on unique Irish grievances.

Since Catholic social critics did not advocate intensive social and economic revision of society, and after the depressions of the 1870s and 1890s demonstrated that personal charity and charitable institutions could not cope with industrial-based poverty, American Catholics and the Catholic leadership turned to trade unionism. The labor movement, they believed, could improve the lot of the worker by opposing the most ruthless of employers while still being antisocialist. Moreover, Catholics already made up a significant portion of union members and labor leaders. Although unions did not keep records of members' religious affiliations, historian Mark Karson, a student of the AFL, found that before 1918 Irish Catholics constituted the largest nationality group within the federation and that a considerable portion of the German-Americans in the AFL were also Catholics. Other analysts of the labor movement agree. Labor economist Selig Perlman noted, "The Catholics . . . are perhaps the majority in the labor movement." Father Peter Dietz, the major labor priest of the progressive period, believed that Catholics made up more than half of the AFL. Peter Collins, a contemporary Catholic labor spokesman, argued that Catholics constituted more than half of all organized labor. Labor economist David Saposs later agreed that a majority of unionists were Catholic.[13]

Karson found that Irish Catholic strength rested not only among the rank-and-file membership of AFL unions, but also among officers of the international unions and the AFL's executive board. More than fifty AFL international presidents were Catholic. Of the eight vice-presidents on the AFL executive board from 1900 to 1918, Catholics numbered at least four during any one year. Although church leadership reinforced adherents' inclinations by supporting organized labor in the late nineteenth and early twentieth centuries, in favoring unionism it took an innovative step. The labor movement still remained unacceptable to the industrial elite and to much of the Protestant establishment.[14]

There were exceptions to the Catholic support of unionism. The closely knit German-American Catholic leadership, generally suspicious of any institution that had an acculturating influence, viewed the labor movement cautiously. At the turn of the century, some of their spokesmen still equated craft unionism with "socialism and anarchy." Green Bay Bishop (later Archbishop of Milwaukee) Sebastian G. Messemer, for example, asserted that "labor unions are all biased toward the principles of socialism." Polish priests sometimes exhibited similar hostility toward organized labor although their parishioners eventually became stalwart union members. After 1900, however, most of the Catholic leadership supported the right to join a union and the right of collective bargaining.[15]

The church was first enveloped in labor controversy with the Knights of

Labor, an attempt at industrial unionism that culminated in 1886. Although Archbishop Elzear Alexandre Taschereau of Quebec obtained a papal condemnation of the Knights of Labor in Canada, American prelates, with some exceptions, defended the group. Patrick J. Conway, vicar-general of the Archdiocese of Chicago, blunted conservative Catholic criticism that secrecy vows taken by Knights of Labor violated the confessional, arguing that union members "practiced secrecy for business purposes." In fighting the condemnation, however, the hierarchy was primarily concerned with protecting the Roman Catholic image in the U.S.–that an American Catholic could practice his legal rights without interference from "foreign influences." Whatever their rationale, when Cardinal Gibbons went to Rome to successfully defend organized labor, all but two of the American archbishops supported him. Church support of the Knights of Labor and of the labor movement in general, prevented the conflict between the church and organized labor that had developed in Europe. As the AFL emerged with a large Catholic membership, and with the federation accepting the conservatism of Samuel Gompers, American Catholic prelates overwhelmingly supported organized labor. The laity and a considerable portion of the clergy echoed the church leadership.[16]

The *Catholic Review of New York* favored unions primarily on the basis that they would enable labor to secure justice with a minimum of strikes. Catholic colonizer and social reformer William J. Onahan, as well as Bishops Spaulding and Ireland, officially endorsed organized labor, although Ireland became increasingly hostile to more militant unionism. Cardinal Gibbons, of course, defended the Knights of Labor at Rome and has since been considered a champion of organized labor. While the Third Plenary Council seemed unconcerned with civil legislation in relation to social reform, they ruled in 1884 that pastors without explicit authorization must not condemn unions. The hierarchy accepted Catholic membership in secular unions providing that the unions were "consistent with truth, justice, and conscience." Few if any Catholic newspapers or periodicals denied that workingmen struggled to better themselves. Both the Boston *Pilot* and the Indianapolis *Catholic Record* particularly supported strong unions. Catholic acceptance of organized labor came at a time when the Protestant establishment, the federal government, most state and local governments, and a large portion of middle class America still condemned unionism. In order to break strikes, vigilantes lynched labor organizers, local governments framed strike leaders, and federal troops imprisoned striking workers in primitive concentration camps.[17]

Pro-union American Catholic spokesmen received impetus from Pope

Leo XIII's 1893 encyclical, *Rerum Novarum*. Although its effect was primarily felt in European Catholic circles, what influence it had in the United States elucidated American Catholic labor trends. With *Rerum Novarum*, Rome attempted to cope with the socioeconomic reality of an exploited European working class. Severe economic conditions resulting from industrial expansion indicated the need for economic reform. This need became especially evident when the depression which began in 1873 proved too much for personal charity. Social and economic reform seemed necessary to significant elements within virtually all major churches.

With the development of industrial complexity and a cyclical economy, a threat arose on the political left. The socialist advance, especially clear in Europe, existed in the United States as well. Leo XIII's encyclical, however, was not simply a sudden pragmatic procedure to counter the upsurge of socialism, as several analysts have implied. Conflict between reform and conservative forces, existing not only within the Roman Catholic Church but also among Protestants, engulfed the entire second half of the nineteenth century. In the social and economic ramifications of this conflict, Leo XIII stood with the liberals before his election as Pope. During his episcopate at Perugia he issued pastorals on the sufferings of the workers and on the callousness of employers considerably stronger and more explicit than *Rerum Novarum*. While Pope, in 1887, he typically stated to one of many visiting groups of workers that should justice, morality, man's dignity, or the worker's domestic life be jeopardized "the State by a right measure of intervention would be working for the common wealth, for it is its duty to protect and watch over the true interests of its subjects."[18]

Although Leo supported reforms that favored the worker, *Rerum Novarum* attacked socialism as an immoral and unnatural alternative to the "utter poverty of the masses." To cope with injustices of competitive capitalism, the Pope sought a system to render obsolete the laissez-faire policies of nineteenth-century capitalism. Socialism, however, deprived the worker "of the liberty of disposing of his wares, and thus of all hope and possibility of increasing his stock and of bettering his condition in life." Leo thus offered a third alternative, one he considered a median between the extremes of socialism and capitalism. His program rested on two principles: private property "for every man has by nature the right to possess property as his own;" and the necessity of the Catholic Church "for no practical solution of this question will ever be found without the assistance of Religion of the Church. It is We who are the chief guardian of Religion." The church would not only sponsor social agencies to help the worker, but more importantly, create a moral and just climate of opinion in which "the Christian inter-dependence of capital and labor" could be realized. The Pope argued that it was "ordained by nature that these two classes [the rich and the poor] should exist in harmony and agreement." And in preventing class conflict, "the efficacy of Christianity is marvellous and manifold," for religion was powerful "in drawing rich and poor together, by reminding each class of its duties to the other."[19]

Leo XIII thus desired a society where rich and poor were united in bonds of brotherly love. Since, however, this stiuation did not exist, the working class should be able, the Pope argued, to look to the state and to its own organizations for material aid. "The public administration must duly and solicitously provide for the welfare and the comfort of the working people." Leo argued that government should take an active part in protecting the interests of the worker. The length of the work day should be regulated not by supply and demand, but by difficulty of the work, "for there is neither justice or humanity so to grind men down with excessive labor." The labor of women and children should be carefully regulated. The employer should be obligated to pay a fair wage, "enough to support the wage earner in reasonable and frugal comfort." The state, however, might not unduly interfere with the market, therefore the wage earner should resort to collective action. To safeguard labor's interests, Leo advocated government protection of organizations of workers and associations of workers combined with employers. Leo compared these latter groups to the guilds of the past, thus tying the present to Catholic tradition. He felt that unions formed solely of workers should be Catholic in composition, or at least neutral, and disassociated with the prevalent left-wing unionism of Europe.[20]

Rerum Novarum, in supporting governmental protection of the worker's right to join a labor union, was a true reform document. Leo also advocated moving away from competitive capitalism to a system based on love rather than competition. He did not outline the system's structure, since the large and diverse audience the encyclical intended to influence necessitated generalities. The intention of the encyclical would presumably have been carried out within the tradition and framework of each given culture.

Unlike some European Catholic spokesmen, the American leadership virtually ignored *Rerum Novarum*'s anticapitalism potential. On the other hand, Americans readily acknowledged the Pope's support of trade unionism. This interpretation of the encyclical conveniently provided a de jure rationalization and official theological justification for American

Catholic emphasis on trade unionism as the avenue for reform.

In the first quarter of the twentieth century, the Catholic leadership continued its approval and support of the conservative unionism of the AFL. John Ryan and Peter Dietz emerged as the most influential Catholic spokesmen on the labor issue. Although Ryan supported organized labor in his speeches and writings, he was not as well known to union activists as he was to the organizers of progressive reform. The union leadership, however, acknowledged his role, as Gompers pointed out when introducing him to the delegates of the national AFL convention of 1906. Matthew Woll, an influential AFL vice-president, accurately summed up Ryan's activities by saying that he "worked on us and for us, as we won our battles, he rejoiced with us." By stating that he worked on the AFL, Woll alluded to Ryan's criticism of the federation. Ryan wanted the AFL to shed its conservative skin and to accept economic reality by supporting industrial unionism and welfare state measures. While Ryan attempted to bring the labor establishment more in tune with the progressive movement, Dietz tried to reinforce the AFL's antisocialism and continued conservatism.[21]

The Dietz position had considerable influence in clerical circles. While the church endorsed the labor movement, its support increasingly became contingent upon labor's repudiation of socialism. Church spokesmen often pointed out that if the AFL veered toward socialism the church would instruct Catholic workers to leave the federation. While the European experience, especially in Belgium and Germany, illustrated that this was no idle threat, American priests, actually started local labor organizations when they believed that socialists had too much strength.

At the turn of the century, Catholic priests in the Buffalo area of western New York formed organizations of Catholic workers to carry out the church's social program and to protect labor against socialism. German Catholics in the St. Louis area began similar projects, mostly on the parish basis. Catholic associations and abortive unions acted only as a threat, not as a dual labor movement. The hierarchy withheld support, for it considered Catholic unions premature. The possibilities of a Catholic dual labor movement, however, could hardly have gone unnoticed by a fledgling AFL still uncertain of its future. Catholic independent unions arose only when socialists dominated AFL locals, for priests organized Catholic labor groups mainly for the purpose of thwarting socialist propaganda.[22]

Antisocialism in the church came from lay as well as clerical sources. During the first quarter of the twentieth century, David Goldstein and

Martha Moore Avery, both lay converts to Catholicism, jointly carried out a self-appointed crusade against socialism. Goldstein and Avery, sponsored by various Catholic organizations, jointly wrote numerous articles, pamphlets, and books. In one particularly influential work, *Socialism: The Nation of Fatherless Children*, they argued that socialists wanted to abolish Catholicism and Christian marriage. They wrote their polemic at the same time the American Socialist party appealed to Catholic workers partly by deprecating contemporary socialist biases against organized religion. Goldstein and Avery aimed their propaganda not only at Catholic workers but also at dissatisfied lay and clerical intellectuals who considered socialism a viable alternative. Avery was also active in the Common Cause Society, a Boston Catholic lay group. As chairman of its legislative committee and later as president of the organization, she helped direct its antisocialist program. The society, however, also supported minimum wage legislation, reduced working hours, employer liability, and child labor laws. Thus it attempted to fight socialism with social reform.[23]

At the same time that Goldstein and Avery carried out their campaigns, Catholic layman Peter Collins, an officer of the Brotherhood of Electrical Workers, editor of its official journal, and president of the Boston Central Union, resigned his labor union posts to devote himself completely to antisocialism. As with Goldstein and Avery, various Catholic organizations sponsored his nation-wide lecture tours. He also authored antisocialist articles and pamphlets. American Catholic leaders lionized Collins, while in the labor movement he became a well-known figure.[24]

The most effective Catholic antisocialist activist was Father Peter Dietz. Before the mid-1920s, the union leadership considered him the church's coordinator for labor affairs. Indeed, Dietz did assume this role, for the church lacked an office of labor relations until the formation of the Social Action Department of the National Catholic Welfare Conference. An alleged statement made by Dietz to a group of Catholic unionists illustrated the theme of his many speeches before labor groups, articles he wrote in labor and clerical journals, and the program he fostered: "If you try anything that could tend to aid the Socialists, the Catholic Church would be compelled to disown the AFL and begin organizing Catholic unions."[25]

Dietz made similar remarks, although not with such clarity, on numerous occasions—even addressing AFL conventions. He did not limit his activities to propaganda. When necessary Dietz engaged in direct action. In 1909, for example, he led a minority of the AFL delegates out of the Ohio AFL convention because the socialists carried a crucial vote.

The German Catholic Central Verein, the major organization of German-American Catholics and an employer of Dietz, fully supported him. It accepted the "safe and sane" AFL as long as the federation clearly opposed the socialists and socialist principles. Its English language news organ, with Dietz as editor, continually attacked the left wing of organized labor. The Verein social reform agency, again with Dietz as director, defined its role as grappling against socialism within the labor movement. Thus it is not surprising that the 1909 Central-Verein convention recommended that the "faithful cooperate with the American Federation of Labor guided as it is by conservatism." At the same convention, the organization's president stated that its function should be to arouse antisocialism among Catholic unionists and to teach them Catholic social principles. At the 1911 convention it was urged that "Catholic workingmen join trade unions whenever possible to combat the propagation of Socialism in the unions." *Central Blatt,* a Verein organ, pointed out that should the left in the AFL come into power "then the movement would be near the danger line, at which time all Catholics will have to halt and at which they would have to leave the Federation."[26]

After leaving the employ of the Verein, Dietz concentrated on coordinating Catholic political activities within the labor movement. In 1910 he founded the Militia of Christ for Social Service. The labor leadership thought of the militia as the formal Catholic spokesmen on labor problems in the United States. Although national union officers officially constituted the militia leadership, Dietz, as executive secretary, directed the organization. Throughout its formative years, the militia numbered about 700 union officials. Although the militia also defended the AFL and supported legislation designed to strengthen conservative American unionism, most of its time and effort were spent fighting socialism. Dietz spoke at numerous labor gatherings of all sorts and sizes. Under the auspices of the militia, he wrote pamphlets, issued a weekly newsletter to both the Catholic and the labor press, and gave personal guidance to many influential Catholics within the labor movement. The militia established a speaker service that sent its own lecturers, antisocialist members of the labor movement and socially concerned clerics, throughout the country addressing various groups.

In 1911 the militia was replaced by the Social Service Commission established by the American Federation of Catholic Charities. Considering the commission's activities and Dietz's role in the organization, historian Aaron Abell suggested that it was essentially an enlarged militia. In later years, however, the Social Service Commission gave up the extensive antisocialist campaigns that Dietz originally intended because "pure and simple" trade unionism was secure in the aging AFL. Dietz's social action career ended in 1923 when his Bishop insisted he return to his Milwaukee diocese. The removal of Dietz from the national labor scene ended his final labor project, the establishment of a labor college. The AFL made this school its National Labor College, but with Dietz's recall the institution failed to survive.[27]

The AFL acceptance of the Dietz-directed institution as the official AFL labor college and the more than sixty national labor leaders, led by Samuel Gompers, who petitioned Dietz's superior to permit him to continue his activities in organized labor, indicated the confidence and rapport that existed between Dietz and the AFL leadership. At a time when the AFL was in its early developmental stage and highly conscious of the threat of dual unionism, those AFL leaders uncommitted on the socialism question could not have been unaffected by the man they believed to be the spokesman for American Catholicism on labor questions. Even the socialists, at the height of their influence in organized labor, admitted the effect of Catholicism on unions. The *International Socialist Review*, for example, stated that the church was virtually "controlling the AFL," and added that "it looks bad for us." Gompers' close association with Dietz and their corresponding labor philosophies— pragmatic, wage-oriented and antisocialist unionism—benefited both priest and labor leader. American Catholicism did not sponsor its own labor unions and the AFL held firm against the socialists. The Catholic, conservative-unionist alliance continued during the 1920s, but the Great Depression brought new commitments and changed emphases for both organized labor and social Catholicism.[28]

CHAPTER TWO

Catholic Spokesmen and Capitalism, 1920–1940

The Man Nobody Knows appeared on best seller lists in 1924 and 1925. In presenting Jesus Christ as the essence of the successful corporate organizer and business promoter, author Bruce Barton symbolized the decade. Middle-class America indeed worshipped at the shrine of the businessman. Although many intellectuals rejected idealization of business, other American spokesmen glorified entrepreneurial success. American capitalism experienced rapid growth. After 1921, except for minor recessions in 1924 and 1927, American industry expanded. A federal agency announced in 1927 that "the highest standard of living ever attained in the history of the world was reached last year by the American people." Technological change accelerated; young industries realized their potential with the development of chemicals, synthetics, autos, electric light and power, and chain stores, among others. New products made life more tolerable, or at least advertisers created the belief that they would. Corporate investment brought higher rates of return, while speculators cheered the continuously rising stock market. From 1923 to 1929, while prices remained steady, corporate profits rose 62 percent and dividends went up 65 percent. Between 1921 and 1929 national income rose from 50.7 to 81.1 billion dollars. For the middle class and the upper middle class, the success of business meant attainment of the good life.[1]

Some of the prosperity of the period trickled down to the worker. Average real income rose about 11 percent from 1923 to 1927, and most immigrants achieved a significant improvement over living standards in their less developed homelands. Immigrants who remained in the United States, those most easily acculturated, could place faith in the future. Other factors, particularly installment buying, helped consumption rise faster than income, adding to the illusion of significant overall economic improvement. As household appliances freed women from some domestic labor, working wives supplemented many family incomes. Between 1920 and 1930 the number of employed women rose 27.4 percent, from 8.3 million to 10.6 million. During the same decade the number of employed married women rose 28.9 percent, from 1.9 million to 3.1 million. By 1930 one employee in four was a woman. The added income of a working wife made a significant contribution to the worker's standard of living. Although the lower stratum of society still faced significant economic problems, popular American opinion shapers refused to take notice while the satisfied middle class watched the stock market rise.[2]

In 1929 the spiral of American economic growth came down in a crash and with it the savings of not only many industrial workers but also many of the middle class. Although the depression forced a lowering of prices, income dropped more significantly—average weekly earnings plummeted almost 33 percent. This drop was compounded by debts accumulated earlier with less valuable dollars. Urban poverty, however, resulted primarily from unemployment. In 1933, thirteen million were unemployed while in 1934, 1935, and 1936 the total fluctuated between ten and eleven million. At the end of the decade nearly ten million remained without jobs. *Fortune* magazine, a voice of the American business elite, estimated that eleven million unemployed workers meant that for one out of every four of those employable (or 25,500,000 people) "regular sources of livelihood [were] cut off."[3]

Statistics themselves do not tell the story, for the methods of compilation resulted in underestimates. Federal sources counted part-time workers as fully employed and did not count farm dwellers who did not receive wages as unemployed, nor persons entering the labor market for the first time, nor those employed by government relief projects at incomes below market rates.

Unemployment was not uniform. It affected the young and the old more than other age groups. Employers laid off black workers before whites and rehired blacks last. The public considered overt employment discrimination against women a positive social step to discourage two incomes in one family. Thus women, especially heads of one-parent families, suffered disproportionately from unemployment. Inhabitants of areas dominated by one or two industries often became another selective group especially affected by unemployment. In some areas of the country virtually all members of a community were without jobs.[4]

The deterioration in hours, wages, and working conditions, along with the high rate of unemployment, reverberated throughout American society. The depression affected the physical and emotional health of the nation. Psychiatrists reported that emotional disorders increased. Annual admissions to state mental hospitals from 1930 to 1932 almost tripled those from 1922 to 1930. The suicide rate also climbed steadily from 14 per 100,000 in 1929 to 17.4 in 1932. The public, however, largely ignored mental health as physical deprivation became a national concern.[5]

Although mass famine did not occur, people did starve. In 1931 New York City hospitals reported almost 100 cases of actual starvation. Philadelphia's Community Health Center found that malnutrition diagnoses rose about 60 percent between 1928 and 1932. A New York City health center revealed that malnutrition patients rose from 18 percent of total admissions in 1928 to 60 percent by 1931. Malnutrition did not necessarily bring on death, but often hunger and under-nourishment led to disease and indirectly to death. Hospital admissions increased for diseases associated with poverty, such as tuberculosis. Clarence Picket of the American Friends Service Committee found schools where over 85 percent of the children were underweight, drowsy, and lethargic. In the South the number of underweight students sometimes comprised 99 percent of the student body. The Federal Children's Bureau admitted that about one out of five children was undernourished; in some parts of the country the proportion increased considerably. Numerous state and local reports contrasting the late 1920s and early 1930s clearly illustrate the increase in malnutrition. In a careful study of New York City, the National Organization for Public Health Nursing found that malnutrition increased from 18 percent in 1928 to 60 percent during the depression. The Community Health Center of Philadelphia in an examination of children reported an increase from 30.5 percent undernourished in 1929 to 41.5 percent in 1932, and the proportion climbed even higher for older children. Studies from other sections of Pennsylvania and Ohio revealed similar problems.[6]

Just as the depression jeopardized the health of the unemployed and their families, it also often destroyed the security of the home. People moved from foreclosed homes or from dispossessed apartments to hovels on the outskirts of the city. Clusters of hastily improvised shacks called Hoovervilles became part of the American urban scene. The poor built them of packing boxes, barrel staves, flattened tin cans, and pieces of corrugated iron. Some were able to insulate their shacks with tarred paper to keep out inclement weather. Men lived in shut-down factories and freight cars. Hoovervilles rose around city dumps, in city and state parks, and on large lots of privately owned property. In Oakland, California, families moved into unused sewer pipes made available by a pipe manufacturer unable to market his product. In New York the homeless slept in subways and in an unused Central Park reservoir. This reservoir settlement became known as Hoover Valley. Open hearth furnaces served as beds for many in Youngstown, Ohio. The California Unemployment Commission described one typical diseased "urban jungle" in 1932. Living in an assortment of shacks were 185 single men and 86 families with 150 children. "Sanitation is ... bad; grounds filthy; no garbage collection; open improvised toilets, inadequate in number. Only one water faucet within half a mile of the camping site." The children of this Hooverville received no formal education since neither city nor state authorities would provide any. As a microcosm of society, the Hooverville became the symbol of American capitalism at bay.[7]

Americans responded to poverty and disillusionment of the depression in numerous ways: some became transients looking for work; others turned to labor organizations to raise wages. In the political realm the vast majority of Americans turned from the party of business to the wing of the Democratic party associated with the progressive movement. The more disenchanted turned to fascist organizations, like the German-American Bund (which had overseas links), or to home-grown varieties such as the Brown Shirts, Silver Shirts, Crusaders, and National Watchmen. More important were the followings of individual demagogues who built movements based on simplistic panaceas, such as Howard Schott's "technocracy," Dr. Townsend's pension plans, or Huey Long's "Share Our Wealth" program.

Still others turned to the political left. In 1932 Socialist party presidential candidate Norman Thomas received 881,951 votes, the party's strongest showing since its peak during the progressive period. In this election the Communist party polled 102,785 votes, not a considerable number but until then their highest total in American history. Given communist intentions of developing a party for the masses, their lack of numerical influence at the polls suggests complete failure. Election figures, however, do not indicate party importance since communists did not seriously attempt to build voting strength during these years. Membership figures better illustrate the party's importance and potential. The Communist party averaged over 40,000 members during the depression. Its cadres willingly dedicated vast amounts of time working for numerous party causes and objectives. The flexibility of party membership made the individual's usefulness more valuable than the equivalent Republican or Democrat to his party; thus 40,000 represented a considerable number.[8]

In addition, the indirect influence of Marxism and the aura of radicalism supplemented direct party activities. Avant-garde intellectuals lauded Marxism during the depression decade. Social scientists and men of letters, including Louis Corey, Sidney Hook, Henry Sigerist, Max Lerner, and Louis Hacker, for example, related Marxism to both history and contemporary America. Literary critics Vernon Calvertson, Granville Hicks, Edmund Wilson, Newton Arvin, and Malcolm Cowley and such creative writers as Theodore Dreiser, Genevieve Taggard, Clifford Odets, John Dos Passos, and James T. Farrell reflected a Marxist outlook. Party members among the intellectuals successfully received support of so-called "fellow travellers" who advanced communist programs—especially those opposed to fascism—supported strikes and the demands of left labor leaders, and publicized violations of civil liberties.[9]

Although the party received significant support from intellectuals in the 1930s, it visualized itself as a worker's party. During the 1920s communists gained a reputation as self-sacrificing, militant organizers through their direction of the Gastonia strike and similar attempts at organizing unskilled industrial workers. In the 1930s, the worker continued to be communism's major concern. Although the party agitated for unemployment relief, established soup kitchens and bread lines, and organized street squads to prevent rental dispossessions, its major involvement continued to be the labor movement.

In the 1930s the party gave crucial aid in organizing the CIO. In directing the new labor federation's mushrooming growth, John L. Lewis, hard-pressed to find experienced labor organizers to fill CIO needs, turned to the communists who had evinced their abilities. The rise of the CIO coincided with a change in the communist international viewpoint, calling for a united democratic front against facism and for the alignment of communists with other democratic forces. As a result of these two developments, zealous young communists and their supporters joined the CIO staff in vast numbers. By the end of the depression, they had significant influence in locals of the electrical, radio, woodworking, fur and leather industries, and the unions of municipal, transport, and maritime industries. Historian Joseph Rayback concluded that as early as 1932 communism "had filtered through a large part of the labor world as the only hope in the midst of despair." He might have added that by 1936, communists, as the dedicated organizers and militant workhorses of their unions, often won the respect and support of the rank-and-file. Communist influence did not result simply from despair; it grew out of the accomplishment of its labor activities.[10]

The massive poverty of the depression, the emergence of an industrial labor movement, and communist influence in the CIO all combined to increase Catholic social concern. Attitudes of the official and unofficial Catholic leadership—hierarchy, prominent clerics, and intellectuals and scholars writing in the more prestigious Catholic press—shifted markedly as the depression affected clerical and lay leaders. Since Catholics constituted much of the industrial and immigrant classes, the Catholic elite traditionally concerned itself with urban poverty. Continued interest in poverty had no new political implications, but provided an avenue for further and deeper questioning of the status quo.

No matter what policy individuals among the American hierarchy advocated to cope with depression poverty, they agreed that unemployed workers faced a severe and unfair plight and that the economic situation furthered communist ends. Speaking for the American bishops at their annual meeting in 1930, Archbishop Edward J. Hanna of San Francisco found that "the United States is suffering the tragedy of millions of men and women who need work, who want work, and who can find no work to do." At the 1931 meeting of American bishops the hierarchy voiced its "deep fraternal sympathy for the millions of Americans . . . [who are] victims of the present industrial crisis." They protested "the most extraordinary conditions which threaten so many of our fellow citizens with want and misery during the coming winter." An official statement of the hierarchal board of the National Catholic Welfare Conference (NCWC) explained that "it would be folly to deny or attempt to minimize the gravity of the situation." They referred to the 1930s as a "period of horror, uncertainty, and suffering." Likewise Pius XI, speaking to the world at large in his encyclical *Quadragesimo Anno*, found living conditions deplorable: "almost all economic life has become tragically hard, inexorable, and cruel."[11]

Pius also castigated communists who he felt exploited economic crisis for their own ends; he attacked their doctrine "which seeks by violence and slaughter to destroy society altogether." The American Catholic leadership similarly linked poverty of the depression with communist advance. "It is to be deplored that the unrest caused by evil already grave and disturbing," the bishops of the NCWC board stated, "should be further increased by designing agitators or by cunning propagandists whose immediate interest is to create turmoil, bitterness, class conflict, and thus hasten a revolutionary situation." "There is a very grave and subtle danger of infection from Communism," a long document on the 1930s issued by the hierarchy argued. "They have as their objective a world war on God and the complete destruction of the supernatural." Within an opening statement analyzing the encyclicals, the American bishops stated "the forces of atheism and neopaganism with their offsprings Communism and despotism are attempting to rob life of all that is spiritual and supernatural."[1][2]

Catholic journalism echoed the anticommunist outcry. Although throughout the 1930s many articles appeared in leading Catholic periodicals lamenting the destitution and misery caused by the depression, as frequently they castigated alleged communist threats. "Hardly a Catholic periodical appears nowadays," a *Commonweal* writer stated, "without at least one vituperative denunciation of Communism." Indeed he was correct; a multitude of anticommunist articles appear in every volume of the period's major Catholic periodicals. Not only did more conservative journals such as *Sign* hold anticommunist views, so did liberal publications such as *Commonweal*. Even the self-professed radical publication, *The Catholic Worker*, had a low-key but definite anticommunist position. Although, in general, Catholic red-baiting was less vitriolic than during the 1920s, it nevertheless continued, virtually having the status of a Catholic party line. The realization of the blight of massive poverty coupled with fear of communism caused American Catholic social leaders to shift their economic and political perspective. They not only continued the general Catholic support for organized labor, but became disillusioned with the capitalist system. No single panacea, spokesman, or institution clearly dominated among the societal alternatives advocated, but numerous spokesmen and several major institutions advocated many methods of change. The anarcho-communist Catholic Worker Movement, Father Coughlin's Social Justice Movement, and, at times, elements of more traditional Catholic institutions, moved in utopian directions. Many American Catholic social leaders thus adopted the stand previously taken by numerous European Catholics, for European Catholic social activists had sponsored reform and even radical movements for half a century. Unlike Americans, Europeans had interpreted *Rerum Novarum* of Leo XIII as a call for massive reform. In the 1930s American Catholic leaders reinterpreted *Rerum Novarum*, abandoning previous emphasis on the document as primarily pro-union and antisocialist. Now *Rerum* was considered a mandate for reform. A new papal encyclical, however, appeared in 1931, updating *Rerum Novarum*.[1][3]

Pius XI's *Quadragesimo Anno* reinforced American Catholic social activist trends. In his statement to a world in depression, Pius XI went further than the innovations of Leo and certainly moved well beyond the conservatism of Pius X and Benedict XV. Where Leo thoroughly condemned all socialism, Pius XI reserved his severity for communism. He depicted socialism as "surely more moderate. It not only professed the rejection of violence but modifies . . . the class struggle and the abolition of private ownership." Pius characterized socialism by stating that it "inclines toward and in a certain measure approaches the truths which Christian tradition always have held sacred." In order to appear wholly consistent with Leo, however, Pius created the fiction that the socialist movement in the 1890s, when Leo wrote *Rerum Novarum*, did not have internal differences comparable to those confronting the radicals of the 1930s. Like Leo, Pius attacked capitalist abuses, but where Leo used more cautious terminology Pius outspokenly advocated change in the economic system. He called for collaboration between worker and employer associations to form industrial corporations. Together with representatives of the state the industrial corporation should "coordinate their activities in matters of common interest toward one and the same end." Instead of conflict between labor and capital, Pius advocated collaboration. Joint industrial corporations and professional associations would cooperate with government to plan economic growth and determine priorities. Thus in place of the old order's economic anarchy, he envisioned economic planning and cooperation. The Papacy therefore moved beyond the conservatism of the two previous popes. It surpassed, as well, in both its anticapitalist spirit and in its desire for a new economic direction, the statements of Leo XIII, himself a papal economic innovator.[14]

The American hierarchy also shifted its socioeconomic emphasis. Contrasting statements of cardinals, bishops and archbishops for the 1920s and 1930s reveal the difference between caution in one period and flexibility in the other. The American hierarchy did not become a hotbed of radicalism. Its changes from the 1920s to the 1930s were more in tone than in political and economic philosophy. The clerical leaders did not suggest drastic change. They advanced social changes they had omitted in pronouncements of the previous decade. In the 1920s the hierarchy had little to say on the basic nature of the capitalist system. They spoke out mainly on persecution of the church in Mexico, on the "Fate of Ireland," on conditions in Russia, and on problems of birth control and disarmament. One of the few statements on American government indicated the church's fear of centralization stemming from harassment of the church by American nativists during the 1920s. The statement, entitled "Paternalism in Government," attacked growing bureaucracy which would "sovietize our form of government."[15]

With the 1930s a change in attitude developed. Shortly after the depression set in, Archbishop Hanna of San Francisco, speaking for the American bishops, saw in unemployment associated with the business cycle "a sign of deep failure in our country." The next year the bishops equated the capitalist system with disorganized "processes of production and distribution." The system, they continued, "has run its course through unlimited individualism and unorganized competition and is climaxed now by an ineffective economic rule." "The greedy capitalists, the tyrannical boss, has had his brutal day . . ." said Cardinal O'Connell in 1931. "Both are guilty of the cause of today's lamentable economic condition." Cardinal O'Connell, a conservative, gave the anarchocommunist Catholic Worker Movement permission to sell its literature at church doors and wrote his approval in the *Pilot*. He also did not hamper the significant aid the Boston clergy gave the worker movement. Acceptance of the general American disenchantment with private enterprise during the 1930s is revealed in a hierarchal statement that "business was shot through with a spirit of greed that led to the perpetration of frauds on the public. . . . Crooked and dishonest practices of stockholders and bankers [are perpetrated] to fleece the public." Cardinal Hayes of New York, calling for a new order based on cooperation and the fair distribution of wealth, had little good to say of the capitalist system which "we can see was built upon a foundation of selfishness, unrestricted competition, and a craving for economic power." Cardinal Mundelein accused American Catholics of being guilty of not taking a proper stand against the old order. "The trouble with us in the past has been that we were too often allied or drawn into an alliance with the wrong side," which he defined as the "selfish employers of labor." He hoped that "the day is gone by. Our place is beside the poor, behind the workingman." Three of the four American cardinals during the 1930s indicated disenchantment with American capitalism. The fourth, Cardinal Dougherty, rarely publicly expounded on social and economic questions. American bishops and archbishops, through their colleagues on the National Catholic Welfare Board, took a similar antiestablishment and anticapitalist position.[16]

Other lay and clerical Catholic spokesmen evinced similar attitudes. Frederick Siedenburg, the Jesuit dean of Detroit University, in his presidential address before the Illinois Conference of Social Work argued that the common Catholic goal should be to "replace the selfishness of the capitalist." He added that "socialization of production and distribution should come about by evolution rather than revolution." Monsignor John O'Grady, a leader in the field of Catholic social work, likewise felt that society needed a "drastic overhauling of the present economic structure." He hoped that *Quadragesimo Anno* would establish the future pattern. James F. Murphy, president of the National Conference of Catholic Charities, Omaha conference, condemned the "ruthless free competition which ends inevitably in economic dictatorship." Yet Murphy also opposed economic centralization and planning. With similar societal criticism, the National Catholic Alumni Federation sponsored meetings to convince American businessmen that capitalism had failed and must be replaced by the papal economic program.[17]

But unity of opinion did not exist, especially concerning goals and the means to achieve them. If it agreed on anything, the Catholic leadership, like American society as a whole, felt simply that something had to be done. Many Catholic spokesmen turned to the New Deal, which they saw as a replacement for capitalism. However, in contrast to the 1920s, the clerical leadership explicitly sought change and expressed disillusionment with the capitalist system.

The Catholic leadership's anticapitalist response to the depression is seen more clearly if one turns from the more cautious statement of cardinals and less colorful consensus of committees to more timely Catholic journalism. Although in the 1920s Catholic journalistic social criticism evolved unevenly, it tended either to accept de facto capitalism or to ignore economic and social problems. In contrast, by the mid-1930s many major Catholic periodicals repudiated capitalism.

Commonweal remained one of the most prestigious Catholic lay publications during these two decades. Its ideological position was neither static nor respondent to any official point of view, but fully reflected the times. In the 1920s, a period when the American public generally retreated from social responsibility, *Commonweal* seldom committed itself on social problems. Although it discussed domestic issues in the broadest generalities, it gave closer attention to the less sensitive European socioeconomic scene. When the journal did speak out on a contemporary domestic problem, it took a conservative position. *Commonweal* admitted the existence of some problems but believed they could be solved through the presumed benevolence of the system. Although *Commonweal* did not question capitalism itself during the 1920s, it considered inadequate distribution of wealth a problem. Yet its view was optimistic. "It is first of all a fact to be noted," *Commonweal* happily pointed out, "that a fair distribution of wealth occupies the minds of an increasing number of the most widely advertised wealthy." It argued that "living conditions in the United States have now reached a point unexampled in the nation's history, as regards to wages paid, ratio of unemployed to employment, and volume of trade." *Commonweal* occasionally admitted economic problems existed. In such cases it offered no remedies or specific indictment, except in agriculture. *Commonweal* bemoaned the plight of the rural poor and advocated more efficient agricultural capitalism through cooperative techniques. Only in the late 1920s did it give some attention to labor.[18]

During the Great Depression, especially toward the end of the decade, *Commonweal* expanded its area of concern. It developed a clear concern for the worker, supported standard reforms, and favored industrial over craft unionism. *Commonweal* became especially critical of the economic system after 1936. From the many responses to an article favorable to capitalism, *Commonweal* printed one by Father Virgil Michel, a noted Benedictine monk who frequently wrote strong anticapitalist attacks. In the late 1930s he became one of *Commonweal*'s leading spokesmen on socioeconomic questions. Of capitalism, he argued that "the system is vicious, both ethically and ontologically." He found that "capitalism degrades men to mere economic factors of cost, to be bargained for at lowest possible market prices." In another typical article Michel depicted the future of capitalism as short and being brought to an end by the depression: "the capitalistic system, or civilization is doomed to extinction."[19]

Commonweal coupled bitter anticapitalist attacks with a general softening of its attitude toward communism, although it still remained essentially anticommunist. The change was in emphasis rather than in position. A priest wrote a moderately anticommunist article in which he concluded that "I think the Communists and I have much in common. I am quite as much opposed to the abuses of capitalism as any Communist." After 1937, a number of such articles appeared, occasionally with a refutation following. In an article entitled "My Communist Friends," for example, the author drew a very sympathetic portrait of several Communists and fellow-travelers. Speaking of non-Bolshevik theoretical communism, another *Commonweal* writer, Martin Lynch, compared communism as "an ideal state" to religious orders. "The Christian doctrine of love," he pointed out, "is the essence of the perfect state of communism." As an alternative to either capitalism or communism, *Commonweal* chose a conglomerate of reforms, some old, a few relatively new, and sometimes contradicting one another. In a single article, *Commonweal* called for support of the cooperative movement in agriculture, Catholic distributism (a highly decentralized economic system based on small producers) and government-controlled monopolies.[20]

The Jesuit publication *America* appeared more consistent than other major Catholic journals from the mid-1920s through the 1930s; yet it also evolved considerably. In the early 1920s *America* retained anticapitalist remnants from its support of reform during the progressive era. A typical editorial in 1921 stated that conditions would improve if the government could "grind to powder, through whatever force it can command, the capitalist system in this country." It argued that capitalism was a major cause of "birth control and the degradation of women to unspeakable depth." *America* idealized the Middle Ages, for "when the craft guilds emerged triumphant, and under the guidance and inspiration of the Church developed the system of a wise distributive ownership, capitalism was doomed for centuries to come." It added that "under the leadership of the same Church the same glorious results could again be accomplished." The major remedy for the system was cooperative production both in industry and agriculture. "We firmly believe," one editorial stated, "that the cooperative movement is one of the most hopeful methods which practical men are offering as a solution of the present day evils."[21]

From 1923 to the end of the decade *America* underwent a significant change. In the first of these years, little appeared on social and economic questions. By 1927, however, it had clearly developed a new position advocating the necessity to live with capitalism tempered by collective bargaining. One article, "Looking for a Catholic Carnegie," enthusiastically applauded the existence of successful Catholic capitalists. In a fitting editorial at the end of the decade, *America* found that "as long as the present Capitalistic system—and we use the phrase in no malign sense—endures, alert, intelligent, and honest managers . . . is probably the best that can be hoped for." *America* conceded that the "system is not ideal, but we do not know what at present, can take its place."[22]

With the crash and the depression *America* shifted its policy. Although it continued to support capitalism, a change in tone is clearly noticeable. As late as 1929 an *America* commentator writing on industry's recognition of unions still assumed that enlightened American capitalists would "one day be glad to endorse the union." In contrast, three years later *America* reported that corporations created misery and suffering among workers and would thus one day bring on communism. If reason failed with these corporations then "suppression of the corporation or business by the state is not merely permissible, but the state's duty." In 1933 an *America* editorial used harsher words. "Capitalism, as we have known it in this country, has ever been a stupid and malicious giant. Even the Depression may have brought it no enlightenment." Capitalism, however, was not to be overturned. It should "be brought up to date, modernized and modified" another editorial pointed out, but the change advocated was to be slow; given the times, this was a conservative doctrine.[23]

Although *Catholic World*, a publication of the Paulist Fathers, had consistently supported liberal causes, its attitudes toward capitalism evolved similar to the more conservative *America*. In the 1930s, however, *Catholic World* presented a more caustic critique of capitalism. In the early 1920s *Catholic World* alternated articles advocating moderate reform with others implying need for more significant change. For example, a series of articles appeared in 1923 supporting minimum wage legislation, a standard progressive measure. In contrast, another more militant piece suggested complete abolition of the wage system. If this could not be achieved, the author, Father James F. Cronin, argued that at least workers should get a greater portion of the profits. More conservative articles also appeared suggesting that labor problems could be solved through individual self-improvement, by "efficient and self-disciplined workers." One essay argued that the worker would advance by "an enlightened and sustained enthusiasm . . . [and] a courage to undertake great enterprises." From the end of 1922 until the beginning of the depression, the *Catholic World* had virtually nothing to say on social questions. The only exception was an occasional article by Father John Ryan, usually on a subject such as temperance.[24]

In the 1930s the *Catholic World* reemerged as an aggressive publication. The capitalist system became its main target. "Capitalism is on the defensive . . . the rest of the world is socialist . . . the United States is a last conservative stronghold," it stated in 1933. It pictured the New Deal as not saving capitalism but replacing it: "President Roosevelt is calling not for a New Capitalism but for a New Deal." During the early 1930s the *Catholic World* felt that the president would undoubtedly receive Catholic support for, "as the Church was not wedded to monarchism, she was also not wedded to capitalism." It associated capitalism with Protestantism: "competition is far more Protestant than Catholic in origin. Catholicism has in mind the welfare of all." "Calvinism," the *Catholic World* pointed out, "in particular might be defined as the religion of 'rugged individualism,' the sort of thing now reprobated and due to be abolished." At the end of the decade an attempt at a judicious summation of the proper attitude toward capitalism appeared in the *Catholic World*. The author concluded, *"a Catholic must favor some public or community ownership* of various forms of property."[25]

Likewise *Catholic Mind* developed a similar approach. A small weekly magazine, it published sermons and speeches, and reprinted complete articles first appearing elsewhere. Very few articles questioning the nature of the capitalist system appeared during the entire 1920s; those that did seemed rather mild. One such rare piece advocated government controls on competition, but the author prefaced his proposal with remarks that "competition in itself is not an evil. It is rather that which gives the spice to a man's life and a fillip to energies that require to be stimulated."[26]

By the mid-1930s articles concerned with social and economic questions changed markedly in both tone and number. "Bourgeoisism is a mark of American society," and the *Catholic Mind* did not mean this in the ameliorative sense, for "the bourgeois spirit is perhaps the fundamental, anti-Christian thing... The Catholic social action movement is at root a campaign to shake off the bourgeois cloak." Ignatius Cox, a Jesuit priest, used a similar approach in a series of articles appearing in *Catholic Mind*. He found that Catholics had been "so unconsciously the victims of the perverted Capitalist ideals in which all of us have been brought up that they defend . . . the utter inequity and wrongfulness of the situation." In his last article of the series he spoke out even more strongly. "The economic situation of the masses today[i.e.] economic slavery," he blamed on the employers and on a system organized "not for men but for the madness of making money." Another author found that "our industrial system has proved a sad failure. It stands condemned as economically unsound." The article concluded that "Catholics should stand with the worker against the system." In 1937, after most of the New Deal gains had been achieved, *Catholic Mind* still felt "that economic and social reorganization is most necessary." It called for further changes to "safeguard the rights of the common man."[27]

Commonweal, *America*, *Catholic Mind*, and *Catholic World* all advocated change to deal with the problems of depression America. They differed in degree of dissatisfaction with the system, on the kind of reform desired, and in assessment of the New Deal. This variation was also true of many less well-known Catholic publications which illustrated similar discontent. Of these *Catholic Action* and other publications of the National Catholic Welfare Conference, *New World*, *Michigan Catholic*, *Pittsburgh Catholic*, *Register*, *Detroit Wage Earner*, New York's *Labor Leader*, *The Catholic Worker*, *Social Justice*, and, at times, the *Catholic Digest* frequently and adamantly criticized the capitalist system. Some of these journals will be examined later when the institutions they represented are studied in detail.

Most prestigious periodicals, the church's intellectual and journalistic spokesmen, and the clerical hierarchy responded to the sudden collapse of prosperity with condemnation of the system they had wholeheartedly supported a decade before. They were hardly unique in so reacting to economic changes, but in that change lies the importance of the response of Catholic spokesmen. Regardless of previous encyclicals or theological nuances, the Catholic leadership responded to the effects of the business cycle in the same general manner as numerous other American institutions. To be sure, the Catholics utilized theological references to support and rationalize the change in viewpoint between the two decades, but, curiously, the change followed the most prevalent trends of American social thought. Secondly, neither prelates nor press responded as part of a Catholic monolith to direction from above. They similarly, but not uniformly, reacted to social needs created by economic blight.

The church leadership, however, may have had one point of view and the local parish priest another. Often a conservative, the priest would likely have more influence over his parishioners than the remote, national clerical reformer. Motivated by fear of communism, many local priests suspected any questioning of the system. In other instances parish priests and conservative bishops simply neglected promotion of Catholic social criticism, discouraged laity from engaging in social action, and attacked industrial unions as communist dominated. Local diocesan newspapers—weeklies and monthlies—also largely remained wedded to the system. Most important, average Catholics read neither journals such as *Commonweal* nor social critics such as Virgil Michel.

Yet workers had some access to Catholic criticism of society. Millions heard Charles Coughlin's radio sermons. Although his message changed over the years, during his early prominence—when Coughlin's following was largest—he took a vehemently anticapitalist posture. Undoubtedly some parish priests leveled their own criticism at the system and fostered views of liberal church leaders. Unlike the Progressive Era, when middle-class social critics aimed many of their barbs at the political institutions of the immigrant poor, critics of capitalism did not threaten those impoverished by depression. Irrespective of local clerical attitudes, Catholic laborers joined CIO unions whether communists dominated them or not and supported seemingly sweeping reforms of the decade through their votes for Roosevelt. Catholic labor did not have to hear an official message of social reform or leadership questioning capitalistic efficacy, for many unemployed workers raised such queries independently.

Whatever the reaction of the laity, Catholic leaders called for social change. Different Catholic institutions issued their own programs, some radical left, some far right, and some moderate reformist. Some organizations attempted to enlist the support of the workers, while others hoped to affect all American Catholics. Few working-class laymen knew of the Social Action Department of the National Catholic Welfare Conference or of its director, the economist, theologian, and social critic, Father John Ryan, but this ignorance did not prevent the conference from doing effective work. Ryan, later called "Right Reverend New Dealer," combined progressive and New Deal secular reform with Catholic social ethics. The most noted reformer in the church, Ryan set the stage for official Catholic response to the Great Depression.

CHAPTER THREE

Social Action and the
National Catholic Welfare Conference,
1920–1940

In the 1930s new Catholic institutions emerged and old ones modified their outlook and programs in response to the depression. The Social Action Department (SAD) of the National Catholic Welfare Conference (NCWC) evolved slowly in the 1920s, but in the next decade added many new activities; thus to a degree it evolved like other Catholic institutions. Yet in comparison the SAD reacted least to the depression, because the department had already fostered reforms during the more conservative 1920s. This apparent untimely reformist outlook resulted from several factors. The department's director, John Ryan, was a leading progressive thinker. Secondly, the NCWC established the department with progressive commitments and a like-minded staff to carry out its goals. The department's organizational apparatus and official purpose gave it enough impetus to function effectually in a conservative climate. Finally, numerous other social welfare institutions continued functioning within the spirit of progressive reform. The department and Ryan himself developed contacts and occasionally carried out joint activities with these welfare agencies—both secular and religious. In closely associating with non-Catholic welfare organizations, Ryan and the SAD portrayed not only a reform commitment but also an ecumenical spirit uncommon at the time. Yet the department's parent institution, the NCWC, grew out of much more parochial Catholic needs.

In August 1917 the American hierarchy established a National Catholic War Council to coordinate Catholic contributions to the American effort during World War I. The NCWC survived the war and in 1922 was renamed the National Catholic Welfare Conference. It dealt with the whole realm of Catholic social interests and sponsored many lay and clerical institutions.[1]

A committee of bishops representing the hierarchy served as the NCWC board of directors, and bishops presided over separate departments within the conference. Initially, Peter J. Muldoon, Bishop of Rockford, took charge of the Social Action Department, which included a subdivision for labor. Peter Dietz helped prod the bishops into establishing the labor-oriented department. Although Dietz wanted to direct it, Muldoon appointed John A. Ryan to the post. Members of the NCWC executive board opposed Dietz because they believed his close AFL association thwarted the objectivity needed to deal with industrial problems, and that with his strong commitment to unionism he would neglect other Catholic supported labor programs, such as cooperatives and copartnerships.[2]

Muldoon thus turned not to labor-activist Dietz, but to Ryan, a progressive social theorist and already the major figure in contemporary American Catholic social thought. The choice of Ryan virtually guaranteed that the SAD would follow progressive lines. The department fulfilled this expectation and in doing so served as one of the many bridges connecting the Progressive Era with the New Deal. The nature of the NCWC, however, severely limited what it could accomplish. Although its administrative board made up of leading prelates had considerable prestige and its announcements seemingly represented the voice of the hierarchy, the board could only act in an advisory manner. The authority of individual bishops within their dioceses remained intact, and could not be overridden by the NCWC. In fact, the bishops did not organize the NCWC as an action agency. It had neither an executive to implement, nor a legislature to make, any decisions. In contrast its Social Action Department operated with more flexibility than the conference as a whole. Although the department emphasized educational work, functioning as a clearing house for distribution of Catholic thought on social and industrial relations, it also became heavily involved in areas such as labor mediation, immigrant aid, and social welfare.[3]

The executive board divided functions of the SAD during most of the 1920s between its Industrial Relations Department, administered by Ryan, and the Citizenship and Social Service Division, headed by John A. Lapp. In 1928 the NCWC combined the two sections under Ryan's direction, and he became the main influence in the Social Action Department for almost twenty years. The SAD did not simply echo Ryan's views. Disagreements arose within the department. At times organs of the department presented the different emphasis of Ryan's assistant, R. A. McGowan. In other instances, opinions of the bishops resulted in a moderating influence on the SAD and on Ryan himself. John Ryan, however, remained the paramount figure in the organization, and his role in great part reflected his own intellectual development.

John Ryan grew up in rural Minnesota. His father, a member of the Northwest Farmer's Alliance—the parent to Populism—subscribed to the *Irish World and Liberator*, which held radical views on land tenure. As a boy John Ryan admired Henry George and populist Ignatius Donnelly. He also developed theological concerns, but his decision to become a priest came after he read *Rerum Novarum*. Influenced by Leo XIII, Ryan decided to spend his life advancing the social gospel.[4]

The young priest quickly developed scholarly interests concentrating on the relationship of theology and ethics to social and economic reality. The worker, as a major victim of society's inequities, particularly concerned him. In Ryan's works before World War I he applied Catholic standards of justice—basically reason, "natural law," and concern for the welfare of the individual—to economic and labor problems. Although before the Great Depression he particularly stressed the role of the individual, Ryan did not neglect society; he viewed it, however, only as it affected the individual. Society's goal should be the good life for the individual. The state should protect individual's rights and promote common good where it could not be achieved by voluntary association.[5]

Relying on *Rerum Novarum* for direction and authority in his first major work, *A Living Wage*, Ryan argued that the worker had a moral right to a respectable living. He called for minimum wages to insure economic justice for the individual. In the early pages of the work Ryan telescoped his thesis. "The laborer's claim to a Living Wage is a matter of a *right*. This right is personal, not merely social: that is to say, it belongs to the individual as [an] individual, and not as a member of society; it is the laborer's personal prerogative, not his share of the social good; and its primary end is the welfare of the laborer, not that of society . . . the right to a living wage is individual, natural and absolute."[6]

Ryan believed that the federal government should foster favorable labor reforms: public-supported employment agencies, social security against unemployment, sickness and old-age benefits, housing projects, and laws guaranteeing the right of labor to organize. He urged the worker to take the initiative in organizing unions to improve his condition. Unionism, however, he considered secondary to governmental responsibility to protect the individual. "Unionism will not by itself," Ryan argued, "obtain a Living Wage for all the underpaid." He nevertheless favored unions, particularly the industrial over the craft variety. Ryan wrote in *A Living Wage* that industrial unionism represented "a splendid opportunity for the workers to create a real brotherhood of labor in which the strong will help to bear the burdens of the weak." In 1910 he elaborately defended the labor movement in an article entitled "Moral Aspects of Labor Unions," prepared for the Catholic Encyclopedia. He presented unionism itself, strikes, boycotts, closed shop, and even featherbedding, as legitimate avenues improving the lot of labor. Ryan accepted such tactics since the rights of the worker to a living wage superseded the rights of capital. He argued that the employer was morally bound not to prevent the worker from achieving a living wage.[7]

In *Distributive Justice*, Ryan's second major work of the period, he moved from the worker to the economy as a whole. He accepted private property, both personal and real. His youthful reading of Henry George did not assert itself, although he felt that ownership of property was limited so that it did not violate the rights of either community or nonowners. Capital had a right to a fair share of the profits after labor received its due; this assumed fair competition. In fact, as a progressive, Ryan fell in the Brandeis camp, arguing for strong antitrust measures to keep corporate units competitive and small.[8]

The worker deserved a reasonable family income supported by minimum wages. Income over the minimum should be determined by productivity, ability, and the good of society. Strong unions would further ensure responsible labor scales. In 1914, two years before publication of *Distributive Justice* Ryan debated with Morris Hillquit of the Socialist party. At this time Ryan elevated the role of organized labor to a major avenue of economic fulfillment, although he deplored the narrow materialism of American craft unionists. Ryan also felt the unions often violated the rights of capital and the public. Thus his advocacy of unions in *Distributive Justice* remained restrained.[9]

To achieve distributive justice, that is, a fair share of the economic fruits and obligations to all society, Ryan turned to private associations, unions, and consumer and producer coooperatives. Government remained passive although it retained its minimum wage and antimonopoly function. Later he added profit sharing and copartnership between labor and management. Ryan condensed many of his ideas in an undelivered speech entitled "Social Reconstruction: A General Review of the Problems and a Survey of the Remedies." Father John O'Grady brought it to the attention of the bishops on the administrative committee of the NCWC. They made a few changes in wording and published it as their own pronouncement. Known as the "Bishops' program," it illustrated hierarchical acceptance of progressivism.[10]

In later years Ryan himself summarized the main points of the program as follows:

> "(1) Minimum wage legislation;
> (2) insurance against unemployment, sickness, invalidity, and old age;
> (3) a 16-year minimum age limit for working children;
> (4) the legal enforcement of the right of labor to organize;
> (5) continuation of the National War Labor Board;
> (6) a national employment service;
> (7) public housing for the working classes;
> (8) no general reduction of housing for the working classes;
> (9) no general reduction of wartime wages and a long-distance program for increasing them, not only for the benefit of labor, but in order to bring about general prosperity through a wide distribution of purchasing power among the masses;
> (10) prevention of excessive profits and incomes through a regulation of rates which would allow the owners of public utilities only a fair rate of return on their actual investment, and through progressive taxes on inheritance, incomes, and excess profits;
> (11) effective control of monopolies, even through government competition if that should prove necessary;
> (12) participation of labor in management and a wider distribution of ownership."

It was a truly progressive document. Ironically, the church hierarchy caught up with progressivism after the movement entered a relatively dormant period. Given the times (1919 on the eve of the Red Scare), the bishop's pronouncement seemed indeed radical to many. Ralph Easley, secretary of the moderate National Civic Federation, spoke for numerous employers when he accused the authors of being duped by "near Bolsheviks."[11]

In the 1920s, the first era of the SAD, Ryan's progressivism did not wane, although he supported organized labor more cautiously than before and felt the times unpropitious for the SAD's advocacy of advanced social change. Ryan, as an individual, continued to advocate higher wages, cooperative decision-making on the plant level, and profit- and stock-sharing plans as a prelude to eventual sharing of ownership. "Industry cannot function successfully," he still argued, "on the basis of the psychological and pecuniary antagonisms which are inherent in our system as it is now operated."[12]

Ryan continued to urge unions to transcend material goals traditionally desired by the AFL and to acquire a social vision. He wanted the AFL to support government measures to aid the worker, including legislation for which Ryan traditionally fought: the child labor amendment, government supervision of bituminous coal, government operation of the anthracite coal industries, and public ownership for Muscle Shoals. Dissatisfied with AFL responses, Ryan became more critical of organized labor than in previous years. "Labor unions should make an honest, sustained, and general effort," he said, "to abolish the practices which they have adopted and fostered for restriction of production." Some of these practices, particularly featherbedding, he declared, were dishonest and others were a violation of charity. A decade before Ryan had defended featherbedding as a protection of job rights which did not significantly restrict production. For the AFL leadership he had little regard, claiming they had "been neither adequate or effective." Although Ryan became more cautious in his support of organized labor he did not weaken his other reformist commitments.[13]

Ryan did not permit the Social Action Department to fully reflect his personal advanced progressivism. In the 1920s the department developed a more conservative stance than the Bishops' Program which, significantly, Catholics virtually ignored during these years. Ryan correctly explained the unwillingness of the SAD to support far-reaching economic changes. "The first obstacle confronting the department is the fact that neither the bishops, the priests, nor the laity are convinced that our industrial system should be reorganized in this radical fashion." Ryan realized that the climate of opinion in Catholic social action circles had changed, and that the Catholic leadership would no longer commit itself to significant social evolution. The department's weak reform stance, however, went deeper than general change in political attitudes. The SAD dissipated its energies in a propaganda campaign defending the Catholic school system, a prime target of nativist groups in the 1920s. Nativists attacked Catholicism by giving government greater powers to disband parochial schools. Thus most of Catholic officialdom supported a diminished government role as a desired principle. Yet many progressive changes implied a strengthening of government.[14]

In addition the SAD devoted considerable effort to immigrant problems. Fighting legal federal discrimination against Catholic migrants from east and south Europe left little energy or finances for reform programs and further weakened commitments to positive government. With the legal nuances of immigrant restriction still being clarified, the NCWC sought to moderate abuses before precedents became institutionalized. Major department concerns now involved defense of immigrants who the changing legislation of the period sometimes barred from entry. When government denied admission with dubious cause, the department often directed and financed appeals.[15]

In 1921 the NCWC established a Bureau of Immigration, under jurisdiction of the Social Action Department. Besides its legal responsibilities, the SAD bureau employed counsellors to assist immigrants at both ports of embarkation and arrival, and to aid them in reaching their American destination. The SAD also helped Americanize immigrants directly by publishing text materials and indirectly by advising local agencies, fraternal organizations, and parochial schools that conducted Americanization programs.[16]

Until 1928 John A. Lapp directed the Americanization program. The department sponsored Americanization schools, published pamphlets and educational materials, and coordinated local Catholic groups carrying out similar goals. According to historian Aaron Abell, Lapp himself equated Americanism with social justice, challenging the view that patriotism meant nationalism. Yet articles discussing the Americanization program in NCWC organs and declarations of local groups often had a nationalistic flavor reflecting the hysteria of the early 1920s. In carrying out the Americanization plan, for example, Joseph I. Breen writing for the NCWC pointed out that "emphasis is laid upon the imperative necessity of teaching loyalty, devotion and obedience to our government, to its institutions and its laws." In Gary, Indiana, eleven Catholic nationality groups were combined into a federation known as the "Loyal Americans." Each nationality subdivision held such titles as Loyal Polish Americans and the Loyal Italian Americans. The constitution of the federation stated: "we declare our undivided allegiance to the Constitution and Government of the United States and declare ourselves unilaterally opposed to any and all theories, principles and practices that are contrary to them." Standard texts used in Catholic Americanization courses stressed a simplistic patriotism at the cost of academic integrity.[17]

If the SAD did not work for major social change during the period, it did not completely neglect labor reform. Ryan was disappointed that he had to put aside more idealistic programs, but the SAD still produced significant services for the worker. It published books and pamphlets promulgating the church's views supporting labor organization. In one year it distributed 4,000 pamphlets to libraries. Department leaders wrote reformist articles in various periodicals, while Ryan and others from the department lectured on such topics as child welfare, labor relations, and credit unions. Department officials gave almost three hundred talks a year. To further the ends of industrial workers, the SAD conducted a weekly news conference on labor matters, often supporting such labor reforms as minimum wage legislation. The department also carried out social and economic surveys to aid dioceses in planning welfare programs for the Catholic working class. Finally, it took part in joint interreligious investigations of significant strikes, particularly in coal mining, textiles, and railroads, usually finding fault with capital.[18]

The department deplored the hostile action of government and courts toward unions and attacked "Red Scare" attempts to associate unionism with communism. Besides denouncing the post war open shop crusade, it urged the AFL to make greater claims on management. The department staff argued that the federation should not limit itself to wage increases but should demand a degree of managerial control, a portion of the profits, and partial ownership. Thus it intended to prod the AFL a bit to the left. Conversely, it supported the conservative AFL position that based wage increases on productivity. In this way, the SAD argued, a unity of interest between capital and labor could be achieved.[19]

Such unity of interest remained one of the prime objectives of Catholic social thought. In order to aid in its creation, the SAD sponsored, beginning in 1922, a number of conferences on industrial questions and labor problems. The SAD brought together capital, labor, and outside experts such as economists, to discuss industrial problems in relation to Catholic principles. Informal debate followed initial talks. The conferences came to no conclusions nor were votes ever taken. Major subjects of interest included wages, collective bargaining, the role of women in industry, and current forms of cooperation between labor and capital. The SAD sponsored a few such conferences in the 1920s. Until 1928 it held just one annual meeting but thereafter expanded to several regional meetings throughout the year.[20]

The Social Action Department in the 1920s failed to work vigorously for the demands of the Bishops' Program of 1919, but did carry out a mild progressive program in an era known largely for its conservative sentiments. In comparison to other Catholic institutions, the SAD appeared in the forefront of progressive activities. Catholic institutions of the 1920s were generally parochial in outlook. The National Conference of Catholic Women concentrated on founding respectable boarding houses and accommodations in private homes for Catholic working girls. The National Conference of Catholic Men planned many programs; few, however, moved beyond a planning stage. Social settlement work continued, but at the periphery of Catholic interests.[21]

With the depression and the change in public outlook the SAD took on new dimensions and Ryan himself underwent changes. More important, as a result of *Quadregesimo Anno,* which many in the Church considered a vindication of Ryan's ideas, his prestige considerably improved in American Catholic heirarchical circles. The SAD could reflect Ryan's reformism with greater emphasis and more telling effect.

Ryan believed that underconsumption and overproduction caused the Great Depression. "The fault lies," Ryan said in a typical letter, "in a bad distribution of purchasing power." His recovery program for the depression grew out of his understanding of its causes. In addressing the National Catholic Social Action Conference of 1937, Ryan outlined his recovery plan most clearly. He called for a three billion dollar public works program in addition to current expenditures. The federal government should finance this program with highly graduated income and inheritance taxes, thereby having a leveling effect on American society. Increased government spending would stimulate consumer purchasing power. "Those who say pump priming has done no good," declared Ryan, "are either lying deliberately or they are too foolish to be left at large." By the end of the decade Ryan had become a thorough Keynsian, advocating deficit financing of government programs.[22]

Ryan also supported legislation to establish a maximum thirty-hour work week. Upon its passage by the Senate, he wrote its sponsor, Senator Hugo Black, "I wish to congratulate you heartily on this astonishing achievement." Ryan argued that the thirty-hour week should be combined with a minimum wage law that would provide "at least $1500 annual income for wage earners."[23]

In supporting the Black bill he went beyond President Roosevelt, but generally Ryan wholeheartedly accepted New Deal programs. He supported the administration's farm policy, government curbs on excessive prices, reduction of interest rates paid by government agencies, greater distribution of ownership, and the National Recovery Administration (NRA), likening the latter to the social encyclicals. He also saw the NRA as the great practical hope for major economic change. After the Supreme

Court ruled the agency unconstitutional, Ryan wanted the NRA reestablished but without the inequities of the original experiment. Thus he demanded that labor be given more power within the NRA. Ryan then advocated a similar NRA for farmers and professionals, overseen by the federal government in order to keep things running smoothly. In addition he wanted little NRAs to fill the vacuum for intrastate industry. He later added to his program the federation of separate NRA economic units to coordinate with one another and with the whole community. Ryan visualized a system of government-directed NRAs planning the economy and coordinating private enterprise with legitimate labor needs. The NRA and similar agencies should regulate quantity of goods produced, prices, employment, wages, hours, training, social insurance, methods of work, capitalization, interest, profits, and credit.[24]

During the depression years Ryan changed his economic attitudes, responding to both the depression crisis and his own increased economic understanding. Government, important in his thought before the 1930s, was now given the primary role in economic reform; he concentrated on society, not on the individual. Virtues of competition and smallness he had stressed in his progressive years he reluctantly replaced by the necessity of regulation and planning. In a letter to a critic he wrote: "Like you, I prefer competition to bureaucracy as a regulator but I would add that I prefer governmental regulation to regulation by private economic despots. You say that you think we have never sufficiently tried out effective competition. I subscribe to that statement also." He added that "it is quite clear that competition and enforcement of antitrust laws provide no remedies in this enormous field."[25]

Like many on the economic left, Ryan assumed capitalism as it existed was doomed. To survive, the system needed vast reform. Of a private discussion with British socialist Harold H. Laski he wrote: "He was quite frank in declaring that he did not believe capitalism could survive. While I did not tell him so that evening, I agree with him that capitalism cannot continue without a radical modification such as that recommended by Pius XI in his Encyclical *Quadregesimo Anno*." He thus supported an expanded NRA and public operation of many basic industries. Ryan, nevertheless, denied that he had become a socialist. "I am not conscious of any changed attitude from the position that I took in my debate with Morris Hillquit. ... What I had to say about Socialism in "A Better Economic Order," is substantially what I have been saying for thirty years or more." However, by the mid-1930s, in all but theoretical issues, it had become very difficult to distinguish between Ryan and the reformist Social

Democratic Federation, except perhaps that Ryan in his understanding of *Quadregesimo Anno* was more millennial than this moderate socialist group.[26]

Ryan consorted with his allies on the secular left, but he felt uncomfortable in their company. In a series of letters between Ryan and William E. Bohn, director of the socialist Rand School of Social Science, Ryan indicated that on at least two occasions he accepted speaking invitations from the Rand School, but canceled them because of opposition from the local bishop. He also backed out of an obligation to speak at a gathering sponsored by the League for Industrial Democracy because, he said, a speech under such auspices "would bring upon me criticism, or at least cause misunderstanding." Though Ryan felt he could not serve on the executive committee of the League for Independent Action, he claimed, "I have the greatest sympathy with the objectives of the League."[27]

Although Ryan's attitude toward socialism did not officially change, he became a more consistent supporter of organized labor. Ryan favored unionism in the 1920s but remained cautious, often critical. This attitude resulted in part from the conservative nature of unionism during the decade. His attitudes toward existing unions, their effectiveness, and their need for economic leverage changed in the depression years. No longer ambivalent in his commitment, Ryan suggested to economist John B. Andrews in 1930 that "the worker needs the union in order to achieve something like equality in bargaining power with his employer," and from this he concluded that "the yellow dog contract is unreasonable" and "the closed shop may be reasonable and necessary."[28] Ryan also defended the sit-down strikes of the period although he disliked them for political and strategic reasons. He granted that they violated property rights, but argued they were not acts of confiscation or larceny, but attempts by strikers to prevent machinery from being operated by strike breakers. Thus, they acted the same as in picketing. He added, "owing to the dependence of the worker and his family upon his present job, his equitable claim therefore might sometimes justify the sit-down strike." He felt that since picketing often resulted in violence, the sit-down strike resulted in less evil, destroying neither persons nor property.[29]

This is not to say that Ryan unalterably opposed labor's use of physical coercion. He argued that workers had a right to use force against the unjust aggression of an employer who refused to pay a just wage or who forced his workers to toil under dangerous conditions. "I content myself with the statement," he wrote, "that employees, as such, have certain natural rights and that they may be defended by 'coercion'."[30]

In the conflict between the conservative AFL and the young, aggressive CIO, Ryan presented himself as officially neutral, although he clearly supported the cause of industrial unionism—a position he traditionally held. Ryan counted among his firends CIO leaders John Brophy and Philip Murray and defended David Dubinsky and Sidney Hillman against red baiters. At the end of the decade, in a sermon delivered before the Association of Catholic Trade Unionists, he stated that this organization should encourage "all legitimate efforts to organize the unorganized, particularly the weakest and lowest-paid groups. The effective form of organization in this field seems to be the industrial rather than the craft union." Although the labor movement had room for both, "undoubtedly, the ideal form would be industrial, inasmuch as it exemplifies the cooperation of the strong with the weak." A letter written for Ryan by his assistant, R. A. McGowan, and intended to represent Ryan's views, noted, "As to industrial unionism, it seems a far better system for mass production workers in factories and for the unskilled and semi-skilled in general. . . . the CIO is making a big drive for organization of unorganized, particularly in the mass production industries it is doing a wonderful job."

In addition, Ryan continued his support for a constitutional amendment limiting child labor. In a letter on the subject, Ryan affirmed "I still hold to the conviction of nine years ago, that the Child Labor Amendment should be ratified by the states and become a part of the Federal Constitution. . . . The necessity for the Amendment is greater now than it was at that earlier time." He also supported a limit on labor injunctions, the Social Security Act, and the Wagner Act.[31]

Ryan served on numerous worker-oriented, prolabor organizations. He was vice-president of National Unemployment League and in frequent communication with its president. He was also a vice-president of the American Association for Labor Legislation, member of the "Citizens Committee to Aid in the Struggle of the Employees of the *Wisconsin News* against Hearst," a vice-president of the American Association for Social Security, and held several federal government labor advisory positions both for NRA and the U.S. Employment Service. Ryan also helped the CIO in its conflict with Mayor Frank Hague of Jersey City, who stated that Catholics could not belong to the "Communist" unions and attempted to keep CIO organizers from operating in Jersey City. Ryan, along with other leading clerics, attacked Hague's persecution of CIO organizers and false accusations against the federation. Thus, like his evolution in economic thought, from concentration on the individual to society and from advocation of competition to controls and planning, he evolved on the labor question from ambivalence and mild criticism to wholehearted support of the labor movement, especially the CIO.[32]

The SAD changed as well during these critical years, but because it functioned as an instrument of the hierarchy, it evolved with greater subtlety than did Ryan himself. In shaking off its lethargy of the previous decade, it reflected Ryan's new attitudes and concerns by shifting emphasis and expanding programs. It did not, however, change direction, but merely expanded the progressive tendencies surviving from the 1920s and adopted new programs pertinent to a new set of social and economic circumstances. The department attempted to aid the worker indirectly through its publications and official statements on strikes, and by bringing labor and capital together to discuss their mutual problems in the light of Catholic social doctrine. It gave direct aid through the training of labor priests and by being represented at labor rallies. In addition the NCWC continued its aid to immigrants.

Most of the publications released by the SAD dealt with the labor encyclicals and the relation of Catholic social thought to the plight of the worker. It dealt in depth with such subjects as unemployment and the role of women in industry. The SAD told women to return to the home, a traditional Catholic viewpoint. This position had great influence during these years since American views of women changed as a result of the depression. In its studies on unemployment, the SAD urged employers to increase wages, reduce hours, and accept collective bargaining with bona fide unions. Following Ryan, the department supported a major public works program and unemployment insurance. Along with representatives from Protestant and Jewish circles, SAD issued joint statements supporting NRA, organized labor, individual unions in specific strikes, the Wagner Act, higher income taxes in upper income brackets, unification of the AFL and CIO, a heavier public works program, a shorter work week, social insurance, and cooperative economic planning.[33]

In the department's attempt to indirectly influence labor relations, it continued the Catholic Conference On Industrial Problems (CCIP) begun in the 1920s. The CCIP held many more conferences, attendance increased considerably, and the content of the meetings changed markedly from the 1920s. The change reflected new concerns growing out of depression America. Speakers concentrated on causes of the economic crisis, need for higher wages and lower unemployment, and efficiency and methods of relief measures. In the early 1930s meetings also stressed charity, but by the middle of the decade, as the inadequacy of philanthropic institutions became obvious, themes shifted to government responsibility for unemployment. Many of the talks indicated the reaction to the depression as speakers supported unions and stressed moral and practical defects of the economic system, emphasizing that capitalism must be reformed through economic planning.

If the CCIP indicated the department's commitment to discussion and indirect change, its clerical labor schools illustrated the department's practical and more immediate response to the depression. The SAD hoped to improve the condition of the worker by providing clerical leadership in local labor causes. It thus trained priests for labor roles by giving occasional classes and, more importantly, by holding several intensive labor institutes designed to educate clerics. Each institute lasted about one summer month and had several purposes: to study the labor encyclicals, understand labor conditions, and review the principles and methods of clerical participation to affect economic life. Labor schools and often individual bishops encouraged labor trained priests to engage in industrial relations work. The urging seemed hardly necessary since they attended these schools for social action training. In the typical summer of 1937, the SAD operated three schools—one in Toledo with fifty priests enrolled, one in San Francisco where thirty attended, and one in Milwaukee with 122 students. The department claimed that in the latter school only space limitation kept enrollment from growing considerably.[34]

The NCWC was most directly involved with the worker through its immigration bureau. In 1937, for example, the bureau assisted 12,348 immigrants in legal action against the United States government. Of 100,000 immigrants interviewed with legal problems, 1,986 were referred to other Catholic agencies for additional attention. A number of the immigrants had been ordered to leave the country. Of the cases that appealed deportation rulings, the SAD won 209 on behalf of the immigrants and lost only eight. This ratio remained consistent throughout the period.[35]

Social Catholicism did not lie totally dormant during the 1920s. With the Social Action Department and its progressive director John Ryan, it inched forward in its attempt to grapple with the problem of industrial reality. With the advent of the depression, and especially after the publication of *Quadregesimo Anno* had added to Ryan's prestige, his prolabor statements took on greater importance. Whether SAD policy or not, they were taken as such, thus giving his declarations the aura of hierarchal approval. When liberal priests spoke before audiences of workers in support of the CIO and denounced accusations that the young federation was communist-dominated, they quoted John Ryan. In the 1930s, Ryan no longer appeared ambivalent about organized labor. He wholeheartedly supported the necessity of an effective labor movement, favored the CIO, and endorsed those New Deal reforms aiding the worker. SAD publications espoused many of his views, as did innumerable other Catholic publications. While Ryan never had the popular appeal of Charles E. Coughlin, to the average parish priest Ryan remained an authoritative voice. His ideas, once considered radical but now legitimatized by Pius XI, were accepted well beyond Ryan's lifetime.

During the depression SAD moved forward into new programs and expanded old ones. Its publications criticized capitalism and supported economic planning. The department expanded the number of industrial conferences in which speakers viewed the system with increasing harshness. It established schools to train labor priests for agitation among industrial workers, an undertaking the department would not have considered in the 1920s. On the whole, however, the SAD illustrated less significant discontinuity with the past than other Catholic social institutions. Most of its programs originated before the depression and merely expanded in response to new needs. Differences existed between the decades; the SAD was less active and had a more conservative stance in the previous decade. The depression enabled Ryan to bring the SAD out of its relative dormancy, but it nevertheless remained a reformist organization and an organ of the Catholic establishment. It took dissident priests and creative laymen to organize a Catholic radical response to the depression.

CHAPTER   FOUR

The Catholic Worker Movement

Some Catholics reacted to economic dislocation by completely rejecting the political and economic system. Peter Maurin and Dorothy Day
stood among those advocating drastic and immediate revision of American
society. These leaders of the Catholic Worker Movement attracted young
idealistic intellectuals and workers. Many of the movement's following
accepted the Catholic Worker ideology, while some used the movement as
an initial training ground, an introduction to other areas of Catholic social
action involvement. Its alumni dispersed among numerous Catholic institutions. Thus the Catholic Worker Movement—the first significant American
Catholic radicalism—had considerable effect on the style, focus, techniques, ideology, and personnel of more moderate Catholic reformism in
the 1930s.

The Catholic Worker Movement considered itself radical, even anarchist, and attempted to combine Catholic reform thought with communitarian perfectionism. The movement had neither an obvious doctrine nor a
party line to clarify its point of view. Its total ideology consisted of a
dualism, the basic philosophy of Peter Maurin and its interpretation and
the sometimes conflicting ideas of Dorothy Day. The movement's overall
ideology synthesized the strands of thought of its two founders.

The roots of the dualism rested in the ideas and intellectual heritage of
Peter Maurin and Dorothy Day. In 1893 Maurin, at the age of sixteen, left
his French agricultural village and became a novice in the Order of the De
la Salle Brothers. After completing his education, Maurin taught grade

school as a brother; after ten years he left the order. This decision reflected an intellectual crisis that climaxed for Maurin in 1899, a year he spent almost entirely in the army.[1] "From this time on," one of his brothers stated, "he became interested in politics and held very advanced ideas on social organization and on pacifism, ideas common today but at that time seemingly subversive of the established Order." Maurin's social concern led him to an active role in the period's ferment. He became politically involved in the strife between the Republic of France and the Roman Catholic Church by joining the Sillon Movement, "the seminal Christian democratic movement in contemporary France," as one historian put it.[2]

The Sillon intended to accommodate the Republic with the traditionally royalist church by stimulating popular Catholic support for democracy. Theoretically, with Catholicism linked to the Republic, France would become a truly Christian democracy. The Sillon attempted to affect the masses through institutes, public meetings, labor unions, and cooperatives. It also established hospices or rest homes to spiritually and physically renew the poor and unemployed. Although the Sillon fostered social reform and political democracy, it had an anarchistic organizational structure. It held no elections and had no specific hierarchy or chosen leadership, but Marc Sangnier emerged the acknowledged leader. Likewise, it lacked an organized membership; a spiritual cohesion existed. The membership stayed together primarily through friendship and devotion. (Although the Sillon evolved, this description coincides with its earlier years, the period in which it influenced Peter Maurin.) When from 1905 to 1906 the Sillon became more political and began to lose church support, Maurin left the movement. In his future social concerns, however, he borrowed much from the Sillon.[3]

In 1909 Maurin emigrated to Canada; he traveled in North America for fifteen years while supporting himself as an unskilled laborer. By 1924 he no longer attended mass and had been out of the church about ten years. he stated years later that at this time anarchist writers influenced him, especially Peter Kropotkin.[4]

In 1925, Maurin's life again took another turn. He had stopped traveling and was deriving a good income from teaching French when he underwent, according to his biographer Arthur Sheehan, a religious experience. Although Maurin did not mention it in his writings, he suddenly and drastically changed his way of life. Maurin stopped charging for his French lessons and let his students pay what they believed the lessons were worth. Two years later he appeared in New York City's Union

Square, "an agitator for Christ." In 1933, Maurin contacted Dorothy Day and began the Catholic Worker Movement.[5]

Dorothy Day had a conventional American Protestant background. Her parents baptized her an Episcopalian, but her family remained little more than nominal church members. Nevertheless, Day concerned herself with religion even as a child, although she left her church while in college. While attending the University of Illinois from 1914–1916 she became a socialist. Of this period Day wrote, "Workers of the world unite, you have nothing to lose but your chains seemed to me a most stirring battle cry." She believed that "religion would only impede my work," and was indeed "an opiate of the people." When her family moved to New York City, she went with them, leaving the university. Shortly thereafter, in the fall of 1916, she found a job on the socialist daily newspaper, the *New York Call*. At this time, at the age of eighteen, her loyalty wavered between socialism, syndicalism, and anarchism. "When I read Tolstoy," she wrote, "I was an anarchist. My allegiance to the *Call* kept me a socialist, although a left-wing one, and my Americanism inclined me toward the IWW movement." She worked for the *Call* through the winter of 1917, also engaging in the pre-World War I peace movement. Day then left the newspaper to work for the Anti-Conscription League, although she did not stay long since the *Masses*, a radical journal, offered her a job as assistant editor. When the *Masses* closed she wrote for its successor, the *Liberator*.[6]

While involved in these leftist adventures, Miss Day nevertheless found herself gradually attracted to the Catholic Church. By 1917, although still not a convert to Catholicism, she attended mass regularly. From 1919 until her conversion to Catholicism in 1927 she associated less with the radical wing of the labor movement than with the bourgeois, left-leaning intellectuals, the so-called bohemians of the period. At the same time, she moved closer to the Catholic Church. In 1925, she gave birth to a girl; her decision to have her child baptized brought Day's marriage to an end because her common-law husband, an anarchist, objected vehemently to any participation in organized religion. In December 1927, Dorothy Day became a Catholic herself. As she moved toward Catholicism she remained in contact with her leftist friends. In fact, the *Masses* printed a story she wrote at the time of the birth of her child. It received international circulation through republication in similar radical journals.

Unlike most Catholics, and especially in contrast to most leftists who converted to Catholicism, Dorothy Day's attitude toward left-wing radicals and radicalism continued to be sympathetic. She did not, however, feel herself part of the left labor movement although she tried to maintain contact with it through her journalism. Upon Day's return from the 1933 Washington demonstration of the unemployed, which she covered for *Commonweal*, Day stated that she prayed for a role for herself, as a Catholic, in the labor movement. A short time later Peter Maurin visited her and together they founded the Catholic Worker Movement.

Her meeting with Maurin changed Dorothy Day's life. "Five years after I became a Catholic," she wrote, "I met Peter Maurin. He was my master and I was his disciple; he gave me 'a way of life and instruction.' " Dorothy Day had a significant influence on the philosophy of the Catholic Worker Movement, but the basic ideas and program out of which the movement grew were those of Peter Maurin.[7]

What did Peter Maurin find wrong with existing society? Why did he become an agitator for radical change? Maurin, who often quoted the French Catholic thinker Leon Bloy on the subject, considered bourgeois capitalist culture essentially anti-Christian. The fundamental problem, Maurin felt, was ethical. Man did not love man, but used him, as material realities preempted spiritual ones. Maurin argued that Americans rationalized this spiritual void as rugged individualism. The entire mentality of the capitalist class system corrupted man. Lack of love did not result in capitalism, but rather capitalism fostered this lack of love. The immoral economic system brought to the surface man's worst potentials. Maurin stated this theme in one of his melodic free verses which he called "Easy Essays":

> "Business say
> That because everyone is selfish
> business must therefore
> be based on selfishness.
> But when business is based on selfishness
> everybody is busy becoming more selfish.
> And when everybody is busy
> becoming more selfish,
> we have classes and clashes."[8]

The capitalist system, Maurin argued, rested on the Protestant ethic and Calvin's endorsement of usury. With acceptance of the Reformation, capitalism could grow to its current evil. Usury continued as a contemporary phenomenon as well, since interest remained a crucial aspect of the capitalist system. Maurin, however, saw the overt evil of capitalism in ramifications of industrialism. The machine not only brought unemployment and underconsumption but also degraded man. It deprived him of satisfaction in work, the creative labor of craftmanship. The machine prevented man from becoming a whole and holy being. The effects of the machine culminated in the depression; in this economic collapse Maurin saw great potential.[9]

He believed that the depression provided a turning point in history, for capitalist contradictions would destroy the system. Capitalism faced destruction, because of the "weight of its own sins," and economically by underconsumption. The system headed for crises and revolution. Welfare capitalism, what Maurin called "the servile state," borrowing the term from Hilaire Belloc, did not provide the answer. Maurin wanted:

> "to make it my business
> to put all business
> out of business,
> including the State business,
> which is big business."[10]

Maurin often argued that the welfare state of the liberal would merely reinforce shoddy capitalism. Only a complete revolution could make crucial changes, yet he wanted a peaceful revolution, a communitarian revolution, and a "Green Revolution." What does Peter Maurin's revolution entail? Before discussing his program it is first necessary to confront Maurin's underlying assumptions. Maurin, however, left no systematic presentation; his ideas must be reordered to be discussed, for Maurin was an agitator, not a consistent philosopher or theologian. Furthermore, his ideas must be gleaned from his "Easy Essays," two of which have been cited above. In these Maurin presented his views through melodic free verse. He not only consciously oversimplified, but freely borrowed ideas if they coincided with his own. Finally, since segments of Maurin's works sometimes vary in emphasis, the question becomes not only what did he really mean, but how did his followers understand and interpret his ideas?[11]

Maurin believed that love united man through work, God, and community; that "to do unto others as others would want you to do unto them" perhaps simplified but explained Christian love. Love emerged as the pivotal aspect of his philosophy. Maurin and Day visualized love as the means of achieving true human and spiritual fellowship. "Love and ever more love," Dorothy Day wrote, "is the only solution to every problem that comes up. If we love each other enough, we will bear with each other's faults and burdens. If we love enough, we are going to light that fire in the hearts of others." But Day did not visualize a sentimental love. To Maurin, Day, and the movement, a life of active love meant difficulty and sacrifice, "a harsh and dreadful thing," as Dostoevsky put it in *The Brothers Karamazov*—a work that particularly influenced the movement's founders.[12]

Love as Maurin understood it implied poverty, a willingness to relinquish material possessions to those more needy. Therefore, the ideal Christian life consisted of voluntary poverty, exemplified by Saint Francis of Asissi. "First of all," Dorothy Day quoted Maurin as saying, "One must give up life to save it. Voluntary poverty is essential. . . . To live poor, to start poor, to make beginnings even with meager means at hand, this is to get 'Green Revolution' underway." Acceptance of voluntary poverty also resulted in greater freedom for the individual. Leon Bloy had drawn the same conclusions as had Dorothy Day. She believed that once people refuse "to worry about what kind of house we are living in . . . we have time, which is priceless, to remember that we are our brother's keeper." Neither Maurin nor Day wrote often of their voluntary poverty, but they and their followers accepted it as their way of life. Twenty years after the movement began Miss Day wrote: "I condemn poverty and I advocate it. . . . it is a social phenomenon and a personal matter. Poverty is an illusive thing, and a paradoxical one." In the same work she clarified this statement by differentiating between inflicted poverty and voluntary poverty, "between the victims and the champions of poverty." "By poverty," Day pointed out, "we do not mean destitution. . . . To us, voluntary poverty has been a mine of wealth and wisdom; a means to an end."[13]

Maurin's understanding of Christian love also led him to accept a pacifist viewpoint. He did not write a great deal on the subject but the movement's interpretation of his position can be seen through its publication, the *Catholic Worker*. It presented two different positions; both involved Roman Catholic theory of justice, which included the criterion of the individual's response to war. Catholic social ethics did not rely on a literal interpretation of the New Testament; the Sermon on the Mount, for example, was regarded as a "counsel of perfection." Social ethics grew out of natural law, and to St. Thomas Aquinas, nature, the basis for a rational grasp of eternal law, grew out of divine reason. A universal standard of conduct could not be equated with nonreasoning love, but sprang from divine reason of the law-giver, and was known to man through reason.

Thus love alone was insufficient for ethical decisions. Human reason was required to decide such questions on the basis of natural law and the peculiar circumstances at any given time.[14]

The *Catholic Worker* usually argued that no war, given conditions of modern destructive techniques, could be a just war. This was set forth most cogently in the 1930s by Right Reverend George Barry O'Toole, a member of the philosophy department of Catholic University of America. During the depression numerous articles deploring the international drift toward war also fostered this view. The *Catholic Worker* also gave its support to pacifists who argued that the individual had a right to follow councils of perfection such as the Sermon on the Mount. This view, however, received considerably less space in publications. As the European conflict polarized the American people, the *Catholic Worker* argued against emotional nationalistic and militaristic responses. Day declared herself neutral in the Spanish Civil War, but primarily found fault with Franco and his fascist supporters. In addition the *Worker* opposed the draft, urged its readers to become conscientious objectors, and reminded them that individuals have a personal responsiblity for whatever actions they might take—that a government law does not override faith and morality. Day and others from the movement went to Washington and testified against the proposed draft before a congressional committee. When Congress passed a conscription act, she encouraged the establishment of an organization of Catholic conscientious objectors. Although Maurin apparently accepted pacifism early in his life, Day spearheaded its thrust in the movement.[15]

Maurin's literal pacifism and daily acceptance of poverty affirmed his philosophy that love constituted a way of life, not just an abstract concept. He believed that love of God was personal and manifested in man's relation to man. The individual himself found God through love of his brothers. Thus Maurin wanted people to take an activist role. Man should do good personally, not indirectly; it might be laudable to contribute to a home for the poor, but that was not enough. Maurin believed that man must open his own home to the poor. Personalism provided the key to the meaning in life. In 1933 Maurin wrote:

> "The Communitarian Revolution
> is basically
> a personal revolution
> It starts with I,
> not with they."

The following "Easy Essay" typifies his approach:

> "To be our brother's keeper
> is what God wants us to do.
> To feed the hungry
> at a personal sacrifice
> is what God wants us to do.
> To clothe the naked
> at a personal sacrifice
> is what God wants us to do.
> To shelter the homeless
> at a personal sacrifice
> is what God wants us to do.
> To instruct the ignorant
> at a personal sacrifice
> is what God wants us to do.
> To serve man for God's sake
> is what God wants us to do."[16]

Maurin called his theology a "personalist philosophy," and he thought of his views as a part of the personalist movement in theology. A number of thinkers with a personalist approach contributed to Maurin's thought. Maurin, and others in the movement, had direct and fruitful contact with both French philosopher Jacques Maritain and American personalist theologian Paul Hanley Furfey, as well as considerable intellectual contact with Nikolai Berdyaev, the Russian émigré philosopher. Many in the movement were influenced by the personalist aspects of Dostoevsky. Personalist thought became formalized in 1932 with the founding of the French journal *Esprit*. It was *Esprit* and Emmanuel Mounier, the leading French personalist, that Maurin mentioned most in his essays of the 1930s—as early as 1933 when the *Catholic Worker* began publishing. Furthermore, Maurin's style of writing could very well have been patterned after Charles Peguy, the intellectual father of Mounier who also used simple melodic free verse. More important, Maurin introduced Mounier's *Personalist Manifesto* to the United States by successfully finding it a translator and publisher. In 1936, Maurin wrote that *Esprit* expounded his communitarian principles.[17]

Personalism considered personality central and understood reality in personal terms. Emmanuel Mounier applied the term "to any doctrine or any civilization that affirms the primacy of the human person over material necessities." In the spiritual realm Mounier saw every person connected in "a unity of mankind" in both space and time. Thus society consisted of spiritual subjects, each of whom had an end in itself and in the whole at the same time. With the acceptance of this personalist spirit as the avenue of Christian love, the common unity of man in the mystical body of Christ was fulfilled, to Maurin, in the practical sense of a conscious existence. The very act of being Catholic included one in the mystical body; but by accepting Maurin's philosophy one lived this existence every day, consciously, in the secular world, not only in the mystical one. Through the individual acceptance of personalism, man could find community. As Day put it, "The living together, working together, sharing together, loving God and loving our brother, and living close to him in community so we can show our love for him."[18]

Spiritual communitarianism implied a secular communitarianism, a desire to live together and work together. Maurin's philosophy of work attempted to apply his theology to the reality of the proletariat and everyday life. As he relied primarily on French theologians for his philosophy of personalism, he once again turned to French theologians for part of his philosophy of work—this time to Etienne Borne and François Henry.

It is true, Maurin argued, that the Fall resulted in the necessity of physical work, but work need not be all pain and drudgery. It could be creative. Day quoted Maurin as stating "God made us in his image and likeness. Therefore we are creators. . . . We became creators by our responsible acts, whether in bringing forth children, or producing food, furniture or clothing." Thus man in his work shares in the joy of creation. Work as the creation of social utility takes upon itself a social value. To work is to do good for others—to love. Work, Borne said, is an experience in brotherhood. Work unites man with man. Ade Bethune, a movement spokesman and artist for the *Catholic Worker* during the depression, wrote that work is for service of man and, therefore, for the service of God. "In the drudgery of his daily tasks he can see the service that united man to man. Work itself is prayer. Work is a gift, a holy sacrifice, offered gladly, in spite of suffering and pain, for the joy of building up brotherhood into the measure of the perfect man."[19]

Work, however, did not mean the assembly lines of a machine culture; it meant the creativity of skilled artisans, or the satisfying toil of the productive farmers. Maurin romanticized manual labor and considered the machine an evil. Work could be a creative act, but only if personal; work could be personal only if creative. The assembly line denied the joy of creativity. Contemporary labor, thus, did not constitute work; neither creative nor a free gift to mankind, it could be bought like a commodity and meant nothing to the worker but a form of subsistence. Maurin called this not work but slavery. Bethune wrote: "Slavery, we held, must be abolished. It is slavery that degrades man not work." Work, in being a personal manifestation of love, tied each person through its social value to each other person. Maurin accepted the Borne and Henry conclusion that work established the bond between the individual, society and the universe—the mortar of the community.[20]

French thought strongly influenced Maurin's philosophy. He attempted to graft the personalism of Mounier to the philosophy of work of Borne and Henry, using the Franciscan concept of love to overcome conflict between personal freedom and duty to the community. The individual who loves as a Christian contributes to mankind on a personal basis, actually carries out activities for other particular individuals at a personal sacrifice. To love is also to desire to work, for work is to create social value and, therefore, to do good. To consciously do good in work is to love, but the love is a love of all, a communal love.

In order for mass man to choose this philosophy of love and to more easily choose good rather than evil, society must be radically changed, for the very nature of capitalism socialized man to act in material self-interest rather than in love of others. Maurin's program attempted to cope with contemporary reality and, at the same time, to develop a new Christian society founded on his basic philosophy.

The Catholic Worker program had three interrelated parts: activities in the stage before societal change, tactics to bring about change, and the creation of a utopia. The movement's program reflected influences of both the Sillon and Dorothy Day. Maurin's use of popular institutes, public meetings, hospices and, in general, the movement's anarchistic style—its lack of organization—reflected the Sillon. Day brought an urban industrial experience into the Catholic Worker Movement ideology. The use of picketing and other measures in aiding organized labor and the general support of the New Deal became part of the movement's rhetoric. If Day's immediate influence suggested contemporary American reality, the ideological influence of Russian anarchist Peter Kropotkin conjured up an agrarian communalist ideal. Although Maurin's program, like those of Hilaire Belloc and Eric Gill, rested on medieval Catholicism placed in the idealized framework of nineteenth-century romanticism, he combined it with the anarcho-communalism of Kropotkin.

Maurin visualized his utopia as a communal, decentralized back-to-the-land movement. Thus, he called his revolution a "Green Revolution." Ideally, he hoped everyone would return to the land and form self-supporting communes. Although the means of production would be communal, Maurin planned a continuation of private property. He wanted each family to own a home and garden; however, economic capital, land, and tools would be held in common. Maurin intended that communes be primarily agricultural; in fact, the system of production would be subsistence agriculture, for any surplus would be given away to the destitute. While each individual would contribute his strength and ability and each would receive what he needed, needs would be modest. Thus, unlike other communal movements, the Catholic Worker commune would not attempt to reach material heights. Subsistence agriculture meant poverty. The means of production seemed to guarantee a lack of affluence. Ideally, the horse and plow and craft production would exist side by side on the land. Like Kropotkin and Peguy, Maurin revealed a dislike for the machine, but, unlike Kropotkin, he preferred to keep the machine out of his utopia.

Although economic problems seemed predestined with this plan, Maurin envisioned each commune to be economically self-sufficient and as independent from American government as possible. He wanted communes loosely federated but still locally autonomous. Since for a time the communes would function in a larger capitalist state he accepted the just laws of the external government. The commune itself, however, would not be ruled by a government; leaders would naturally arise from the association of individuals.

How did Maurin's romantic communal image work out on Catholic Worker farms established during the depression? Colonizers adhered to Maurin's general ideals, but responded to their own particular situations, for neither Maurin nor Day set policy at actual worker communes, nor did they want to. Maurin felt each commune should be truly independent and should respond to the needs of its own community. When asked for a specific communal plan, he responded, "I don't give blue prints." Each commune was owned, administered, and financed independently. Although local communal leaders often solicited advice from Maurin and Dorothy Day, the founders gave philosophical direction but extended no controls.[21]

By the end of the 1930s, several Catholic Worker Movement communes functioned, and approximately a dozen more arose independently but worked closely with the movement. Martin Paul, the director of the Catholic Worker group in Minneapolis, helped start the Holy Family Farm at Rhineland, Missouri. The founders of the Philadelphia Catholic Worker house rented a large farm in Oxford, Pennsylvania, and used it for many years. The Burlington urban Catholic Worker unit operated in conjunction with a commune in Colchester, Vermont. The Boston group established St. Benedict's farm in Upton, Massachusetts. At Cape May, New Jersey, Akron, Ohio, and South Lyon, Michigan, small independent communes sprang up to restore the idea of community.[22]

Individual Catholic Worker communes seemed patterned after the New York farm. They also appeared to emulate the New York commune's uncertain beginnings. The New Yorkers first attempted to cultivate a vegetable garden on Staten Island. This was superseded by a 28-acre farm situated about seventy miles from New York City near the town of Easton, Pennsylvania. During its first year, 1936, the farm had less than five acres plowed and most of that by a neighbor. Catholic Worker settlers worked the remainder with a two-horse plow pulled by an old truck. Although the settlement had some cows, chickens, and pigs, the main produce consisted of vegetables. The second summer the commune rented an adjoining farm of 44 acres and expanded.[23]

James Montague and Joseph Zarella managed the commune during its early years, while Paul Toner, a Catholic Worker from Philadelphia, directed much of the agricultural work. Legal title to the property rested, Day said, in the hands of "the leaders of the movement" as trustees for the *Catholic Worker*, the movement's newspaper. Original capital came mainly from donations. The settlers worked the farm both communally and privately. Each member of the commune cultivated land held by all, as well as a plot given to him for his "exclusive and permanent use." The community, however, had final control over all property sales. If a member permanently left the settlement his land reverted to the community.[24]

Staff members, residents, and people who visited for short stays of a weekend to several weeks did the actual daily labor. Each contributed according to his own conscience. Slackers were officially accepted along with the others. The extreme toleration of the group may be seen in the case of an asocial resident who lived alone on the commune but still caused continous friction. Besides being an alcoholic who seldom worked, he periodically stole the commune's meager tools, residents believed, to finance his drinking. Neither personal, legal, nor communal action excluded him from the farm. He lived there taking what he felt he needed from the common storehouse of goods until he died an old man.[25]

Although the commune had a permissive policy concerning work distribution, disputes nevertheless arose over how much work an individual was required to do. Some permanent members of the New York commune claimed that others did little work, and they disapproved of the policy of providing hospitality to the many farm visitors, often students. Guests sometimes consumed communal produce but did only token work. The commune, nevertheless, continued its open policy. Maurin encouraged young intellectuals to visit the commune, which could then serve as an avenue for their ultimate involvement. He stressed the role of the scholar on the land, who, Maurin felt, would become a whole person and better scholar through physical and craft labor. Like Kropotkin, Maurin argued that on the land the scholar would be manually educated and the worker would become a scholar. Scholars are seldom thought of as the most productive form of agricultural labor. One might conclude that the commune was economically unsound.[26]

Given the sources available it is difficult to measure the prosperity of Catholic Worker communal life. Since it served as a recuperative center for the sick who had sought help at the New York City Catholic Worker Center, the commune operated efficiently enough so that residents ate well, at least by depression standards. Also it attracted a large number of temporary visitors who stayed short periods of time. The management gave unconsumed produce to the New York house which distributed it to the unemployed. Thus, unlike most traditional communal movements, the Catholic Worker settlement did not attempt to reach any material heights. In this, of course, it followed Maurin's philosophy that in being poor, though not destitute, one could be truly free. Following Maurin's point of view the commune never stressed material consumption; still there was adequate food and living space.

Visitors and workers lived in communal buildings and ate together in a large dining room. Thus, Maurin's plan that each family would own its individual house did not work out in the New York case. Because of lack of capital, a single family could not long occupy any new separate structures. Perhaps the joint living experience of the Catholic Worker New York settlement house also stimulated adoption of the more communal course. There seemed little dissatisfaction with the arrangement. Evidently enough were content with the system to keep a New York commune in operation from the 1930s to the present. Other communes emerged and died. Yet the members recall the communal activities with fondness. William Gauchat, for example, one of the founders of the Cleveland group, typically felt that life on his commune was "never uncomfortable . . . we felt poor and we were happy there." Given the objectives of the movement, however, the communal system failed. The New York commune never attracted large numbers of people. Nor did a large back-to-the-land movement develop. Those in the movement liked the idea of a return to the land; but the communes remained, as Joseph Zarella—a member of the New York commune—pointed out, mostly theoretical since the great majority in the movement felt more concerned with immediate problems. The communes became, Zarella said, "second houses of hospitality."[27]

Establishment of houses of hospitality emerged as the second plank in Maurin's program. These urban settlements, originally providing a central focus for the Catholic Worker Movement until the utopia could be achieved, became a major Catholic Worker institution. Like the hospices of the Sillon, the Catholic Worker institutions served as urban refuges feeding and housing the poor. Maurin hoped they would replace some government welfare institutions. Thus the needy would be helped personally by those who cared—hospice residents who themselves accepted a life of voluntary poverty—not by impersonal governmental agencies.

The Catholic Worker hospices, Maurin believed, would have numerous practical functions. They could serve as vocational training schools, Catholic reading rooms, seminaries, Catholic instructional schools, and as meeting places for discussion groups. Maurin expected that hospices would bring the church back into the practical everyday life of the people. He often repeated,

"We need Houses of Hospitality
to bring the bishops to the people
and the people to the bishops."

The hospices would further the ends of the movement by providing future training to scholars and the other laymen who would live there while serving on the staff; they could also channel workers to communal farms, which in turn would support hospices with food from their surplus.[28]

Maurin hoped that these practical ends would be short-lived. As mainly a stopgap measure to cope with the depression and as a means for bringing about a communal society, the hospices theoretically would eventually close. They would no longer be needed. Maurin believed that in the future, while voluntary poverty might exist, none need be destitute. But because of the depression destitution existed, and the theoretically secondary activity of building hospices as a stopgap measure dominated the movement during the 1930s. At these urban settlements the unemployed could live along with Catholic Worker staff; together all would ideally take what they needed from the common storehouse of goods while giving what they could of their time and abilitiy to society. Once established, the houses went beyond being urban refuges and avenues for rural communalization. They became gathering places for Catholic dissidents, intellectuals, and radicals. Here young Catholics read, argued, tested their views in informal debate, and came into contact with some of the major American Catholic social thinkers of the period: Virgil Michel, John A. Ryan, and Paul Hanley Furfey, among others, visited frequently. The young intellectuals became motivated in various reform and radical directions and stimulated considerable Catholic social action. They still carried out daily hospice work of procuring food by begging at neighborhood markets and of housing the poor.[29]

The New York house remained the most important since other houses used it as a model. Most houses accepted Day's attitude that houses should be small enough to allow considerable personal contact. The New York house also developed a spontaneity that many of the later houses adopted. Day did not want the house to have the formal aspect of a mission. Thus no one preached to men forced to listen on empty stomachs. At the New York house people could read, talk, eat, and sleep if space was available. As the movement became more established the New York hospice grew although it did not develop a bureaucratic structure.[30]

The first house of hospitality in New York City began as a cooperative apartment in a condemned tenement. It housed three men of the Catholic Worker group. A cooperative apartment for unemployed women followed a short time later. A store, office, dining room, and kitchen housed several more; Dorothy Day's own apartment which she and her daughter shared with several women and one large apartment that accommodated fifteen women became movement residences. Donations from laymen, revenue from canvassing, and contributions from either individual priests or from parish collections paid the rent. Since these resources could not keep so many places operating at one time, the movement replaced them with one small old house, the Charles Street house. The clientele lived on the upper floors while the staff published the *Catholic Worker* newspaper and movement pamphlets on the first floor and in the basement.[31]

In the spring of 1936, the Catholic Worker Movement received the use of a building, the Mott Street house, one block from New York's China Town. It had twenty rooms and several other apartments that the movement could use in an adjoining building. Two stores on the ground floor served as the dining room for the unemployed, reading room, editorial print shop, and kitchen. The main building provided sleeping rooms, one floor for men and two for women. Sometimes stores and offices also served as bedrooms. In addition several Catholic Worker staff members had their own apartments or rooms elsewhere and spent their days working at Mott Street.[32]

The Catholic Worker house remained at Mott Street throughout the 1930s. This unlikely headquarters, full of neighborhood children, lines strung with laundry, radios blaring and countless discussions going on, managed to feed breakfast to one thousand people a day in addition to its regular residents and staff members.[33]

Hospices arose in other parts of the country, emulating the New York house. Day, however, did not extend her administration beyond the New York unit. Each local group operated and financed itself independently. Nina Polcyn described Catholic Worker units as autonomous but "similar in spirit." William Gauchat experienced a similar independence. When his group wrote to New York for help in solving problems he was consistently told "we can't give you any advice—you will have to work it out yourself."[34]

Thus each hospice concentrated on a program particularly needed in its area or suited for its staff. The Boston group ran a bread line for men, feeding over two hundred daily. In St. Louis, a priest, Timothy Dempsey, established a house which aided thousands over the years. Average daily meals for the month of April 1935, the only figures appearing in *Catholic Worker* for this hospice, indicate the St. Louis hospice fed over 2,700 daily and distributed 700 baskets of food a week.[35]

Washington, D.C., had several Catholic Worker houses. One, established to aid black unemployed, included among its founders Father Paul Hanley Furfey, the personalist theologian. Another Washington house, St. Christophers Inn, served as a sleeping quarter for transients. The Blessed Martin Home in Washington was virtually a one-man operation. Dorothy Day described it as dilapidated, with falling plaster, protruding slate, and paper hanging from the wall. The floor sloped in the unheated structure, yet manager of Llewellyn Scott housed forty-five men a night during the winter of 1938–39.[36]

In Harrisburg, Pennsylvania, the house of hospitality sheltered evicted women until the Catholic Worker staff could find them new homes. In Akron and Chicago main efforts went into feeding hungry children. The Detroit group, in addition to feeding six hundred daily and participating in demonstrations, established a workers' school. The Pittsburgh house, discussed separately in a latter chapter, fed over 800 a day and operated a clinic. A 1939 survey conservatively estimated that the movement fed at least 5,000 daily.[37]

Each Catholic Worker group thus went in its own direction without being hampered, controlled, or administered by the parent group in New York. Lists of worker institutions appeared in the *Catholic Worker* for 1938 and 1939. In 1938, twenty-two houses existed in the United States with nineteen cells, primarily places for discussion servicing a few Catholic Workers. In 1939 three houses were added, bringing the total to twenty-five; cells fluctuated between thirteen and sixteen, and there were four farms.[38]

Convincing others to accept his philosophy and program constituted the third aspect of Maurin's program. Like many a radical, positive of the righteousness of his ideology, Maurin felt that in the intellectual confrontation of ideas, dissidents would be converted to the Catholic Worker Movement. To carry out this "clarification of thought," Maurin advocated public meetings similar to those held by the Sillon. All radicals, intellectuals, and interested workers could attend. He also urged the establishment of a Catholic Worker labor school and "agronomic universities" where his agricultural ideas would be taught.

Maurin's propaganda had its traditional side as well. He advocated establishing a low cost Catholic radical newspaper which would present his ideas and publish his "Easy Essays." A newspaper could disseminate his thought to a wider audience than could most other avenues of influence. The newspaper, called *The Catholic Worker,* covered all aspects of what Day considered the workers' main concerns: the labor movement, racial problems, politics, the church and encyclicals, war, and general Catholic labor activities. It had a homespun quality achieving intellectual intimacy with its readers. Articles on the commune tended to be personal and gossipy. Day, in her column, often discussed her family and friends within the movement. Her columns seemed to be directed to an in-group of subscribers; nevertheless, the number of readers increased considerably during the 1930s. By the end of 1933 the *Catholic Worker* had reached a circulation of 20,000. By the end of the depression, circulation reached 125,000.[39]

In addition to its newspaper, the movement used other propaganda techniques. Street-corner meetings proved popular. Soon after the movement began, two college students spoke for the movement and distributed newspapers on a Manhattan corner. Eventually the New York group held street meetings on a regular basis three times a week. Sometimes Maurin spoke on a corner or in New York's popular gathering place for radicals, Union Square. Frequently he prearranged for hecklers to attack his opinions, thus giving him the attention he needed to draw a crowd.[40]

Maurin advocated organized public discussions as part of the propaganda program. The Manhattan Lyceum, at that time primarily a communist and socialist meeting place, hosted Catholic Worker conferences on a regular monthly basis. In conjunction with these gatherings the movement attempted to establish a labor school, a common adjunct of worker-oriented organizations in the 1930s. At first, classes were held almost daily. They consisted of a talk or two preceded and followed by discussion. Professors at local universities lectured without pay, and sometimes writers or clerics spoke. In the middle of the decade, however, the labor school held more formal sessions only one evening a month. Maurin found that the popularity and spontaneity that he desired for the schools did not last. The idea, however, did not die in the 1930s. Other units of the movement established labor schools, and some ran summer schools for college students.[41]

The synthesis of Maurin's personal philosophy and program into the ideology of the Catholic Worker Movement resulted from his organizational collaboration with Dorothy Day and her subsequent influence on the movement. While at first Day did not fully agree with Maurin's ideas, he succeeded in winning her to most of them. She never accepted all his views, and her role as the institutional leader in the movement made her ideas as significant as Maurin's. The program of the movement, although not its basic underlying philosophical assumptions, thus became a synthesis of Maurin's agrarian, romantic, Catholic anarchism and Day's American radicalism centered around the role of the industrial urban worker. On most issues, Day compromised with reality more willingly than Maurin. Thus, Day supported movements or conditions that she believed would bring about an improvement in the socioeconomic conditions of the worker, even though they conflicted with one of Maurin's specific ideological points. This gave the Catholic Worker Movement a broader and less doctrinaire framework.[42]

Although the staff highly respected Maurin as the ideological leader of the movement, Day's personality was more overwhelming. Nina Polcyn, one of the founders of the Milwaukee group, and for a time associated with the New York unit, described Maurin as "an intellectual with a non-stop mind" who was "harder to be with" than the warmer Day. Zarella felt that Day's vibrant personality helped explain the movement. "There was nothing I wouldn't do for her." Day's charisma must be coupled with Maurin's lack of emphasis on the labor movement, a panacea for many intellectuals in the 1930s. In addition, Day's consistent dedication in making decisions and organizing the daily routine thrust her into the forefront. As Day put it, in a letter to Richard Deverall of the *Christian Front,* "I have charge of all the practical details of our existence." Thus many Catholic Workers looked to Day for direction. Perhaps most important, because of Day's experience as a journalist, she became editor of the movement's paper. Her administrative leverage, personality, leadership qualities, and urban labor orientation led to a pragmatic approach in the *Catholic Worker.*[43]

Differences which initially arose between Maurin and Day on minor matters indicated larger conflict. As early as May 1, 1933, when the movement distributed the first issue of the *Catholic Worker* Maurin criticized the newspaper. It consisted of articles on such topics as white racism, the labor movement, and child labor. "Everybody's paper is nobody's paper," Maurin said. He wanted to print almost exclusively his own essays, to omit labor union news, to include more religious material, and to title it *The Catholic Radical.* Day's decisions on the nature of the paper prevailed; Maurin left New York City and had his name removed from the editorial staff. Maurin's absence, Day wrote, "gave me an uneasy feeling, reminding me that our paper was not yet reflecting his thought."[44]

Maurin and Day disagreed most strongly on the role of organized labor. In 1936, Maurin wrote:

> "And organized labor
> preys into the hands
> of the capitalist. . . .
> by treating their own labor
> not as a gift,
> but as a commodity,
> selling it as any other commodity
> at the highest possible price."

Maurin, who never belonged to a labor union, believed that organized labor, like all reforms, only supported the shoddy system. Another of his "Easy Essays" emphasized this attitude:

> "Organized labor,
> whether it be
> the AFL
> or the CIO
> is far from knowing
> what to do
> with the economic setup."

He did not favor the use of strikes and often said, "strikes don't strike me," although he sympathized with the sit-down strike, which he considered a type of passive resistance. Maurin had little faith in labor leaders, who he believed often organized for their own benefit, not for the working class. Maurin argued that only return to the land would cure unemployment permanently, while works of mercy should apply to immediate needs.[45]

Dorothy Day, however, continued to support organized labor. "Both unions and strikes and the fight for better wages and hours," she wrote, "would remain my immediate concern." In contrast with Maurin, Day visualized the labor movement and the strike as viable temporary means for dealing with immediate material problems. She felt that, "when we were invited to help during a strike, we went to perform works of mercy, which include not only feeding the hungry . . . but enlightening the ignorant and rebuking the unjust." She also believed that when participating in strikes "we are reaching the workers when they are massed together for action. We are taking advantage of a situation." In a movement pamphlet Miss Day argued that strikers "are fighting for the right to be considered partners. . . . They are fighting against the idea of their labor as a commodity, to be bought and sold."[46]

Promulgating Day's point of view, the *Catholic Worker* strongly supported organized labor and regularly reported labor views. It asked the readers not to buy specific products or patronize particular concerns. The *Catholic Worker* urged Catholics to organize within these unions and to fight for social justice. A 1936 editorial clearly illustrated the movement's point of view: "*The Catholic Worker* does not believe that unions as they exist today in the United States, are an ideal solution for social problems. . . . We do believe that they are the only efficient weapon which workers have to defend their rights as individuals."[47]

The Catholic Worker movement's position on unionism went beyond rhetoric. It took an active part in the struggles of the 1930s. "Hardly a week went by," according to one participant, "that we were not engaged in picketing or helping some union organize." The Catholic Worker group participated in its first major strike in late 1934 and 1935 as department store employees in Manhattan walked off the job. The strikes affected just two large establishments, S. Klein and the Ohrbach Department Store. Although the issues at S. Klein were resolved quickly, the Catholic Worker Movement picketed Ohrbach's with the workers and carried signs quoting papal support of unions. Since the predominantly Catholic police regularly arrested picketers not belonging to the Catholic Worker group, Day's followers became the bulwark of the strike. Enjoined by the courts from picketing, the Catholic Worker group practiced civil disobedience by violating the injunction. In addition the movement's staff attended strike meetings and informed the workers of Catholic thought regarding strikes, picketing, and nonviolent techniques. In the meantime the *Catholic Worker* told its readers not to patronize the department store. "You are not upholding social justice if you disregard the plea of those workers." During the strike the movement worked closely with local communists, a repeated situation which inevitably led to criticism within the church. Day defended the justice of the issues the communists raised. " 'The truth is the truth,' writes St. Thomas, 'and proceeds from the Holy Ghost, no matter from whose lips it comes.' "[48]

The Catholic Worker Movement displayed its heaviest strike activities of the era in supporting leftist Joseph Curran's National Maritime Union. The young union appealed to the *Catholic Worker* to help in housing and feeding some strikers in May 1936. The movement immediately accepted fifty men at the Mott Street house. Before the strike ended the Catholic Worker Movement rented a store in the strike area, using it as a reading room and free soup kitchen. The soup kitchen, operated by workers Bill Callahan and Cyril Echele, served coffee and sandwiches at almost any hour. The movement also performed its usual services of picketing with Catholic-oriented placards. The strike seemed settled and the seamen returned to their ships. Then in November the strike again erupted and continued into 1937. Once more a Catholic Worker waterfront branch became a resting place for idle seamen. Conveniently located around the corner from strike headquarters, the store was filled to capacity with seamen from early morning until midnight. Picketers could relax and read Catholic newspapers and magazines. More important, the movement fed thousands of strikers, which resulted in a $3,000 debt; yet the store remained open, even after the strike had ended, feeding more than 1,000 persons a day until the men again went back to their ships.[49]

The Catholic Worker group in Pittsburgh particularly aided the labor movement, especially the CIO's Steel Workers Organizing Committee (SWOC). Father Charles Owen Rice, the local Catholic Worker leader, spoke to overflow crowds at the immigrant meeting houses where large numbers of Catholic laborers gathered. Concurrently, his supporters distributed the *Catholic Worker* at ethnic social halls. Father Rice and his associate, Father Carl Hensler, led their staff members on steel worker picket lines and encouraged workers to heed SWOC speakers.[50]

The Catholic Workers also picketed with the seamen and demonstrated before the ships. Movement placards declared "Unionization is favored by the Pope!" and "The Church backs a living wage!" Police broke up the picket lines, often clubbing demonstrators. Unlike the S. Klein strike, Catholic Worker participants also became victims of physical confrontation. At the strike's conclusion, many ships' crews acknowledged Catholic Worker support by voting to contribute funds to the movement. Some seamen stayed permanently with the movement.[51]

Sometimes the Catholic Worker Movement negotiated with management concerning a labor dispute. A New York City department store chain, for example, laid off a number of nonunionized saleswomen without severance pay. The women had been employed there from twelve to twenty years. The Catholic Worker Movement offered to join the women in picketing the company's stores, and then met with company officials threatening them with public attacks both in the *Catholic Worker* and from the lecture platform. The firm agreed to provide severance pay for some workers and to take back the rest.[52]

These instances typified the movement's labor activities. It harassed numerous other companies involved in labor disputes; the National Biscuit Company, Borden Milk, Heinz Corporation, Loose-Wiler, and American Stores of Philadelphia were some of the more well-known. Marble workers of Vermont, fishermen of Boston, sharecroppers of Arkansas, auto workers of Michigan, textile workers in Massachusetts, brewery workers in New York, printers, librarians, and meatpackers were just some of the striking workers who sought and received moral support, press space, and countless thousands of meals from Catholic Worker groups throughout the country. At least one company, Borden Milk, responded by placing advertisements in the *Catholic News* and *Brooklyn Tablet* (a major Catholic newspaper) attacking the Catholic Worker Movement. The continued support of the Borden strike caused the *Catholic Worker* to lose an order for 3,000 subscriptions from a New York Catholic secondary school.[53]

Dorothy Day thus added organized labor to Maurin's ideological attempt to deal with the immediate needs of the depression poor. To judge by the space accorded to it on the front page of the *Catholic Worker,* organized labor's role equaled that of the hospice during the depression years. But Miss Day's innovations did not end here. The Catholic Worker Movement founded a Catholic Union of Unemployed headed by an ex-communist, Timothy O'Brien. The movement also spent considerable effort in moving evicted families. It transported furniture, found new apartments and, when a family was settled, provided clothing and additional furniture. To coordinate these kinds of activities, the movement organized a number of neighborhood councils patterned after Communist party unemployed councils.[54]

The attitudes of Day and Maurin toward the New Deal also illustrated differences between the two founders. Maurin strongly veered in a distributive direction. He idealized the commune and advocated smallness in government, capital, and labor in the intermediate stage before a communally based society could be established. In speaking of public assistance to the unemployed, he said, "it is not the function of the state to enter into these realms. Only in times of great crisis, like floods, hurricanes, earthquake, or drought, does public authority come in." He had little sympathy for the New Deal:

> "We try to put patches
> to the existing social order
> and call it a New Deal.
> Having no School of Catholic Social Studies
> we let college professors carry on costly experiments
> at the expense of the taxpayer."

He opposed government in business for it created a welfare state: "state business" is just another "big business." He was equally unsympathetic to key New Deal programs; Dorothy Day quoted him attacking the NRA as "experimentation without theory in back of it. Let's try—let's try! Bump your head against the wall and then find it's hard. Try everything but your door—and only then the door . . . one fool on the land—the other on industry. Attempting something without trying to get at the root of things."[55]

The *Catholic Worker,* on the other hand, usually supported the NRA and the other measures of the New Deal. An editorial in the September 1933 issue stated that the *Catholic Worker* had become "more and more enthusiastic about NRA," and that NRA "is following the lines laid down by Pope Pius XI in his encyclical 'Forty Years After'." The editorial gave enthusiastic support to the Roosevelt administration and ended with the statement that "we can only work and pray the administration will succeed." In a *Catholic Worker* article, Rev. Francis J. Haas, a member of the NRA labor advisory board and a prominent labor-oriented priest, told the individual worker that he had the duty to himself and to his fellow men to join his union and support the NRA. Contributor Henry J. Foley reiterated this a month later. "The NRA is the most intelligent and forward-looking effort made in a generation to bring back prosperity." His only criticism was that the NRA did not go far enough, and he offered measures to make it more effective. Other articles continued in this vein.[56]

In view of Maurin's program, the differences with Day were indeed profound. Where these differences occurred, Day's point of view prevailed. A synthesis in the program of the Catholic Worker Movement from Maurin's utopian, communalist agrarianism to a more practical concern with the immediate needs of the worker resulted from this ideological dualism. Maurin's basic philosophy remained untouched. His followers began to carry out his program by establishing decentralized communes and urban hospices; but the movement supported unions and big government as well.

The Catholic Worker Movement tried to influence the lives of the worker and the effectiveness of the labor movement. It is difficult to measure its success, though considering the totality of problems in depression America, it obviously had meager influence. Yet throughout the depression various Catholic Worker houses did feed thousands and shelter and clothe a significant number. Its other involvements—such as opposing racism, anti-Semitism, and anti-Catholicism in Mexico; aiding alcoholics; holding art classes for slum children; finding apartments for the homeless or helping move evicted families—provided a measure of hope for some during the depression. Catholic Worker groups helped in many strikes and at times contributed to a settlement favorable to the workers. Total achievement in these areas, however, could not have been great. The movement supported the CIO by aiding in organization. It also provided the young federation with propaganda in its conflict with the AFL. CIO growth, however, was unrelated to the Catholic Worker Movement.

The Catholic Worker Movement did not make a concentrated attempt to affect Catholic social reform, yet its greatest influence was in that area. In stressing the disparity between the practices and discrepancies of American life when compared to the social ideals of the church, the movement attracted young discontented Catholics with a radical bent who otherwise might have filtered into the secular left. "The Catholic Worker proved to be the last refuge for many who were on the brink of leaving the Church," a chronicler from within the movement put it. Moreover, the Catholic Worker Movement provided a source of direction for social Catholicism and an early avenue of involvement for Catholic radicals who later moved in other, usually liberal, directions. Thus the Catholic Worker Movement stimulated numerous Catholic social institutions. William Callahan organized the first American branch of Pax at Mott Street. Pax eventually became the Association of Catholic Conscientious Objectors and ran forestry and hospital camps in New Hampshire, Illinois, and Maryland during World War II. At the kitchen table of the Mott Street house, John Cort organized the Association of Catholic Trade Unionists with several other members of the Catholic Worker Movement. Many independent labor schools and Interreligious Friendship Houses as well grew out of the Catholic Worker Movement.[57]

A number of liberal Catholic journalists and publishers received their early impetus from the Catholic Worker Movement during the depression. In addition to the New York City newspaper, Catholic Worker Movement newspapers were published in Baltimore, Chicago, England, and Australia. The *Canadian Social Forum,* the first *Christian Front,* and the *Source* also came out of the Catholic Worker Movement. For example, John Cogley, later editor of *Commonweal,* began his activities in social action causes leading the Catholic Worker units. Cogley ran the movement's hospice in Chicago and edited the Chicago *Catholic Worker.* Edward Willock, cofounder of *Integrity,* and Edward Marciniak, founder of *Work,* received their apprenticeship in the Catholic Worker Movement. John Cort, an extremely prolific writer on social Catholicism, and social critic Michael Harrington both were members of the New York group. The *Catholic Student's Digest* was specifically launched by the New York house.[58]

The Catholic Worker Movement may have done little to affect the labor movement directly, but its contribution to the development of social Catholicism in America supported a climate of opinion favorable to organized labor. More important, it rekindled Catholic social reform activities, relatively dormant for over a decade, and began a tradition of antiestablishment, American Catholic activism. Those results of the Catholic Worker Movement are to a degree ironic, since neither the labor movement nor the social reformism of groups and individuals that grew out of the Catholic Worker Movement represented Peter Maurin's goal of communitarian society. Nevertheless, from the Catholic Worker Movement grew many of the Catholic institutions dedicated to working with the industrial worker. Not only organizations like the Associations of Catholic Trade Unionists and the Catholic Radical Alliance emerged from Catholic Worker beginnings, but many individual priests also responded to the movement's call to activism. Some priests wrote for *Catholic Worker,* others provided the movement with funds, while still others bought and distributed copies of the newspaper. Many clerics, stimulated by the Catholic Worker Movement, became involved in other labor activities, sometimes becoming free-lance labor agitators.

CHAPTER FIVE

The Labor Priests—
The Contrasting Approaches of Charles Owen Rice and John P. Boland

Although the Catholic Worker Movement consisted primarily of laity, numerous priests supported its programs. Some wrote for the *Catholic Worker;* others supported the movement by speaking at meetings, operating hospices, collecting funds, distributing newspapers, or participating in discussions at Catholic Worker centers. Much of this clerical interest reflected genuine excitement for Catholic Worker programs. On the other hand, some priests rejected the movement's ideology but used the movement as a convenient vehicle for contemporary involvement. Other clerics ignored the movement but, nevertheless, reacted to the depression by promoting labor activities. Some labor priests responded to needs in their working class parishes, while others sought out workers. An article in the Catholic labor-oriented journal, *Christian Front,* urged priests to accept a labor vocation. The author believed that clerical participation at union gatherings "draws workers to unions."[1]

Priests and sometimes hierarchy followed such advice by actively engaging in labor agitation during the depression. Although European labor priests earlier supported social reform, and an occasional American cleric had worked closely with the labor movement, during the depression American Catholic clergy chose a far more extensive involvement in the labor movement than at any other time. In the last two years of the depression, the *Labor Leader,* a New York City Catholic labor newspaper, cited more than twenty-five highly active priests who had heavily involved themselves in labor activity.

Labor-oriented priests responded to the depression in several ways. Some spoke at union organizational rallies and meetings, often for the CIO, thus attempting to counter the statements of Catholic priests hostile to the new federation. Others acted as union chaplains or even became full-time labor activists. This support gave the CIO the aura of legitimacy in an era when employers used red-baiting as a primary antiunion tactic. The appearance of a priest, or occasionally a bishop, on a union platform often assured Catholic industrial workers that communists did not dominate the union seeking their support. Labor priests also functioned as delegates to union conventions, as educators operating labor education schools for workers, or as arbitrators and mediators during labor disputes.

Father John Monaghan, advisor to the Association of Catholic Trade Unionists, formed a speakers' bureau of priests to coordinate clerical prolabor propaganda. The bureau sponsored talks not only at union gatherings but also at meetings of Catholic lay organizations. Monaghan also established a national institute, the Social Action School, to educate labor priests in public speaking and labor economics, generally concentrating on social questions. Much of the faculty consisted of prominent clerics known either for their social work or as analysts of social reform. While the media reported only statements of the well-known faculty, virtually all its instructors advocated reform of the capitalist system. Father John P. Boland, one of the outstanding faculty members of the Social Action School, supported labor management partnership agreements and industrial planning to replace the competitive economic system which he characterized as "blind, stupid stagnation." Father Raymond A. McGowan, second in command of the Social Action Department of the National Catholic Welfare Conference and a prominent Catholic writer and social analyst, also taught at the school. McGowan advocated establishment of a cooperative society based on shop committees, industrial councils, and national economic planning. He hoped a copartnership of labor and management based on rational planning would simultaneously repulse government expansion and replace capitalism.

James McNicholas, Archbishop of Cincinnati, also established clerical labor education programs for his archdiocese. He appointed specific priests to study labor questions and then to actively assist in the labor movement. In Chicago the highly influential Monsignor Reynold Hillenbrand arranged classes for priests from the industrial districts. After attending lectures and seminars directed by labor leaders, the priests engaged in community organizing, particularly aiding the labor movement.[2]

Although the Catholic clergy established schools for their own enlightenment in trade union affairs, this did not remain their emphasis in labor-oriented education. Priests also taught at schools designed for future labor leaders among the working class. Individual dioceses and independent Catholic lay groups, such as the Catholic Worker Movement or the Association of Catholic Trade Unionists, sponsored labor schools of this kind. Occasionally a lay group working jointly with the local diocese operated a labor school. Most successful of the latter were Catholic labor schools of Detroit. No matter how schools were administered, faculties consisted primarily of clerics. Course material centered on parliamentary procedure, Catholic industrial ethics and labor encyclicals, labor economics, and sometimes labor history. One analyst of social Catholicism estimated that over five thousand attended Catholic labor schools yearly. Since the students were often minor union officials there was strong potential for Catholic influence.[3]

Given these educational activities of concerned Catholic clergy, it is not surprising that numerous priests became known for their close alliance with organized labor. Charles A. Maxwell, spiritual advisor to a local Steel Workers organizing committee, was the first honorary member of the United Steel Workers. He had been appointed to his chaplaincy by John A. Duffy, Bishop of Buffalo, New York, also a strong labor supporter. Father William J. Kelley, educational director of the AFL in Buffalo, administered the education program of 40,000 members from 130 local unions. Auxiliary Bishop Bernard Sheil of Chicago enthusiastically supported organized labor, especially the CIO. Under his guidance the pro-union newspaper *Catholic Labor* began publishing, and the Catholic Youth Organization aided union organizational attempts. Sheil himself helped labor by appearing at union rallies and endorsing union demands. The CIO believed that Sheil's role in the Newspaper Guild Strike of 1937 countered anti-CIO conservative Catholic support. On the national level, Robert Lucey, shortly to become Archbishop of San Antonio, Texas, consistently supported the CIO. The federation published and widely circulated pamphlets quoting his statements. Typically, in a letter to John Brophy, executive director of the CIO, Lucey stated that "in the Province of God a bitter day has dawned on the teeming masses of people. By enormous efforts the Committee for Industrial Organization is lifting labor from its lethargy."[4]

In numerous industries but most particularly in steel, CIO organizers acknowledged the aid of labor priests. Carey E. Haigler, then a CIO organizer, acknowledged that "there were many instances of Catholic Church priests helping to a great extent." He especially considered the church in New Orleans "very helpful," undoubtedly having in mind the work of Father James Drolet who helped organize most of the city's CIO locals. Brendan Sexton of the United Auto Workers considered some of the local priests "reactionary" but found that "most were quite close to their congregations and friendly to the union." He found this was also true of many priests of ethnic congregations who aided the nationality societies (usually church sponsored) in actively supporting union organizational drives. Irwin L. De Shetler, another CIO activist of the period, believed that "most churches were afraid to have their facilities used because of the fact that their main contributors were the Corporations and members of the Corporations." Nevertheless, he observed that "many individual Catholic priests . . . [gave] their personal support to organizing drives all over the country." It is impossible to measure the effect of such diverse activity on national scale. A greater understanding of the labor priests' role may be derived from comparing in depth two prominent labor priests, Charles Owen Rice and John P. Boland, whose styles and immediate goals were notably different.[5]

Pittsburgh had a tradition of clerical labor activity. Even in the 1920s when Catholic social activism barely existed, Pittsburgh could claim one of the few labor priests of the decade. Father James Cox, known as the "Pastor of the Poor," helped labor organizational attempts and devoted time to working class causes. The emergency of the depression and the inability of the federal government to deal with poverty outraged the concerned priest. In 1932, he organized 15,000 people for a "hunger march" on Washington. Cox then enrolled 50,000 unemployed workers in an organization and threatened to form a Jobless Party if neither the Democrats nor Republicans brought relief to the poor. The optimism following nomination and election of Roosevelt, however, ended Cox's threat. After the demise of the Jobless Party idea, Cox appeared once more on the national political scene. He led a group to Washington, D. C., in support of the Townsend plan, met with the President, but received no commitment. Cox then dropped from the national spectrum.[6]

Although his political pronouncements and meandering in party allegiance made local news, his main energies centered around a free soup kitchen sponsored by his church. Cox is reputed to have served over two million free meals, distributed half a million baskets of food, and provided medical care for thousands. Because of Cox's preoccupation with feeding the unemployed, he spent virtually no time aiding trade union activities. In fact, while other Catholic groups and individual clerics gave considerable aid to the union in the Pittsburgh Heinz Corporation strike of 1937, Cox supported management. He had consistently accepted Heinz products donated to his soup kitchen. Cox apparently felt that such a generous firm would do little wrong. His attitude toward the Heinz strike revealed his underlying ambivalence toward organized labor. Although he labored for the poor and he considered himself a "union man," Cox continually denounced labor in the 1930s for being dictatorial and corrupt. Obviously, his status as a labor priest declined measurably.

Although Cox received national attention, in Pittsburgh labor circles he was completely eclipsed by Father Charles Owen Rice, a young, dynamic priest. Rice, through dedicated and innovative work, emerged as the major labor priest of industrial Pittsburgh during the depression years. In fact, Rice became so close to the CIO leadership that he became known as the "Chaplain of the CIO."[7]

Rice was born in New York City. After his mother died he went to Ireland and lived among relatives for seven years of his boyhood. At age eleven he returned to the United States and joined his father in Pittsburgh. Rice later attended Duquesne University and St. Vincent's Seminary, where he was ordained in 1934. Rice seemed destined to labor activism. His schoolmaster uncles with whom he lived in Ireland were concerned with rebellion, politics, and religion. Years later Rice said of his family, "we were definitely hung up on the Irish struggle for justice." Like many Irish radicals in America, his initial hostility to the establishment stemmed from British oppression of the Irish Catholics. The Irish revolutionary movement gave Rice not only an outlook which reached beyond conventional assumptions of American society but also an empathy with the exploited. To be a nationalist in twentieth-century Ireland was to be a democrat, an economic reformer, a revolutionist, and a Roman Catholic.[8]

"I am a radical, a Catholic radical," Rice often pointed out. "I believe that the present social and economic system is a mess and should be changed from top to bottom." He branded Catholic "friends of the present system" as "traitors to Christ." Rice did not outline any truly radical ends for society other than his commitment to the socioeconomic visions of the major papal social encyclicals, *Rerum Novarum* and *Quadragesimo Anno;* rather, he stressed his allegiance to labor unionism, particularly the emerging CIO. Summarizing Catholic doctrine on labor unions, Rice said in 1938, "Labor unions are good things for the workmen. Those who interfere with the workers right to organize, in whatever fashion, are doing wrong and commit grave sin." Like other labor priests he argued that the "worker has a right to join a union, moreover, he has a Duty to do so." Rice based his unionism on religious commitment. "As a Catholic priest I am profoundly interested in social and economic reform, especially . . . labor unions. I am so interested because of my Christianity. Christ's concern for the poor and the exploited is clear command to all His followers to be concerned for them. Unionism," he declared, "is the Christian thing."[9]

Rice favored the CIO, but not uncritically. "I find fault with the CIO chiefly because it does not go far enough. . . . But it is young and in time will develop an adequate social philosophy." Likewise, Rice's close associate and fellow Pittsburgh priest, Carl P. Hensler, hoped capitalism would be moderated through left-wing unionism. "The union especially cannot remain a mere fighting machine," he stated at a National Catholic Social Action Conference, "its role must be enlarged from bargaining over wages and hours to sharing in the conduct of the whole industry."[10]

In order to achieve his reform goals, Rice, assisted by Hensler and Monsignor George Barry O'Toole, in 1936 led other priests and laymen in forming the Catholic Radical Alliance (CRA). The organization began as an outgrowth of the Catholic Worker Movement. Each Catholic Worker unit independently responded to the needs of its area. Some groups spun off completely, forming separate organizations. The Catholic Radical Alliance reflected this galloping autonomy of the Catholic Worker Movement. For a time Rice considered the alliance a unit of the Catholic Worker Movement. He often forwarded progress reports to the movement's outlet, the *Catholic Worker,* pointing out that the "Pittsburgh branch has been prospering." But the CRA never had the radical goals of Maurin. Influenced by the Catholic Worker Movement, it carried out much of the movement's program, especially the establishment of a highly successful house of hospitality. During the depression, however, the CRA concentrated on industrial unionism as its overreaching concern. In describing the alliance in later years, Rice stated, "we stood for unions, we stood for freedom of workers to join associations, we called for modification of the social and economic system and we were very strongly pro-peace." By modification of the socioeconomic system Rice meant commitment to the social encyclicals, a less radical alternative than Maurin's communalism.[11]

The alliance spent most of its time aiding the labor movement. In 1938 Hensler and Rice taught at a Steel Workers' organizing committee summer school. The two labor priests also organized their own labor classes and discussion groups, but made their main contribution to organized labor during the 1930s by defending the CIO when anti-union forces accused it of being communist controlled.[12]

Attacks upon the CIO came from all quarters. When the papal publication *Osservatore Romano* published an interview with Martin Carmody, Supreme Knight of the Knights of Columbus, in which he accused the CIO of being "completely directed by Communist forces," Rice immediately sprang to the federation's defense. He replied that the "statement is simply untrue. . . . By your ill-advised statement and your wild charges, you do no service to our order, which numbers among its members many high officials of the CIO." Likewise, Rice responded to Monsignor Fulton J. Sheen's slurs against organized labor. "Monsignor Sheen was definitely unfair to labor in inferring that labor is responsible . . . for the violence that has characterized American industrial disputes." Rice offered to personally show Sheen that "fight after fight . . . was . . . provoked by organized capitalist thuggery." In this statement Rice also defended the CIO's use of the sit-down strike. In a speech republished in the trade union press, including the front page of the *Textile Worker,* Rice lauded the CIO as a "good thing, it is a healthy, growing movement." He added that "it is not Godless, Communistic, or un-American. It has its roots in Christianity and Americanism." He denied that the CIO had any communists in positions of importance. "I have not seen one decent piece of evidence that would tie a front rank CIO leader to the Communist Party." When conservative AFL official John P. Frey implied before the House Un-American Activities Committee that CIO director John Brophy was a communist, both Rice and Hensler testified that he was a devout Catholic. Frey backed down. Brophy expressed his appreciation to Rice, "for the fine support and cooperation you gave me." Rice argued "that charges of Communism laid against the CIO are ill advised and asinine, especially when they come from Catholics." He added that such accusations enhanced the communist image by presenting them as leaders of a forward looking, sound, and necessary movement. He added that the "CIO is a bulwark against Communism. It is not perfect, it is American and Christian, fundamentally."[13]

Rice and his alliance took part in numerous CIO organizational drives during the 1930s. After hearing of a strike, the alliance contacted strike leaders to, as Rice put it, "tell them what we can do for them." After determining the justness of the strike, the alliance offered "to speak for them, to authorize the Alliance to carry signs proclaiming our support, and to issue statements for them." The Steelworkers of Western Pennsylvania received the bulk of CRA support. When the CRA, led by Rice, went to Youngstown, Ohio, during the Little Steel Strike, they faced problems with local Catholic clergy. "We were unfavorably received," Rice related later, "by the priests of the community." In many major cities, such as Philadelphia, Boston, and even Pittsburgh, Rice opposed anti-union clerics. In such instances, Rice propagandized his view of Roman Catholic responsibilities in labor actions and he defended the CIO. On the other hand, he often found clerical supporters, as in Johnstown and Wheeling where pro-union priests made Rice's job easier.[14]

Rice dramatically portrayed his approval of the CIO organizational drives by personally engaging in strike activities, a highly unusual practice for a Catholic priest at this time. He picketed during the Pittsburgh Heinz Corporation strike of 1937. During steel industry confrontations he often spoke to overflow crowds at immigrant meeting houses and had his fellow supporters distribute Catholic labor literature. In the late 1930s, Rice gave aid to the Aluminum Workers Union, Paper Workers, Hotel Restaurant Workers, American Newspaper Guild, Auto Workers, United Mine Workers, Teamsters, Laundry Workers, Amalgamated Meat Cutters, Fraternal Order of Police, Amalgamated Clothing Workers, Bakery Workers, Retail Clerks, Warehouse Men and Mechanics, and Transport Workers Union. He worked with hospital, river, and communications workers, as well as teachers, to improve hours, wages, and working conditions through labor organization.[15]

Like John Ryan, Rice attempted to help the CIO in its conflict with Mayor Frank Hague of Jersey City, New Jersey. Victor Pasche, secretary of the Newspaper Guild, in a letter requesting Rice's support, described Hague as "virtual absolute ruler of Hudson county . . . who has consistently tried to identify his antilabor activities as good Catholicism, and uses his position as self-appointed defender of the Church to have his police beat up and drive out peaceful organizers." Rice immediately joined the New Jersey Civil Liberties Union, the vanguard in the fight against Boss Hague, and he established a subcommittee of the civil liberties group in Pittsburgh. Most important, he issued public statements to counteract Hague's misuse of Catholicism. "Understanding that Mayor Hague professes Christianity," Rice ironically asked, "I wonder how it is that he can reconcile the teachings of Christ with his brutal tactics." Condemning Hague's practices, Rice argued that "it is but a hollow sham to profess Christ and at the same time to war against His justice and charity." The CIO and the Civil Liberties Union widely circulated these statements in Jersey City. Hague, however, successfully blocked Rice's intention of personally confronting the Mayor's forces in Jersey City. Hague used his influence with Archbishop Walsh who made it clear that he did not want Rice engaging in politics within his diocese.[16]

Rice's Catholic Radical Alliance expanded beyond organized labor activities. Like its parent, the New York-based Catholic Worker Movement, it established a house of hospitality as a refuge for the poor, that both housed and fed the unemployed. The Pittsburgh St. Joseph House, once an orphanage, outgrew similar undertakings within the Catholic Worker Movement. Thirty people staffed the three-story building which housed alliance offices and classrooms for worker education. From here the alliance sponsored a radio program, fed over eight hundred daily, slept three hundred nightly, and operated a medical clinic. At times the number sheltered reached nearly eight hundred, with men sleeping on floors and eating the inadequate amount of food the alliance could provide. The organization began a farming commune in the spring of 1938—"a weird effort," Rice later called it. The farm established in Indiana County, Pennsylvania, depended primarily on one man, Frank Hensler, brother of Rice's collaborator. It dissolved shortly after World War II because, as Rice later explained, "they couldn't get other people interested and because an investment in chickens turned out badly." The alliance also sponsored a peace group reflecting the Catholic Worker Movement's pacifist orientation. Rice, however, influenced by the famous German exile priest, H. A. Rheinhold, accepted the necessity of armed conflict in order to stop the advance of Nazi Germany.[17]

In 1938 Rice established within the alliance a unit of a new national Catholic labor organization, the Association of Catholic Trade Unionists (ACTU). Like the alliance, the ACTU grew out of the Catholic Worker Movement but severed its connection with the parent organization. The ACTU followed an adamant anticommunist ideology at odds with the more moderate Catholic Worker Movement. The alliance had also taken a stronger anticommunist position than the Catholic Worker Movement, but its techniques differed from those of the ACTU. Although the Catholic Radical Alliance refused to cooperate with communists, in the 1930s it rejected red-baiting, a standard ACTU tactic. Nevertheless, the alliance accepted an ACTU unit within its fold. Eventually, alliance ties to the Catholic Worker Movement withered away and Rice affiliated his group with the national ACTU. The implications of the ACTU-CRA merger would not be felt until later years. In the late 1940s and 1950s the alliance, known then as the Pittsburgh ACTU, concentrated on fighting communist influence in labor. It thus lost much of its Catholic Worker orientation. The attempt to force communist unionists out of the labor movement, however, played little part in the depression goals of the alliance. During the 1930s the CRA concentrated on sublimating the supposed communist threat in order to help the CIO attract cautious Catholic workers.[18]

In keeping with his support of industrial unionism, Rice wholeheartedly endorsed the Wagner Act as a logical defense for the worker. Although he favored most other New Deal objectives, he occasionally came into conflict with Washington reformers. Ironically, this led to close ties between Rice and the Roosevelt administration. In 1938 Rice opposed urban renewal in a lower-middle and working-class section of Pittsburgh. He felt that destruction of a stable community of small homeowners and subsequent imposition of a public apartment house complex in an already crowded neighborhood, was unfair, immoral, and harmful to stable family life. Thus, Rice formed a tenants' association and brought the matter to court. He did not successfully block the project, but on the average local residents received $1,000 more for their homes than the original figure offered by the government. In later years Rice became chairman of Pittsburgh's Fair Rent Committee. This community action group processed thousands of complaints against the Public Housing Authority and other government agencies during the boom town atmosphere of wartime Pittsburgh. Rice eventually held numerous government positions in housing, went to New York and set up the Brooklyn Rent Control System, and became OPA Rent Control Director for Western Pennsylvania.[19]

Although Rice was never as radical as the name of his organization implied, he worked closely with the labor movement during the Great Depression, becoming one of the most active labor priests of the decade. While many other clerics carried on similar activities, the industrial complexion of the Pittsburgh area thrust Rice into the focus of national attention; and, in the perspective of the cautious immigrant workers of the area, Rice appeared well ahead of his clientele. When Catholic lay organizations did respond to the needs of the depression-ridden city, Rice and his band of priests met the challenge. After naming the organization Catholic Radical Alliance, thus achieving immediate notice, Rice proceeded to carry out genuine, serious, and, for a priest, innovative social action activities. Thus, in contrast to the conservative image of the church, and especially compared to some outspoken anti-union clerics, Rice seemed more radical than he was.

Rice was no revolutionary, but was willing to use militant means to reach short-term reform objectives. Thus he stepped into the forefront of strike activity to aid the labor movement and worked to feed the poor. Once he was given notoriety as a radical labor priest and backed his commitment with solid activities, the CIO continually called for his support to counter conservative ethnic suspicions of the new labor federation. Rice, the logical defender of the CIO in Western Pennsylvania, thwarted attacks of hostile clerics who accused the CIO of being communist. During the 1930s Rice provided a service to the worker and especially to the labor movement. Although in the late 1940s and early 1950s he supported removal of communists from positions of influence within organized labor, during the 1930s he helped create an effective, popular, and united CIO.

Rice personified one kind of labor priest of the 1930s—young, committed to change, and willing to agitate in the streets for the worker and the labor movement. Like other labor priests he supported the reforms of the New Deal and, like a select few, was appointed to office by Roosevelt. As a government administrator and as unofficial chaplain of the CIO, he had access to national figures; yet Rice did not lose sight of the individual worker. His main focus continued to be the poor, the worker, and the local union; government work remained an obligation of secondary importance.

Other labor priests concentrated on the relationship between organized labor and government. Because so many priests had prolabor associations, both state and federal Democratic administrations appointed clerics to government positions involving the labor movement. Father Francis J. Haas, author of numerous pamphlets, articles, and books favorable to unions, emerged the most notable priest serving New Deal labor agencies. President Roosevelt appointed Haas to the National Labor Board in 1933 where he chaired the majority of NLB cases from the time of his appointment until June 1934. In a personal tribute to the priest in 1935, the President described his services as "invaluable." In that year the administration assigned him to the three-man Labor Policies Board of the WPA. He also served on the NRA's Labor Advisory Board from 1933 to 1935, and on various planning and relief boards. As a federal labor mediator he settled hundreds of labor disputes from 1935 to 1943. Roosevelt sent Haas, as a presidential trouble shooter, into some of the most controversial and violent strikes of the period, including the Minneapolis Teamsters strike of 1934, the New Jersey textile strike of 1937, and the Allis Chalmers conflicts of 1938 and 1941. Haas, as a major clerical writer on social questions and as a New Deal official, gave his pronouncements on labor a two-fold tone of authority. Writing in the *Catholic Worker,* Haas argued that the worker had a duty to himself and to his fellow men to join a union.[20]

Other Roman Catholic clerics took similar if not as influential roles. Father William A. Bolger and John W. McGuire were members of the

Chicago regional labor board. Father McGuire, president of St. Victor's College, successfully mediated several controversial strikes. He had considerable confidence that government would change the exploitive traditions in American business. "It is no longer right to have any employer say—'I am not going to let anyone tell me how to run my business!' . . . Organization and reason is coming into industry." Father Fredrick Seidenberg was vice-chairman of the Detroit regional labor board; and Father Louis Hershon, vice-president of the Cleveland regional board and chairman of the Toledo regional board. James F. Cunningham served in the garment industry as chairman of the advisory board of the dress code authority. President Roosevelt appointed Edward T. Hanna of San Francisco as chairman of the National Longshoreman Board. Peter M. H. Wynhoven, editor-in-chief of the New Orleans archdiocesan newspaper *Catholic Action in the South*, served as chairman of the New Orleans regional labor board. Governor Gifford Pinchot appointed Pittsburgh's colorful Father James Cox to the Pennsylvania State Commission for the unemployed, while President Roosevelt named Cox to the state recovery board of the NRA. Monsignor John A. Ryan, the major American Catholic social thinker of the early twentieth century, held numerous labor positions both in private and public fields. He was vice-president of the National Unemployment League and vice-president of the American Association for Social Security, and held several federal government advisory positions relative to labor.[21]

If Charles Owen Rice personified the labor activist priest, John P. Boland perhaps represented the effective, government-involved labor priest. Boland did not have the national reputation of Haas, but like other priests in government he became well known and well liked in labor's official circles.

John P. Boland, son of a grain shoveler on the Buffalo docks, spent much of his life with the American worker. Upon entering the Roman Catholic priesthood, Boland became pastor of an immigrant Italian working class parish in Buffalo. He was chosen vice-president of the National Catholic Industrial Conference, which primarily engaged in discussion, dialogue, and analysis of contemporary urban, labor and economic problems. A keen observer of the labor scene, he eventually completed two unpublished volumes in labor history. Within Catholic circles Boland was considered an expert on labor problems. In 1937 he planned a course of study for the Association of Catholic Trade Unionist's labor school. He also became "moderator" of the floundering Institute for Social and Economic Problems, which he shortly revitalized.[22]

Boland's labor background brought him to the attention of New Dealers as well as politicians from the New York state Democratic organization. In 1934 Boland was named regional director of the National Labor Relations Board, holding that position while administering two parishes. In 1937 New York governor Herbert H. Lehman asked Boland to become chairman of the State Labor Relations Board (SLRB). The *Buffalo Times* urged his appointment, finding "Boland ... endeared ... to organized labor." The endorsement of the Buffalo Central Labor Council illustrated the validity of the *Times*'s statement. Holding a full-time job as SLRB chairman from 1937 to 1942 forced the priest to give up his pastorates, although not all of his nongovernment interests.[23]

During these years, Boland managed to continue in worker education. In 1939 John A. Duffy, Bishop of Buffalo requested Boland to establish a labor school. Boland organized and became director of the Diocesan Labor College which offered courses in industrial ethics, public speaking, parliamentary procedure (for greater effectiveness at union meetings), and labor law. It charged no fees and teachers volunteered their time. In 1939 the College enrolled its first class of seven hundred workers.

Boland, government administrator and church educator, developed a prolabor attitude despite his commitment to impartiality as chairman of the SLRB. Yet his official role affected his outlook, for he remained moderate and supported traditional government change. Ultimately, Boland's own interpretation of *Quadragesimo Anno* determined many of his labor views. He sought establishment of a confederation of unions, employer associations, and organizations of farmers and consumers to solve the economic ills of the depression and ultimately to change American society. He believed such a system could be established without major governmental control. Government might lead or coordinate, but its role, he felt, must be limited and the economy, although cooperative, essentially could remain in private hands. Inter-industry cooperation and effective representation of consumer and union within the economic decision-making apparatus, Boland argued, could plan an economy for permanent prosperity and human dignity. Boland considered this approach the best compromise against extremist alternatives. "The state should follow neither the individualistic nor the collectivistic theories regarding its duties." He added, "its course may well be down the middle road." Boland felt that "both industry and unions have been long on militancy and short on statesmanship," and now they should make the compromises necessary for a sane economy. He viewed the National Industrial Recovery Act as a step in this direction. It could lead to co-ownership of the means of production "and the finest in correlative planning and performance."[24]

Like many liberals, Boland viewed section 7a of NIRA as the "Magna Carta for labor." He looked favorably upon unions and argued that Pius XI, in *Quadragesimo Anno,* supported them: "his teachings with reference to union organization and membership are fairly well known." Some Catholic theorists, however, suggested that unions increased class conflict and thus were not supported by the encyclical. Boland carefully constructed an argument against this position. He asserted that not only did economic conditions of the worker improve from "collective negotiations," but so also did "the moral-religious position of the worker." He believed that "removal of existing antagonisms between employer and employee is another conclusion budding right out of free omnibus bargaining." Thus collective bargaining, rightfully carried out with such proper governmental supportive services as mediation, would lessen class conflict by bringing order and peace into the labor market.[25]

In his statements, therefore, Boland strongly supported collective bargaining and endorsed unionization efforts. He declared, the *New York Times* reported, that "collective bargaining had now become so firmly a part of the social fabric that no intelligent employer should any longer oppose it." Boland believed that collective bargaining prevented workers "from offering one another ruinous competition." In a New York state fair speech he pleaded with employers to accept collective bargaining. Boland claimed that "nowhere on earth but here are collective bargaining and all it implies still regarded as objects of deepest suspicion."[26]

Collective bargaining as a means to lessen class conflict became, to Boland, a tool of stability and conservatism. "Talking things over, discussing the middle ground," Boland believed would dispel the "cloudburst of riotous revolution threatening the whole industrial world." In a speech before the Central and Trade Labor Assembly of New York, Boland continued this theme. "Collective bargaining presupposes belief in the wage system." He argued that collective bargaining "must not include . . . the Revolutionary assumption by labor of management's rights." If to improve working conditions union leaders sought "a new economic system . . . they betray their trust." In a panel discussion Boland suggested that "industry and labor can see eye to eye . . . and they must here if America is to live." He also pointed out that in England collective bargaining "is good business" and that "we may well reach the same conclusion within the next few years." Boland best summed up his collective bargaining philosophy in 1939. "High wages for men and fair profits for management are not self-contradictory . . . the road to the highest possible wages that industry can pay must also be the road to the fairest possible profits for industry itself."[27]

If the purpose of collective bargaining was to create inter-class harmony and justice, then disruptive forces must be viewed with caution. Strikes "like war, should be labor's last weapon." He particularly criticized the sit-down strikes of the decade as "of fast-waning vogue and unhappy memory." Unlike John Ryan and Charles Owen Rice, Boland considered sit-down strikes "quasi-confiscatory occupation of another's property." Speaking before labor gatherings he also attacked communist involvement in organized labor, and frequently stressed that "the very system of private ownership of property, will bring immediate reforms."[28]

Since Boland used collective bargaining to enhance class harmony, he thoroughly supported the organization of labor and often attacked anti-union employers, whom he called "social illiterates." Boland challenged anyone to prove that "labor is more to blame than industry for the industrial ills of today." He could be dramatic in his support of unionism. "When the cry of the laborer for a just wage and reasonable working conditions is heard . . . it is the manly, startled clamour bewildered cry of part of me, of part of you . . . it is demand for inalienable rights." He could also be philosophical. "The right to organize flows from our very origin. It is a natural right." In all, he supported the "complete unionization of all industry."[29]

Boland believed a strong united labor movement would lead to class harmony. He thus lamented "the disastrous split into two movements" as "deadly." Although he felt that "the 'voice of government' was frankly on labor's side," he opposed government controls over unions arguing that "in the nature of things these should be defined by labor itself and not forced upon it from without." He believed government should not curb the right to strike even in defense industries.[30]

Boland also supported the legislative program of organized labor. He lauded the Wagner Act as an important breakthrough, and, in reaction to attempts to change the act, Boland publicly argued for its retention. He pleaded for five years to test the act and claimed that all changes proposed were "premature" and showed "deep seated bias." Boland similarly asked for further trial for the State Labor Relations Board (SLRB), debating the issue over New York radio. He often stressed the number of strikes averted by the SLRB and he likewise met with laborers themselves to prevent industrial conflict. Thus since labor relations boards and state mediation services not only aided organized labor but also promoted class harmony by preventing unnecessary conflict, Boland defended their preservation.[31]

Having a prolabor attitude while simultaneously serving on an impartial state board might have presented Boland with some difficulties. He alluded to this conflict in a 1938 article stating that "the Labor Board has to be above the very hint of attachment to either party," but he admitted that "it might lean to labor wherever the facts warranted it." His pro-union attitude posed less of a problem since Boland ultimately wanted to preserve private investment, prevent needless strikes, and promote class harmony. It is not surprising that both business and labor found him an effective and empathetic public official. In his home city, the magazine *Buffalo Business* stated that Boland had "a personal understanding of the problems of management as well as men." Herbert Lehman, governor of New York, considered Boland "an ideal public servant." New York attorney general John Bennett praised Boland as having "done much to bring peace and tranquility to labor relations in this state." In an unusual gesture the AFL and the CIO joined to sponsor a dinner in Boland's honor. Such labor leaders as William Green, president of the AFL, and James B. Carey, secretary of the CIO, lauded Boland. His respect in the labor movement could be further seen in Boland's over one hundred honorary union memberships.[32]

John P. Boland's depression labor activities lasted from the mid-1930s until his return to parish work in 1942. He typified one wing of the decade's labor priesthood—the conservative idealist. Like many an idealist Boland desired a harmonious cooperative society envisioned in the encyclicals. To bring his societal ideal about, Boland supported a conservative gradual development of class harmony through cautious union activity overseen by impartial government boards. Yet like Father Charles Owen Rice, the militant activist and organizer, Boland remained close to reality. Both men represent different thrusts of the labor priest movement, yet they jointly symbolize the contemporary socially committed cleric.

A *Christian Front* article urged priests to become labor activists. The author asked "does a priest of a local community realize how great an opportunity he has to help his workers organize? . . . His very appearance at the meeting of almost any local union is looked upon as a mark of health." Rice responded to social needs with this kind of activism, although he also did much more. The article further urged priests to work for labor quietly by writing and oratory. "It may well be one of the missions of priestly thought and speech to challenge the anti-unionism of the Rotarian." Boland took the quieter road; he worked with little fanfare and wrote, spoke, and aided labor through government service, always hoping to be a moderate force promoting class harmony. Labor priests responded differently to the poverty of the period. Cardinals such as Mooney, Stitch, and Mundelein; Bishops such as Sheil, Boyle, Duffy, Haas, McNicholas, and Lucey; Monsignors such as John Ryan, Joseph Smith, and Ligutti; Fathers Boland, Rice, Monahan, Drolet, Masse, Corridan, Higgins, Shortell, Carey, Smith, Hammond, and Cox exemplify the labor priest. Stimulated by institutions such as the Catholic Worker Movement, as well as by the obvious needs of the day, Catholic priests turned to the labor movement in greater numbers than ever before, making their influence felt in different ways. In reflecting the inner change of Roman Catholicism and its reaction to economic crises, they also mirrored the flexibility within the evolutionary process.[33]

The Catholic Worker Movement inspired many labor priests, although they often remained independent of the movement, or joined other institutions. The most well-known American cleric of the depression decade, Father Charles Coughlin, created his own institutions based on his politics and personality. Coughlin's national political role and his involvement in presidential politics has obscured his worker-oriented activities and ideas. Although not a labor priest, Coughlin attempted to significantly influence the worker and the labor movement.

CHAPTER SIX

Charles Coughlin and the Labor Movement

Father Charles Coughlin, the "Radio Priest" of the 1930s, became the first American Roman Catholic cleric to build a large national political following. Historians have studied his political activities; however, his relationship to the worker and labor movement and his attempts to organize labor have remained largely unexamined. Yet these interests of Coughlin, important in themselves, elucidate other more controversial questions concerning his ideological commitment, for his worker-oriented activities can best be understood in relation to the changes in his political perspectives.[1]

Coughlin joined the predominantly working class Detroit diocese in 1923, and three years later was assigned to a new parish at Royal Oak, an impoverished suburb on the edge of the city. Royal Oak's active Ku Klux Klan unit harassed local Catholics. Responding to Klan threats, Coughlin broadcast his sermons over a local radio station. Increasing popularity of the medium, lack of significant religious radio competition, and Coughlin's own melodious voice resulted in a gradual growth of his radio audience. By the end of 1929, Chicago and Cincinnati stations carried his sermons. A crucial acceleration in his career came in October 1931 when Coughlin attacked Herbert Hoover's ineffective attempts to stimulate economic recovery. Detroit seemed ready for strong words. By 1931 the auto industry laid off 213,000 workers, forcing over 210,000 on relief rolls while approximately 150,000 left the city in search of work. Coughlin's audience reacted to his condemnation of Hoover by sending large numbers of supporting letters. He chose to direct this political tangent into a major thrust. In a short time Father Charles Coughlin emerged a public figure.

Soon after moving into politics, Coughlin became concerned with the worker's plight. Although his arguments underwent a metamorphosis by the end of the decade—a change reflecting the evolution of his public ideological commitment—the worker nonetheless, remained one of his central concerns. In Coughlin's first statements directed to labor, he called upon workers to unionize to avoid further exploitation by the capitalist system. The worker, Coughlin argued, had his "hands tied by the manacles of disorganization; neither you nor I," he said, "dare find too much fault with him. He is more sinned against than sinning." He interpreted the social encyclicals, *Rerum Novarum* and *Quadragesimo Anno,* as pro-union documents, arguing the church specifically taught that workers had not only a right to join unions but a duty to do so. As he stated in one sermon, "in his struggle for recognition of labor unions the laborer is absolutely on the side of the angels." Coughlin advocated a guaranteed annual wage to insure working class families sufficient income. If a guaranteed wage necessitated government regulation of the economy, Coughlin would gladly support it. "For while it is unjust for labor to demand excessive profits, it is the business of government to protect labor and see that profits are justly distributed." He advocated state intervention to prevent a work day in excess of eight hours, and, if necessary, to establish the four-day week in times of economic crisis; "but pay the laborers," he maintained, "so that they can live for seven."[2]

In November 1934, Coughlin summed up his views on wages. Labor should receive an annual wage to live in decency according to American standards. "Instead of the hourly wage contract, there should be a contract of copartnership not in the ownership of the business, but in the profits of the business." To achieve this goal, government should supervise labor relations of employers, ensure "that work will be provided for all those who are willing to work, and . . . regulate the wage scale." In addition, labor should be given a voice in management. He believed, however, that a dynamic and legitimate labor movement could solve the major problems facing the worker.[3]

In the quest for permanent recovery, Coughlin advocated an inflationary panacea overshadowing both union activity and industrial reform. He saw unionism as only one strategy and, like church unionists in Europe, felt strikes should be used sparingly. "If you must strike," he often stated, "strike . . . not by laying down your tools, but by raising your voices against a financial system that keeps you today and will keep you tomorrow in heedless bondage." He did not, however, exclude the necessity of occasional just strikes.[4]

Although Coughlin supported the right to organize, he did not support the AFL which, he felt, failed as the vanguard of labor. He pointed out that the AFL organized a small minority of workers, mainly the highly skilled, and neglected the mass of industrial labor. Thus Coughlin attacked the "class bigotry" of the AFL, adding that the federation charged high dues in order to keep out unwanted industrial workers. Doubting both the morality and the efficacy of craft unionism, he supported the industrial alternative. "Unions must be formed of men who can be bound together not according to the position they hold in the labor market," Coughlin argued, "but according to the diverse function which they perform in society. All postmen in one union, all steelworkers in another union, all automotive workers in a third union."[5]

Elements in the AFL attempted to censor Coughlin shortly after his public attacks on the federation. They accused Coughlin of building his church with nonunion labor and using a nonunion printer. Coughlin replied that he distributed the construction work to his own parishioners who needed work. He claimed that he paid them above both NRA and union scales, and invited the AFL to unionize them with his suppport. The printing, he claimed was donated, but henceforth it would be done by a union shop. William Green, president of the AFL, thwarted federation attempts to censor Coughlin. In a letter to the priest, Green considered him "most sympathetic and friendly to the organized labor movement." Delegates of the Michigan Federation of Typographical Union convention, however, adopted a resolution withdrawing their "moral and financial support" from the Radio Priest. Frank X. Martel, president of the Detroit AFL, answered Coughlin's radio rebukes and called the priest "the principal racketeer in the United States."[6]

Coughlin's conflict with the AFL involved more than its failure to organize industrial workers. Its ineffectiveness in organizing auto workers of Detroit particularly disturbed him. Coughlin felt that the AFL horizontal structure precluded effective organization in the industry; he also believed that in lieu of a reasonable structural framework the AFL attracted members with extravagant wage goals. Coughlin, not realizing that unions bargained by making heavy demands often rescinded during negotiations, felt that excessive objectives added to labor capital conflict. Thus, in a sermon supporting the right to organize, Coughlin attacked AFL demands as "shallow bravado."[7]

Coughlin's hostility to the AFL and his caution regarding strikes left him open to charges of being an apologist for company unionism. His belief in mutual dependence of labor and capital further implicated him. Indeed, he considered a sophisticated union an advantage to the company: "Had the motor manufacturers been in the least intelligent they would have helped organize a friendly and efficient union years ago, instead of fighting against the laws of God and the natural laws of man." The epithet "company unionist," however, was a misnomer. Like the church unionists in Europe, he accepted, at this stage of his career, *Rerum Novarum*'s position that social Catholicism should not aid class conflict but should build bridges between the classes. The European labor clerics taught that strikes should be avoided, if possible, and dialogue between economic interests substituted. Yet European Catholic unions, although least militant on the continent, still remained independent of company control. Likewise, Coughlin condemned company unionism. As he reported in one of his Tuesday night lectures, although Coughlin believed that unions ultimately benefited employers, this "did not indicate support of company unions." He added that auto workers should withhold support from the AFL for "all auto workers should be in one union." Coughlin, in supporting industrial unionism and attacking the elitist, conservative AFL, took a position similar to other American social reformers of the early 1930s. Likewise, Coughlin's political and economic views reflected his social reformist outlook during the first four-and-a-half years of the depression.[8]

Although Coughlin counted left-wing socialists and communists among his foes, he directed a major thrust against capitalism and individualism. The industrial potential of capitalism, Coughlin argued, "has been increasingly perverted. . . . The wealth created by machines has gone in appalling disproportion to the owners of machines." In 1933, he noted "the inescapable conclusion that . . . the wage system and . . . industrial system have been inefficient and are now obsolete." Coughlin believed that "the cycle of uncurtailed mass production with its hiring and firing, its up-seasons and down-seasons has been finally completed." In another sermon given in February 1934, he identified modern capitalism with individualism and private ownership, and stated approvingly that Catholicism insisted on a dual aspect of ownership, public as well as private. He believed that a few individuals had great influence over capitalism through their control of private banking. The church, Coughlin said, absolutely condemned this concentration of wealth. His sermons pointed out that in the future contemporary anarchistic individualism "shall of necessity give way to the finer teachings that were cradled in the crib in Bethlehem." There would be a struggle between love and capitalist exploitation, between those "who are imbued with the idea that Christ's charity toward our fellow men must pre-dominate as against those who will cling tenaciously to uphold man's individualism." He argued that "the slavish philosophy that a man can be hired or fired from his occupation which pays him on an hourly basis is doomed."[9]

Coughlin's attitude toward industry also reflected his reform position of the early 1930s. He called for "socialized capitalism," urging that Catholic doctrine does not simply defend "private enterprise but also upholds a definite public ownership and public supervision." "We maintain," declared Coughlin at the end of 1934, "that principle that there be no lasting prosperity if free competition exists in any industry. Therefore, it is the business of government to legislate not only for minimum wage and maximum working schedule to be observed in industry, but also curtail individualism, so that, if necessary, factories shall be licensed and their output should be limited." It is the duty of government, he argued a short time later, to limit profits in any one industry and to see the worker reasonably paid.[10]

Of New Deal government agencies, Coughlin gave the National Recovery Administration limited support as an institution with potential. "This act as it stands is not the end but only the beginning of a huge industrial modification to be brought about by the government." In an interview with the *New York Times,* he stated that the NRA operated slowly but that perfections could not be expected overnight. At the same time he criticized and tried to prod the NRA further. With the exception of his inflationary panacea, Coughlin criticized the NRA in a manner similar to others on the moderate left. He argued that labor did not get its due under the capitalist-dominated agency which "must gradually lower the hours of weekly labor to no higher than 30. . . . Second it must gradually increase the minimum wage to approximately eighty cents per hour . . . capital and industry must learn to share more equitably their profits with labor." Like many, he felt "this National Recovery Act is only an infant without teeth."[11]

Coughlin's views were consistent with those of numerous social reformers. He supported public works, social security, and regulation of stock exchanges. Even his inflationary panaceas echoed similar approaches by many progressives within the Democratic party. Thus, it was not surprising that when conservative Catholic prelates attacked Couglin in the early 1930s, Monsignor John A. Ryan, the leading Catholic progressive, and

Dorothy Day, the spokesman for Catholic radicalism, came to his defense. Of course, Coughlin had considerable liberal support outside the church. Roosevelt patronized him and some of the President's halo could not help but brighten the priest's path of influence. Fifty-nine congressmen and six senators officially endorsed Coughlin's appointment as an advisor to the London Economic Conference. Even socialist Upton Sinclair, in his attempt to capture the governorship of California as a Democrat, sought Coughlin's support.[12]

Coughlin's social reformism became clouded by late 1934. From then to the end of 1936, Coughlin became ideologically inconsistent and ambivalent. This resulted from his growing disenchantment with the New Deal, culminating with his reluctant split with Roosevelt in 1935. Coughlin then decided to build a third party to achieve his inflationary goals and remain politically influential. But first he had to keep, and even increase, his following—a difficult task for an enemy of the popular president. Thus, the period from 1934 to 1936 was an uncertain transition for the Radio Priest. While Coughlin would eventually accept de facto facism, in this interim period of intellectual meandering he indicated this future tendency.

Coughlin began his shift from the mainstream of social reformism when he organized the National Union for Social Justice. Ironically, it began as a lobby for social reform dependent on the electoral procedure for its influence. Yet it revealed Coughlin's dictatorial traits, soon becoming an authoritarian political organization completely controlled by Coughlin.

The National Union of Social Justice (NUSJ) never had room for a democratic opposition. In a 1934 sermon outlining his plan for NUSJ, Coughlin stated "that anyone who is not willing to accept them [Coughlin's principles] in the entirety is not welcome in this Union." And, indeed, when he established the organization, Coughlin placed all power in his own hands. Upon election of the president, he alone selected the committee that nominated all candidates for the board of trustees. Thus, Coughlin, to whom the constitution had delegated all significant operating powers, controlled the board of trustees, the only practical counterveiling power within the organization.[13]

This autocratic hold did not diminish Coughlin's support among the membership. His resolutions at conventions usually passed unanimously. One which was sponsored from the floor in 1936 and brought the fascist salute from many members indicated the tone of Coughlin's support: "We endorse *our leader's* stand with regard to labor. We unreservedly commend *our leader's* stand on the annual living wage."[14]

Coughlin clearly illustrated his dictatorial powers within the NUSJ in his endorsement of William Lemke, his Union party presidential candidate in 1936. He found Lemke "eligible for endorsement by the NUSJ" without calling a convention or securing a mandate from the membership. In late 1935, he merged his Social Justice Movement with Townsend's pension followers and remnants of Huey Long's Share-the-Wealth program. Coughlin, in searching for a base of continued support, permitted many of his previous commitments to flounder or be compromised. In his sermons he moved away from labor and attempted to attract the middle and lower middle class, or those who were members of these groupings before 1929.[15]

In his attempt to capture the middle-class vote and at the same time distinguish himself from the president, Coughlin abandoned advocacy of large scale economic planning and supported competition between small economic units. In February 1935, he told his audience that he wanted "to save small industry, to protect to a degree the medium-size industry and to eliminate the danger of big industry." He planned to tax large corporations into submission, "to provide fair competititon, and thus protect small industry from being forced out of business." A month later, he indicted the New Deal because the Sherman anti-trust laws, "which were designed to curtail the growth of monopolies and trusts," had been set aside. During the Union party 1936 presidential campaign, he verbally flayed the financial and industrial capitalists. While Coughlin had never favored these groups, now, moving in a new direction, he idealized competition between small economic units. Yet he remained reluctant to sever his following among labor. Coughlin reflected his ideological shifts and compromises in his remaining labor activities during 1935 and 1936.[16]

When a new independent industrial union of auto workers, the Automotive Industrial Workers Association (AIWA), came to Coughlin for aid and counsel, he became its principal advisor and sponsor. Although he continued to orient his radio sermons to appeal to the middle class, he did not reject potential support from the industrial work force.

The AIWA grew out of an unsuccessful AFL attempt to organize the industry through federal locals. The organizing drive resulted in the emergence of several splinter groups. Of these groups the AIWA became one of the more important. It eventually claimed a membership of between seven and ten thousand, largely confined to the Dodge division of Chrysler Corporation.[17]

Coughlin first spoke for the AIWA at a meeting of ten thousand workers at the State Fair Coliseum in Michigan. He announced plans for organizing "a single vertical union of all the automotive workers of Michigan," and made a number of recommendations: a minimum annual income of $2,150 as the financial goal; caution in regard to strikes ("If you are contemplating a strike," he said, "do not enter it unless it is on a sound economic basis"); and a detailed plan for the elective structure of the union, (even suggesting the dues rate). Because of his blessing and the tone of his remarks, the union soon became known as Coughlin's union.[18]

It was not Coughlin's union, but he had formidable influence in it. In later years, statements of the original AIWA leadership depreciated Father Coughlin's role. Richard Frankensteen, secretary of the AIWA, stated that "Father Coughlin never sat with our executive board. He never had a meeting with us." Richard Harris similarly stated that Coughlin "did not act much in the role of an advisor."[19]

Coughlin had, however, an important role. In an interview in which John A. Zarembra depicted Coughlin as an eventual traitor to the AIWA, Zarembra admitted weekly meetings occurred at Coughlin's home between the priest and AIWA leadership. "I, Dick Frankensteen, Cousens, Harris, Ross, McIntyre, and many others; we would sit there and discuss matters." The AIWA dedicated its first annual publication to "our advisor and supporter Father Charles E. Coughlin, the friend and educator of the mass." The statement followed a full-page photograph of Father Coughlin that appeared on page one. The eventual image of the AIWA as a "semi-company union" when men like Frankensteen were bona fide union leaders perhaps resulted from Father Coughlin's restraining influence. Even Frankensteen admitted Coughlin's effect in building the organization membership: "on the strength of his name and his program at that time, we organized a lot of people." Richard Harris conceded that "unquestionably his name and prestige did give us an impetus," and John A. Zarembra found that to "the Polish workers . . . what Father Coughlin said was infallible. . . . We had die hards to the last because of Father Coughlin."[20]

At the end of 1935, Coughlin began moving apart from his independent union allies. The AIWA struck the Motor Products Company in mid-November. Coughlin, who argued that industrial conflict should be the last resort, reacted by ignoring the organization. More important, as a self-appointed spokesman for the alienated middle class, he was uncomfortable supporting an active industrial union. At any rate, he did little to help the AIWA. As Richard Frankensteen put it, "We were sadly disappointed by the fact that Father Coughlin, who had professed himself to be our friend, either went on a vacation or refused to speak out for us. . . . Father Coughlin just let us down cold. He did not do a thing for us. I think he made one public statement and that was all."[21]

The final break came shortly afterward. Zarembra claimed that the rupture resulted from a conflict of interest. Coughlin had been in contact with General Motor's executive Lawrence Fisher (Fisher Body of G.M.), whose mother belonged to Coughlin's Royal Oak Parish. Coughlin, Zarembra related, admitted to the Friday night group he would have to withdraw his support of the union or his parish would lose sizable Fisher contributions. Coughlin chose Fisher over his erring union followers; the following Sunday he attacked the AIWA and publicly broke with the group.[22]

In 1936, the year of the Union party campaign, Coughlin's labor strategy remained cautious. He tried to offend neither his labor nor antilabor supporters. Coughlin's newspaper outlet, *Social Justice,* featured many articles on the worker and labor movement. "Labor News Round-up," consisting of labor movement material from different parts of the country, appeared regularly.[23] Although in 1935 Coughlin had supported the Committee on Industrial Organization, he attacked labor and Governor Murphy of Michigan during the CIO auto strikes of 1936. For the most part, in 1936, Coughlin seldom spoke out concerning labor, and when he did he tempered his criticism with empathy. Even William Green and the AFL escaped Coughlin's wrath during the Union party campaign.

With the overwhelming defeat of the Union party in 1936, Coughlin's antidemocratic tendencies, already evident in his Union for Social Justice, came to the fore. Coughlin had said earlier that the depression not only placed capitalism on trial but "truly, democracy itself is on trial." With the defeat of the Union party and a clear victory for Roosevelt, Coughlin apparently concluded that he had given the democratic system its chance and it had failed.[24]

Nevertheless, it remained tactically difficult to break away from the moorings of democracy. Could he keep what following remained after 1936 if he moved to the political fringes? Would his superior, the newly installed Bishop Edward Mooney, permit him necessary latitude if Coughlin greatly differed from American consensus? These uncertainties caused Coughlin to modify his authoritarianism with lip service to democracy.

By late 1937, however, his ambivalence ended. Coughlin moved in a clear authoritarian direction thoroughly outweighing any remaining indications of democratic commitment. He emphasized that in the United States procedural democracy could not work because a financial conspiracy perverted it. As he put it in one sermon, "in reality, this is only a democracy in name. ... Eventually," he continued, "Congress became devoted to safeguarding the monopolies of finance and industry.... This is because the wealthy command the lawyers and the lobbies." He stressed the decadence of the party system. "I am appealing for a restoration of American democracy delivered from party-ism." He continued, in another sermon, "our lamentable condition is the direct result of the inefficient party system of politics ... some reorganization is necessary for a system of government which fails to govern." His official journal, *Social Justice*, like other rightist publications, attempted to give its attacks on democracy the respectability of tradition. The "United States Never Was a 'Democracy,' " announced a headline in 1939. "Since when did the United States become a 'democratic' form of government?" the article asked. "Since when was 'democracy' substituted for 'republic' as established under the Constitution?" Coughlin himself, although more restrained than his spokesmen, pictured the Constitution similarly. He argued that true democracy was impossible unless Congress followed the Constitution, but Congress refused to accept its proper constitutional role.[25]

The radio priest coupled his attack on the American party system with apologetics for Hitler. At one point, a column appeared in *Social Justice* entitled "Hitler Speaks," consisting of quotes from Hitler's works and writings. *Social Justice* closely parroted Nazi anti-Semitism after 1938, including the republication of the spurious "Protocols of Zion." In addition, *Social Justice* depended upon World Press Service, a Nazi propaganda agency, for a major portion of its news. While at times Coughlin mildly criticized Hitler, both Franco and Mussolini—the latter, *Social Justice*'s "man of the week"—fared better. Although Coughlin wrote Mussolini as early as 1933, not until 1938 did Coughlin indicate to the Italian dictator his support for Italian fascism. Coughlin invited Mussolini to submit an article to *Social Justice* because "so much misunderstanding has been created by the unfriendly press in America." He suggested that Mussolini "clarify your attitude toward the Jews, toward the national question and toward any other point you wish to make clear." Even though Coughlin could not know the exact content of the Italian dictator's remarks, the priest pointedly added that "*Social Justice* ... will be happy not only to publish your article but to support it editorially." The Italian ambassador to the United States then telegrammed Rome endorsing Coughlin's request. When Coughlin emerged as the moving force behind the Christian Front—which he visualized as a storm-trooper-like spearhead group uniting

right-wing organizations—the Italian ambassador further endorsed Coughlin in a letter discussing Christian Front activities. He found that Coughlin's position "is today favorable to both Italy and fascism."[26]

The Christian Front's inability to develop any important dimension is
immaterial in achieving an understanding of Coughlin's thought. He urged
his followers to gather into "platoons" which would be affiliated directly
with him. In June, Coughlin announced the establishment of the "Million
League," made up of platoons: "at the proper time, *Social Justice* platoons can be merged into a great thinking army that can swing our
teetering nation back to unity and right thinking." In July 1939, Coughlin
reaffirmed his support of the Christian Front and continued essential radio
propaganda. *Social Justice* declared that the Christian Front would operate
as a "defense mechanism against Red Activities and as a protector of
Christianity and Americanism." After a radio address denouncing the
"poppycock of democracy," Coughlin declared in *Social Justice* that his
Christian Front "will fight you (the Jewish-communist-banker conspiracy)
Franco's way if necessary . . . units of the Christian Front have formed and
are forming in New York City and elsewhere. Does that mean anything to
you Bolsheviks?"[27]

Members of the Christian Front apparently believed that they were
indeed a defense mechanism. Numerous reports indicate physical harassment of their opposition. Mayor Fiorello La Guardia of New York City
received charges, mostly from Jews, complaining of Christian Front meetings and annoyances. However, the group did not direct its hostility only
at Jews. Members of Roman Catholic organizations hostile to Coughlin
also suffered abuse from his followers. Father Charles Owen Rice, head of
the Catholic Radical Alliance, reported that Coughlinites broke up his
meetings. Members of the Catholic Worker Movement had similar problems. William Gauchat, founder of the Cleveland Catholic Worker group,
reported Coughlinite threats. Joseph Zarella, active in the New York City
unit, related similar harassment.[28]

While Coughlin scorned the political structure and his followers often
reacted violently to what they considered unpatriotic, the Radio Priest
seldom specified the kind of system he preferred over democracy. In a
March 1938 radio sermon Coughlin did outline an ambiguous governmental program. He proposed to abandon the two-party system. Instead of
congressional elections, he would "substitute the system of 'Corporate
state elections'." Each industry would have delegates in Congress with
equal representations for owners, management, and labor. Thus, for example, the steelworkers, owners, and managers of the steel industry would

each be represented separately in a House of Representatives. The House would elect the president and sponsor legislation. The Senate would be made up of two representatives from each state, one from labor and one from capital. This body would simply approve or disapprove legislation originating in the House. Congress alone would regulate money and "safeguard the functioning of the law of supply and demand" to end unemployment and hunger. In addition, Congress should settle "with finality all questions arising between capital and labor" that could not be settled by the parties. The role of the president remained unclear, but the source of power lay in the House; having two representatives from capital for every one for labor would insure its control by the capitalist, who would, therefore, also control selection of the president.[29]

A complementary article appeared in *Social Justice* less than a month later. The article related Coughlin's theory to existing practical government and perhaps clarified his image of the presidency. The article, which supported with the fullest exuberance "Salazar's Corporate State," was entitled "Portugal—God's Gift to Reformers." It visualized the president as dominating his appointed cabinet, and his one-party assembly. That the Salazar regime was a dictatorship was well known and fully acknowledged. Speaking of Salazar the article ended, "Perhaps his action will lend inspiration into whose hands the destinies of nations have been committed." During these years Coughlin often praised and defended European dictators, but he did not completely endorse their systems as did this major article in *Social Justice.*[30]

Coughlin's new industrial plans called for a system similar to NRA, but in his new approach even more power resided in private enterprise than did under the New Deal agency; he placed less power in the hands of labor. Thus, in contrast to the early 1930s when Coughlin considered NRA a good program but criticized it for not giving enough power to labor and government, he now proposed to weaken these sectors in their relations to private enterprise. This change did not represent a confusion but simply a logical aspect of Coughlin's political complexity. Given Coughlin's extremist political direction by 1937, he had worked out a new labor formula consistent with his public ideology. Coughlin wanted government to organize American workers into a single government-controlled association that would be directed by the Secretary of Labor. He wanted to eventually obliterate autonomous unions by placing them under the capitalist-controlled government. The labor agency would be similar to those established in Fascist Italy and Nazi Germany.[31]

Although Coughlin remained hostile to the AFL, the CIO, with its affiliate the United Auto Workers, became the greater evil after early 1937. "Subjected to an avalanche of hostile criticism from my fellow clergymen, I was forced to withdraw from the UAW. Immediately, it fell into the hands of radicals." Coughlin believed that the radicals and "dictator" John L. Lewis dominated the CIO. "Lewis," Coughlin said, "is an unilateralist which means that the entire world must bow before him." At the same time that Coughlin attacked democracy, he attacked the head of the CIO as undemocratic. "Certainly the laborers did not elect John Lewis, nor will John Lewis and his conferers permit the laborers to vote for any of the high officers simply because John Lewis does not believe in democracy." Coughlin went further. He insisted that a Catholic could not belong to the "Communist"-controlled CIO.[32]

Coughlin rejected both the AFL and the CIO, and reluctantly saw no possibility of the Department of Labor directing relations between management and labor. So, with the CIO having organized both General Motors and the Chrysler Corporation, Coughlin turned again to independent unionism. This time the objective was Ford. In June 1937, Coughlin attempted to start his own independent union of Ford workers which would work closely with capital. He attempted to convince the Ford management that an independent union would be beneficial to company and worker. Ford Motors could establish retail commodity centers to sell necessities to its workers at cost, thus creating with very little capital outlay both good will and a greater real income for its employees. The union, being independent, would be weak in relation to the giant company and would be controlled by the understanding Coughlin. Most important it would preempt organization by the CIO, a threat both Ford and Coughlin feared.[33]

Using this approach, Coughlin established a "Workers' Council for Social Justice" at Ford. Coughlin injected anti-Semitism, by now one of his major themes, into the auto scene, as his union excluded all "non-Christians." The union group, calling itself the Ford Brotherhood of America, began to solicit members. Three Ford workers who headed the brotherhood took leaves of absence from the firm in order to organize. Management, however, did not respond favorably. Harry Bennett, Ford's labor relations director, ordered the workers to return or face dismissal. A meeting held for the potential members brought forth very little support, and Coughlin's followers returned to work. The union died by the end of the month.[34]

Coughlin made a second attempt at Ford two months later. This time Coughlin arranged through Homer Martin, the president of the UAW, a meeting of Martin, R. J. Thomas of the UAW, and Coughlin himself. The priest offered his aid in a UAW attempt to organize Ford. Coughlin stated, according to Thomas, that while he would not use his radio sources to help the UAW, he would use his newspaper. In addition, Coughlin said that he would arrange meetings of priests to support the union and he offered the use of a building for the union's local headquarters. Coughlin considered his major contribution his ability to arrange a meeting between the Ford management and Martin. This could be done, Coughlin believed, through a Ford vice-president, one of Coughlin's parishioners. However, Coughlin based his aid on one qualifiaction, that the UAW withdraw from the CIO. Thomas rejected the idea but Coughlin favorably impressed Martin, who continued his communication with the priest.

Thomas found Martin's enthusiasm surprising. Apparently Thomas did not know that Martin had unsuccessfully sought Coughlin's support: "I listen at every opportunity to your broadcasts and have done so since you started," Martin wrote in early 1935. "I love you and your cause which is the true cause of Christ and Humanity . . . I solicit your interest in our cause." He closed the letter with a request for one thousand membership blanks for Coughlin's NUSJ. A month later he wrote, "we appreciate and love you for what you are doing in behalf of the people of our nation." A short time later he added, "I have been urging the people of my own union to join the National Union for Social Justice." A few days after Coughlin launched his campaign for the AIWA, Martin still used the same approach. "I . . . will be happy to do anything in my power to help the cause here in the state of Missouri. I have a weekly broadcast over WLBF in Kansas City, and in that broadcast have done all I could to promote the Union of Social Justice." Coughlin, however, paid little attention to Martin at this time. By 1937, the priest changed his stance. However, it was too late for him to use Martin in the CIO, for a new coalition within the union forced Martin out of the leadership.[35]

From 1938 to the end of Coughlin's public career, his labor movement activities continued in the same trend that began in 1937, but with slight variations. He attacked the existing labor federations, but now the CIO and John Lewis received particularly abusive beratement. Coughlin stated in many radio sermons that he opposed the CIO because it refused to break with communism. The CIO had adopted "the Soviet pattern . . . the pattern of the CIO is un-American, unsound and undemocratic," stated *Social Justice*. *Social Justice* attacked the CIO as anti-Nazi, but with "no corollary battle against Communism. *There has, in fact been a constant policy* of Communist coddling." Lewis was the major villain, "a labor dictator at the head of a strange organization." The CIO, according to Coughlin, had no constitution and did not believe in the autonomy of its affiliated unions. In accordance with the anti-labor line, Coughlin discontinued the labor section in *Social Justice* and gave up his attempts to attract major grassroots support among organized labor.[36]

Although Coughlin began to deemphasize his labor activities, he did not completely divorce himself from his labor supporters. He continued his intervention, particularly in the auto industry. In the 1939 UAW-Chrysler strike, Coughlin attempted to start a "back to work movement" in order to end what he called "the outmoded persecution of Chrysler." The union thwarted him partly by enlisting the aid of the Association of Catholic Trade Unionists (ACTU), which countered Coughlin's claims that the CIO was an anti-Catholic, communist-controlled organization. At a rally of 40,000 workers, Monsignor John S. Mics attacked Coughlin. The Reverend Raymond S. Clancy, executive secretary of the Archdiocesan Labor Institute, refuted Coughlin in detail in a radio program sponsored for this purpose by the ACTU. While the UAW defeated Coughlin in this instance, he remained an annoyance for the union by supporting his followers in the local union elections. As late as 1940, UAW convention delegates defeated a proposal to elect officers by referendum because they feared it would strengthen Coughlin's forces.[37]

In other parts of the country, Coughlin's labor followers continued to be active. They were influential among the predominantly Irish Catholic New York City transit workers. Large numbers read the New York pro-Coughlin Catholic newspaper, the *Brooklyn Tablet,* and Coughlin's own *Social Justice* also circulated among transit employees. The New York transit social justice group attempted to break a contract between Michael Quill's Transport Workers Union, then a left-oriented union, and the Interborough Rapid Transit Company. On February 7, 1939, Coughlinite Thomas W. Stack directed an unauthorized strike. Work crews deserted a number of trains in response to the lay off of temporary employees to make room for veteran workers who had lost their jobs when the city demolished an elevated subway division. Actually, the transit social justice group had few traditional trade union goals in the walkout. Rather, it attempted to test Coughlin's strength vis-a-vis Quill's dominance of the Transport Workers Union.[38]

Support during the strike apparently heartened the Coughlinites and although Coughlin no longer had great influence by 1940, the subway workers set up a Christian Labor Front as a subdivision of the Christian

Front. The labor group, led by Joseph and Harry Thorne, never received major support and the unit dissolved.[39]

In contrast to these conflicts with the CIO, after 1938 Coughlin revised his opinion of the AFL. He considered it the better of the two federations. "Green Denounces Reds but Lewis Pampers Them," announced the headline of an anti-Lewis article in *Social Justice.* Coughlin described the AFL as a "well organized, well officered and thorough-going American labor group." The priest's inconsistent praise stemmed from his support of the UAW-AFL, which he viewed as battling his old enemies in the Detroit CIO; Coughlin argued that "when it became apparent that the unskilled laborers in the automotive industry had lost their autonomy and had refused to recognize Communist leadership, the AFL stepped in." Homer Martin, now head of the AFL auto union, received particular praise in *Social Justice:* "the Homer Martin UAW in a sense is farther advanced than any labor union in America." The headline on the front page of one issue read, "AFL auto union will draw thousands," and was accompanied by a large flattering picture of Homer Martin and William Green.[40]

This is not to say that the AFL itself became immune to Coughlin's attacks on organized labor. *Social Justice* accused "the CIO and the AFL of taking over the government of the United States. . . . Why does not the press of the nation publicize that Harry Bridges, the coddled Communist of labor, is at the head of the 'goon squad' in Washington?" Republishing an article by Westbrook Pegler, *Social Justice* presented the view that unwilling captives constituted the membership of both federations. "These organizations are not American labor, but by the studied design of some union bosses and through the ignorance of others [they want to create the system] . . . which the nation is fighting to destroy."[41]

At the end of the decade, Coughlin's labor position differed considerably from his stated views during the early years of the depression. He evolved from a supporter of organized labor, especially the industrial union concept of the CIO, to an enemy of organized labor and especially the CIO; from a self-appointed anticapitalist spokesman for the worker to an anti-union redbaiter; from the foe of a too conservative AFL to an inconsistent supporter who often viewed it as pink tinged; from a supporter of legitimate unionism to an advocate of government-controlled labor associations.

Why these vast changes? The answer lies in the evolution of Coughlin's public political and economic attitude in relation to his momentary political ambitions. While Coughlin had inconsistencies, they did not mask a basic ideological shift that occurred between the early and late 1930s. His financial views remained the one crucial area where his basic position did not change. He continued throughout the 1930s as an outspoken inflationist, although at times he modified the device used to inflate the economy. However, in other ideological areas he moved from a mild reformer to, by the end of the decade, a de facto fascist.

He revealed his authoritarian attitude as early as 1934 with his outline of the Union of Social Justice; his followers in the union accepted his complete direction. But since Coughlin desired national influence through the electoral process, he tried not to alienate the mass of voters and thus held his fascist tendencies in check. The election of 1936 not only destroyed any use Coughlin had for the electoral process but also revealed the hard core of his following. With each swing away from the mainstream of social reformism, he lost a portion of his supporters. After the break with Roosevelt and the Union party failure, he kept the most alienated, uneducated and extreme followers. Those who had faith in Coughlin as a personal saviour could be depended on to remain with the priest. The hard core following permitted his adventures into the extremities of fascism at the end of the depression and during the first two years of the 1940s.

Much of Coughlin's later labor activities must be seen in light of his facist point of view. If by fascism we mean a dictatorship, one-party rule, regulated capitalism controlled in a large part by the capitalist, and an emotional nationalism to sublimate class conflict (in Coughlin's case based on anti-Semitism), Coughlin's position after 1938 was fascist. It was not a copy of a distinct European model. He blended corporate thought with traditional populist symbols, thus making his views more palatable to Americans. Coughlin's inflationary panacea firmly wedded him to the American past.

Coughlin may have been an unconscious fascist, not even admitting it to himself, just as he may have been an unconscious anti-Semite (he claimed to be neither), but, nevertheless, by the end of the era Coughlin's position had become de facto fascism. Indicative of the change was the attitude of previous defenders. Catholic reformers and New Deal liberals now spoke out against Coughlin, his causes, and his activities.

Given Coughlin's public adjustment to a fascist viewpoint, it is not suprising that at the end of the decade he advocated government direction, and complete government control, over trade unionism; and that he considered both the AFL and CIO evil, especially the more radical CIO. His political commitment did not preclude the existence of unionism, especially if it would be nationalistic and sublimate class conflict. Thus, it appeared logical for Coughlin to approach Ford, particularly given Ford's anti-Semitism and his rightist views concerning European politics. Coughlin's position on the Chrysler strike in 1939, his attacks on Lewis, and his support of the 1939 New York City transit strike typified his antileft attitude during this period. If he could not build a new force in organized labor, at least he could harass and oppose what he considered a communist-dominated unionism.

Coughlin's labor activities and ideas followed definite trends. From 1929 to late 1934, he favored industrial unionism and was hostile to the capitalist apologist and craft-oriented AFL, from early 1935 to the end of 1936, he was somewhat ambivalent, still officially favoring industrial unionism but relinquishing his support of the AIWA when it most needed him. He showed mild hostility to the CIO. For the most part in 1936 he said little concerning organized labor, yet *Social Justice* made efforts to interest labor elements. From 1937 to 1942, Coughlin's most thoroughly fascist period, he consistently attacked the CIO. Although the more conservative AFL fared somewhat better, Coughlin's ultimate objective was no longer industrial unionism but government-controlled labor associations. Nevertheless, he continued his labor interest and activity. His labor pattern was more consistent than his political meandering. However, to fully understand his labor activities, Coughlin's public ideological commitment must be considered. While confusion exists, especially because of Coughlin's reluctance to give up lip service to democracy, the basic difference of his ideological pronouncements from the early depression to the end of the decade cannot be masked. Coughlin's shift from a social reformist position on labor to an authoritarian anti-labor one was meaningful considering the polarization of his public political and economic views.

Coughlin's interest in the CIO was generally mirrored by Catholic spokesmen, but his point of view was not. Likewise, organized labor was concerned with the Catholic leadership's point of view since Roman Catholics constituted a large proportion of the industrial work force.

CHAPTER SEVEN

Catholicism and the CIO

Charles Coughlin's hostility to the CIO, contrasted with support by other Catholic institutions such as the Association of Catholic Trade Unionists, illustrated the differences among the Roman Catholic leadership. What of the rank and file, particularly the Catholic working-class ethnic communities? No hard data is available concerning the ethnic makeup of Roman Catholic union members. However, a cursory examination can be made for several groups given attention by labor economists and ethnic historians. The Irish and Germans provided the bulk of Catholic AFL members and leaders, while a more complex Catholic conglomerate belonged to the industrial unions of the CIO. The unskilled and semiskilled CIO Irish filtered into all major CIO unions, but conspicuously undertook leadership roles where they numerically predominated. This was particularly true in public and private municipal transportation, perhaps because of Irish political leverage on the local level. Michael Quill's Transport Workers Union, for example, originated from two sources: the clubs and social groups of Irish Republican Army exiles who had organizational savvy and a relish for political intrigue, combined with the organizing efforts of the Communist party. Although CIO organizers recruited pro-union Italian-Americans in large numbers, Italians were less likely than the Irish to have reached union leadership levels by the end of the 1930s. In many industries employing Italians—particularly in garments, hats, furs, and the other needle trades—the Eastern European Jews who came out of the social democratic tradition or in some cases the communist movements had the experience and ideological commitment to move more quickly into union hierarchy. The CIO did not successfully penetrate other industries, such as shoe manufacturing, where Italians worked in large numbers, while in still other industries Italian-Americans constituted a marginal ethnic unit. Those who entered the AFL building trades and other skills found the union leadership already in other hands, often the Irish. Although individual Italian-Americans managed to hold important local union posts in the 1930s, they had considerably less success than the unskilled Irish of the CIO, to say nothing of the skilled Irish of the AFL.[1]

Labor historians have generally assumed that union organizers found it especially difficult to enlist Polish-Americans in the union movement. However, a recent study analyzing Polish and Lithuanian miners in earlier years (before 1903) convincingly pictures the Poles as staunch union members. It might seem reasonable, then, to assume that those unions finding it difficult to organize Poles operated in industries where the labor movement faced roadblocks unrelated to the ethnic make-up of the work force. Organizers in the 1930s, however, did find Poles a more difficult union target than other ethnic groups working in the same industry. In the auto industry, for example, John A. Zarembra found Poles reluctant to join auto unions; but Poles readily enlisted in the independent Automotive Industrial Workers Association when advised to join by Father Charles Coughlin. Once unionized they became firm but conservative supporters. Len De Caux, editor of the *CIO News* and a chief aide to John L. Lewis, considered the Poles hard to sway. Union organizers in steel, such as John Sargent and George Patterson, agreed that the Poles were one of the most difficult ethnic groups to recruit in the heavily Polish Gary-Chicago area, but that once organized they fit into the union structure and made steadfast members. The Poles rose slowly to leadership positions. Indeed, the United Mine Workers, which organized the heavily Polish steel industry, placed its own people into the new union's hierarchy; while in other unions such as in the UAW, various political factions manuevering for control staffed their organizations with firm allies. The Poles had to wait their turn and prove themselves, which they did in time. Considerable research needs to be done concerning Poles, Italians, Irish, Croatians, Lithuanians and other Roman Catholic groups, particularly investigation of the ethnic effect on union structure and ideology, and of factors promoting unionization or retarding it among particular ethnic groups.[2] Unions undoubtedly took ethnicity into consideration when organizing, just as they took the religion of potential members into consideration.

The CIO realistically considered the church position important because so many unionists and potential union members adhered to Roman Catholicism. Just how many CIO members were Catholic remains unclear. Accessible figures of the religious make-up of organized labor, particularly the CIO, do not exist. Philip Murray, speaking before the Council Against Intolerance in America, said: "None of our CIO statisticians, we are happy to say, can furnish the figures as to how many Negroes, Jews, Catholics, or any other category of human beings we number in our membership." Competent scholars and observers did, however, make impressionistic estimates. According to John Brophy, the first executive director of the CIO, Catholics made up "the largest creedal body" in the federation. Historian Marc Karson, writing of the progressive period, felt that Catholics did not quite constitute a majority of the labor movement but were the largest religious group within it. Martin P. Mayer, writing in the late 1940s, estimated that at that time one-third of American unionists adhered to Catholicism as did one-fourth of all labor leaders.[3]

More precise figures may be derived from studies done in the middle 1940s. Although religious surveys of union membership were not completed during the depression, there is little reason to assume that creedal make-up of the CIO drastically changed. The most complete study distinguished between AFL and CIO membership and therefore is particularly applicable. This work gave the percentage of CIO members among American Catholics, not the percentage of Catholics in the CIO. In order to find the Catholic percentage of the CIO, the number of cases surveyed in the CIO was divided into the number of cases of American Catholics who were members of the CIO. A resultant 29.3 percent of the CIO were Roman Catholic. Following the same procedure for the AFL, results indicated that 29.7 percent of the AFL was Catholic (see Table 1).[4]

A similar picture emerged when the leadership of the CIO, the federation of particular concern in this study, was analyzed. A 1946 *Who's Who in Labor* surveyed the backgrounds of approximately 4,000 union leaders. Although the *Who's Who* appeared after the depression, it is the only such source available; and almost all the union leaders included in the 1946 survey had been active in the 1930s.

A questionnaire sent to union officials listed "church affiliation" among its questions; respondents did not, however, have to answer this query. A random sample of 400 of the original responses was selected for analysis, and of these, 295 labor union officials had answered the question of church affiliation. Table 2 shows the distribution of the responses. It is significant that of the 133 CIO leaders who answered the question of church affiliation, 52 were Catholic—almost 40 percent. Even if only a

TABLE 1. RELIGIOUS DISTRIBUTION OF UNION MEMBERSHIP

National Sample		Not union members		Union members, federation not specified		CIO members		AFL members		Union members, not AFL or CIO	
Cases *12,167*		*Cases* *9,865*	*%* *81.1*	*Cases* *176*	*%* *1.4*	*Cases* *739*	*%* *6.1*	*Cases* *1131*	*%* *9.3*	*Cases* *256*	*%* *2.1*
Roman Catholic	2,400	1,727	72.0	44	1.8	228	9.5	337	14.0	64	2.7
Methodist	2,157	1,846	85.6	22	1.0	83	3.8	161	7.5	45	2.1
Baptist	1,405	1,175	83.6	31	2.2	81	5.8	92	6.5	26	1.9
Presbyterian	964	843	87.4	14	1.5	33	3.4	56	5.8	18	1.9
Protestant, smaller bodies	889	741	83.3	6	0.7	53	6.0	71	8.0	18	2.0
Lutheran	754	607	80.5	13	1.7	42	5.6	83	11.0	9	1.2
Episcopal	589	510	86.6	3	0.5	27	4.6	36	6.1	13	2.2
Jewish	537	415	77.3	7	1.3	51	9.5	53	9.9	11	2.0
No preference	469	348	74.2	7	1.5	44	9.4	62	13.2	8	1.7
Protestant, undesignated	469	351	74.8	12	2.6	39	8.3	54	11.5	13	2.8
Christian	390	335	86.0	2	0.5	10	2.6	36	9.2	7	1.7
Congregational	378	334	88.4	4	1.4	11	2.9	22	5.8	7	1.8
No answer or "don't know"	302	242	80.1	3	1.4	17	5.6	30	9.9	10	3.3
Latter Day Saints (Mormon)	178	148	83.1	6	3.4	6	3.4	16	9.0	2	1.1
Christian Scientist	137	114	83.2	0	0.0	5	3.6	16	11.7	2	1.5
Reformed	133	118	88.7	2	1.5	6	4.5	5	3.8	2	1.5
Atheist, agnostic	16	11	68.8	0	0.0	3	18.8	1	6.2	1	6.2

Source: Wesley Allensmith, *Information Service*, May 15, 1948.

TABLE 2. Religious Affiliation of Labor Leaders

Total	AFL	CIO	Independents	
Roman Catholic	99	43	52	4
Episcopal	8	1	4	3
Methodist	36	21	14	1
Baptist	31	16	14	1
Lutheran	18	12	5	1
Congregational	10	4	3	3
Presbyterian	23	15	8	0
Jewish	3	2	1	0
Protestant or Christian	27	21	6	0
Others (29 denominations)	39	13	26	0
Totals	294	148	133	13

NOTE: Of the 400 questionnaires sampled, 294 answered the question of religious affiliation; 99 (33.6%) answered "Roman Catholic."

minute number of Catholics did not answer the question, the percentage of union leaders who were Catholics seems quite significant: the potential for Catholic influence was great. (Almost 30 percent of the AFL leaders answering the question of religious affiliation were Catholic as well.) Among the presidents of the CIO in the 1930s a number of Catholics appear as leaders of significant unions: Philip Murray, steel workers; James Carey, electrical workers; N. A. Zonarich, aluminium workers; Joseph Jurich, Fisherman's Union of the Pacific; Samuel Jogan, marine engineers; Hayward Broun (a convert), American Newspaper Guild—to name just a few. Others, such as Michael Quill of the Transport Workers Union, were most likely nominally Catholic during these years. Of the original CIO executive board established in 1938, three of the five members were Catholics: Philip Murray, one of the vice-presidents and in 1940 elected president of the federation; secretary-treasurer James Carey; and general director John Brophy. All three were concerned and committed Catholics.[5] All three eventually became active anticommunists—Carey earlier than the others. But in the 1930s their social Catholicism led to a reformist path and alliance with the CIO left.

Philip Murray, born in Scotland and son of an Irish miner, migrated to this country where he followed his father's occupation. His rise in the United Mine Workers eventually led to the presidency of the steelworkers. According to Charles Madison's biographical study of several labor leaders, Murray at an early age "took his Catholic religion affirmatively and accepted the labor encyclicals of Pope Leo XII as his goal." *Rerum Novarum* seemed to impress Murray in later years even more than *Quadragesimo Anno.* In an article discussion the moral responsibilities of organized labor, Murray's analysis echoes the views of Pope Leo XIII. At times Leo is quoted, at other times he is paraphrased. Murray found that "there is no difference in essence between the reasoning of Pope Leo and the reasoning of the modern labor organization." In speaking before the ACTU, Murray suggested his personal relationship between religion and labor. "I am one of those who believe that a labor movement . . . can't very well live without a soul. That is a necessary part of the infinite decree that all of us . . . must have the inspiration [and] values of the spirit of the soul."[6]

During and after World War II Murray advocated an "Industrial Council" plan clearly reflecting the papal encyclicals. Father Rice, a close friend of Murray, stated in later years that "Murray and McDonald both wanted to follow the encyclicals and be influenced by them." In late 1940 when Murray suggested adoption of industry-wide defense councils to President Roosevelt, the Michigan ACTU claimed the plan "very closely approximates the pattern of 'modern guild' organization advocated by the Popes and by American Bishops." When an article in the *Catholic Digest* misinterpreted Murray's position, Carl Weber, president of the Detroit ACTU, responded that "Murray's 'industrial council' plan is regarded by many Catholic authorities as the most American application of the 'vocation group' or 'modern guild' idea advanced by Pope Pius XI." He named several prominent prelates who highly praised Murray's plan as well as "other prominent and trustworthy interpreters of Catholic social thought." Weber also pointed out that the plan "was embodied in the official re-employment program of the 1944 National CIO Convention." The ACTU not only correctly interpreted Murray's position but had personal correspondence with the CIO chief in which he complimented the *Wage Earner* for being "one of the first newspapers in the country to recognize the importance of establishing industry councils as the basis of economic activity." Father George G. Higgins, in his syndicated column

"The Yardstick," stated that Murray "happens to concur with the social encyclicals of the Popes." Higgins claimed that he knew Murray well, and indeed, Murray responded to the column by writing Higgins a letter of appreciation. It is interesting that Murray belonged to the Knights of Columbus, the Ancient Order of Hibernians, and the Catholic Conference on Industrial Problems. The Catholic hierarchy sponsored the latter conferences through its subsidiary institution, the National Catholic Welfare Conference. He also served on the Advisory Council of Notre Dame; spoke often at Catholic University, where he deposited his papers; and frequently accepted honors from Catholic groups such as the Association of Catholic Trade Unionists. Both Murray's statements and institutional obligations indicated a strong Catholic commitment.[7]

John Brophy, executive director of the CIO, similarly had a Catholic background which carried over to his labor activism. In his autobiography he spoke of the local priest in the community where Brophy grew up: "He was the unselfish missionary, kind, humble, and hard-working—a true miner's priest. . . . His example has been one of the primary supports of my faith." In his early years Brophy interpreted social Catholic thought in what was considered a radical manner. As a result he faced constant harassment by conservative Catholics. Brophy defended the integrity of his Catholicism, which he felt his radicalism enhanced. In a letter to the *Pittsburgh Catholic,* he stated: "I have done what I could to aid in lessening the burdens of my fellowmen. That I believe to be Christian and radical, really radical—not red." To *America* he wrote: "I am a radical, Yes, I admit it,—in the sense of the word. I am as radical as the Encyclicals on Labor by Pope Leo XIII and Pius XI. I am an exponent of CIO policies and programs . . . such a program is not communism, even if the Communists now support it, but thoroughly in line with Catholic doctrine." To a heckler at an ACTU rally, Brophy answered, "Yes, I am a Catholic and because I obey Catholic teaching I go forward in my chosen calling to fight against greed and privilege." Interviewing the CIO director for the *Christian Front,* Richard Deverall was taken aback by Brophy's strong religious commitment. Expecting to interview a communist apologist, Deverall wrote, "we left that man Brophy with the feeling that we had met an outstanding Catholic layman." Father Rice, who knew Brophy well, agreed. He found him a "magnificent character."[8]

Speaking before Catholic audiences, Brophy related the social encyclicals to CIO organization drives. Interpreting Pius XI to the national Catholic Social Action Conference in 1938, Brophy argued "that all of us, priests and laymen and all interested in humanity go with the workers and help them achieve their immediate and practical needs, their just legitimate desires for a better and more decent way of living." This, he said, must be done immediately for "our church wants and demands the problems of the social order be thought about now." His speech ended by quoting Archbishop Robert E. Lucey's statement that it "is the duty of working people to join a bona-fide labor union." Brophy, calling on the encyclicals for support, repeatedly argued that it was a Catholic duty—a religious obligation—to support the CIO. "The Labor Encyclicals were a call to action," he said, "let us have action."[9]

James Carey rose to the position of secretary-treasurer of the CIO from the presidency of the United Electrical Workers. Like Murray and Brophy, Carey was a conscientious Catholic; in his later years he became the Association of Catholic Trade Unionists' most active ally in the labor movement. In an article for the *Religious News Service,* Carey tied his Catholicism closely to his labor thought by picturing religion and labor as having similar goals. Like Murray, Carey held membership in several religious institutions. He was a director of the National Conference of Catholic Charities, a trustee of the National Conference of Christians and Jews, and a member of the executive committee of the National Religious and Labor Federation.[10]

The two non-Catholic members of the CIO executive committee were accessible and friendly to Catholic clergy. Sidney Hillman, often praised by his friend, labor priest Francis Haas, invited Haas to give a major address before the Amalgamated Clothing Worker's Convention. According to John Brophy, most of the leadership of Lewis' United Mine Workers was Catholic. Lewis himself in a famous dialogue with Archbishop Lucey, replied to the prelate's point that the Pope wanted the workers to join in the management of industry: "I have read the encyclicals and I use them too, but I don't dare advocate worker's sharing in management just now. It would create a furor and I would surely be put down as a Communist."[11]

It can be reasonably assumed that possiblities of Catholic church influence existed in the CIO. Although labor leaders might personally understand their commitment in Catholic terms, they did not, however, successfully promote the ultimate aims of Catholic social doctrine. This can be explained in part by the church ambivalence toward the CIO, manifested in constant internal disputes over whether the CIO—the only realistic labor vehicle for social change—deserved support. Secondly, the CIO itself concentrated on organizing members and sublimated its ideological emphasis. Even organized communists with clear-cut goals did not build mass union support for their ideological position. The task of organizing receptive workers after many years of organizational failure diverted attention from ideological ends.

On the question of whether or not to support collective bargaining and labor organization, the Catholic social leaders were less ambivalent. With few exceptions, they encouraged Catholics to join the unions and to participate in union affairs. The institutions already discussed—Catholic Worker Movement, Social Action Department, labor priests of various viewpoints—all advocated union membership. National Catholic publications echoed the general posture of favoring unions and collective bargaining. *America,* for example, found unions necessary. "Without it, the worker will continue to be exploited, either directly or through the company unions." It believed that the Catholic worker should "consider it his duty to join a union." Although it did not consider the existing AFL perfect, *America* felt the federation should "be used until something better can be provided."[12]

Virgil Michel, writing in *Commonweal,* took a stronger position. Arguing that the "labor movement is possibly the most vital and important movement of the day," the author declared it the "duty of the Catholic laborer today . . . [to provide] whole-hearted support of labor organization . . . is not merely something which the Catholic church accepts as an inevitable development of our industrial society, it is something which she whole-heartedly approves . . . which she earnestly commends to worker and management alike." The article further agreed that priests who discouraged union activity "are derelict in a duty which the highest authority of the church misses no occasion to emphasize." Likewise the *Homiletic and Pastoral Review* published a pro-union article by Archbishop Lucey. He suggested that "devotion to the welfare of the laboring classes automatically includes the union." Lucey argued that "the priest may not be lukewarm towards unionism. Considering the circumstances of our time, he must be dynamic for organized labor." In a stronger statement he declared that workers "are living in a condition of economic servitude. They must be organized and set free."[13]

Numerous Catholic leaders involved with labor, such as Dorothy Day, John Ryan, R. A. McGowan, M. C. Gowan, John Cort, Francis Haas, and Charles Owen Rice, publicly set forth similar views. Even Charles Coughlin supported the principle of unionism. Those few rejecting collective bargaining tended to be either agrarians or utopians having little faith in the future of industrial society and were primarily escapists from contemporary reality.

To accept the desirability of unionism and collective bargaining usually meant support of federal legislation necessary to permit establishment of stable unions. However, Catholic spokesmen on labor questions viewed section 7a of the National Industrial Recovery Act with caution. Theoretically the section intended to protect the rights of labor within the cartelized economy which the act intended to establish. The National Labor Board, however, recognized employer directed and financed company unions as legitimate bargaining agents. Although bona fide unions expanded under the auspices of 7a, company unions grew at a faster rate. Labor-oriented Catholic leaders responded to 7a in the same manner as prolabor non-Catholics.

At first, there was enthusiasm over the potential represented in the act. Many clerics joined NRA regional boards, with Father Haas of the National Labor Advisory Board as their dean. Soon, however, Catholic social critics pointed out the National Recovery Administration's shortcomings. Section 7a, argued McGowan, Ryan, Rice, Haas, and others, did not go far enough. It protected neither the worker's right to organize nor the union's right to collective bargaining; instead it spurred company unionism.[14]

The Wagner Act, although it lacked the economic implications of the unconstitutional NRA, replaced section 7a of that act with more encompassing protective legislation. The Wagner Act created a new National Labor Relations Board, whose rulings could be enforced by the courts, and empowered it to protect the right of all workers in a given jurisdiction to organize and bargain collectively. The Wagner Act also empowered the NLRB to protect workers from "unfair" employer practices such as interference with the rights of workers, support of company unions, use of hiring or firing to discourage union membership, discrimination against workers complaining to the board, or refusal to bargain collectively with worker representatives. With very few exceptions the Catholic social leadership wholeheartedly supported the act, perhaps with even less caution than labor movement spokesmen. The bishop's administrative committee of the National Catholic Welfare Conference urged its acceptance by Congress. John Ryan publically endorsed the bill, using his congressional influence to spur its passage. Labor priests such as Rice and lay leaders such as Dorothy Day echoed the bishops. After its passage, Catholic labor activists such as labor priests Boland and Monaghan defended the act against proposed changes.[15]

The Wagner Act, in providing some protection for the worker, ensured the labor movement's ability to organize the industrial sector of the north and west. No longer could employers easily and openly fire workers because of union affiliation. The conservative AFL had never taken advantage of unionist sentiment in mass production industries. Even if the craft unionists had been willing to make the effort of organizing the unorganized, it is questionable how much success they would have had while unemployment remained great and government refused to protect the worker's right to organize. Since government intervention in labor affairs had almost always benefited capital, the AFL pursued a defeatist approach. It assumed that future intervention, in the long run, would also hurt the worker. Thus the AFL did not politically work for protection for the newly organized. Furthermore the AFL had organized craft unionists, and this elite of labor had little desire to recruit immigrant or black unskilled laborers. Many union spokesmen believed the unskilled to be inferior and inherently unorganizable. The AFL had not only rejected the principle of labor solidarity but completely accepted a simplistic capitalist framework. The Federation committed itself to "more" for its clientele, primarily highly skilled native-born workers. Convinced by their leaders, and by society at large, that "more" was the best, right, ethical, and American way, many skilled workers believed they had little reason to support union drives intended to create better conditions for outsiders. Finally, the archaic AFL structure of autonomous and competitive craft unions significantly hampered any attempts to organize the unskilled industrial work force. Since the craft unions would consider neither structural changes for themselves nor more industrial unions in the AFL, their organizational tactics had little chance of success.

The successful industrial unionism of the CIO changed the history of American labor. To confront the complex and economically ponderous corporate giants, all workers of an industry, irrespective of skill, combined together effectively. An ideological commitment reinforced this structural pragmatism. Unlike the AFL leadership, the CIO leaders committed themselves to organize the unorganized. This spectre of dual unionism not only served as an organizational stimulus to the old guard of the AFL, but added to the zeal of CIO activists. In addition the Wagner Act provided security to industrial workers who already had accepted the desirability of organization. Thus the CIO organized such basic industries as steel, auto, textiles, oil and shipping. By 1937 the young federation claimed a membership of more than 3,700,000. When this is juxtaposed to the less than 3,000,000 members of all trade unions just four years earlier, the scope of organization is more clearly realized. By the end of the decade, American unions had over 8,000,000 members.[16] Thus the CIO surged

forward in its organizational thrust. Although led by politically conservative John L. Lewis, socialists and, more important, experienced communist
organizers carried out the daily tasks of signing up workers, administering
locals, and directing strikes. Soon the rank and file elected young communists to leadership positions of many CIO unions.

Undoubtedly in response to communist influence in several unions,
some Catholic hostility to the CIO developed. This reaction was high-
lighted by the conflict between the CIO and the AFL. Since an alternative
existed, clerics hostile to the CIO but favoring the principle of collective
bargaining supported the more conservative AFL. Yet in the early 1930s,
before the CIO emerged as a problem for Catholicism, most Catholic
spokesmen had considered the AFL, as *Catholic Charities Review* put it,
too "slow to adjust itself to existing business conditions. . . . This attitude
of the federation is due to the conservatism of the craft organization." The
prestigious lay journal, *Commonweal*, put it more strongly: "the count
against the A.F. of L. is that, after the crash, it refused to acquire common
sense." The periodical accused the federation of not working "for the true
interests of the American working man . . . the federation is today in a
state of decay." *Commonweal* further scored the elitism of the AFL,
which "jealously guarded the privilege of "skilled labor." The Jesuit
journal *America* reluctantly attacked AFL ineffectiveness. As early as
1930 it scorned the AFL for having "no worth-while program and no great
leaders." It later suggested that "the A.F.L. is on its way to the bone-
yard . . . under its present administration." It wanted "the President of the
American Federation of Labor [to] tell us of well-considered plans for the
formation of more labor unions." *America*, like other Catholic periodicals
concerned with labor, believed the AFL horizontal craft structure obsolete. "The Federation can no longer afford to ignore [the industrial
union]. . . . Should it lose this chance for leadership, another opportunity
may not be afforded." On the eve of the birth of the CIO, *America*'s
support for industrial unionism became very cautious, for it feared a split
would result in radicalization of the labor movement. *America* questioned
whether "there would be no more disappointment were the horizontal to
be replaced by the vertical union." But it added that "a fair trial of the
industrial union might be of immense advantage to workers."[17]

When the CIO emerged Catholic leaders and publications deplored the
labor movement's cleavage but supported the energetic new federation.
However, the emergence of significant communist activity in the CIO
frightened many Catholic spokesmen. When the CIO began using sit-down

strikes, an anti-CIO Catholic bloc developed. Between September 1936 and June 1937 nearly a half-million workers occupied plants in such industries as auto, rubber, textiles, and glass. This tactic, previously used by the IWW and by radical unions in Italy, questioned traditional assumptions concerning private property. Catholics of both conservative and liberal persuasion became alarmed.

Jesuit Joseph N. Fichter, writing for the *Catholic World*, stressed that "it must be blatant to any thinking man that the method is wholly illegal. . . . Staying in a man's factory when he doesn't want you there is legally termed 'criminal trespassing'." He related sit-downs and the CIO to communism by claiming that John L. Lewis "employs not only a Communistically inclined organization, but likewise a Communist tactic, the sit-down strike." In a follow-up article entitled "Socialism: Communism: C.I.O.," Eugene Huber depicted the CIO as heir to the socialists and IWW. He argued that "the tactics permeating the entire organization conform to approved method of Marxism—the utter reliance upon force or the threat of force." He condemned sit-down strikes as "partial insurrections aimed at vulnerable points accompanied by invasion of properties that do not belong to it." The popular Catholic newspaper, the *Brooklyn Tablet*, declared that the sit-downs were led by "a radical disturbing element with a definite link to communism." Father Edmund A. Walsh described the tactic as a communist "alien importation." A *Sign* editorial attacked Lewis for "indifference to the inroads Communism has made in his organization"; but it praised the CIO for organizing the unorganized and suggested that without it economic misery "would breed Communism even faster then the CIO." Thus *Sign* urged Catholics to join the CIO unions and "direct this movement according to the sound principles of Catholic sociology." If *Sign's* criticism represented a halfhearted break with the CIO, the *Guildsman* symbolized the other extreme. Not only did it attack the CIO but almost alone the *Guildsman* condemned organized labor as a whole as well as the system of collective bargaining. "Union recognition means submission of employers and employees to the authority of the highest union official." It also connected organized labor to the supposed communist threat. "Is the present drive for unionization meant to serve revolutionary purposes? Even if not, the further question would remain: Is Labor's right to organize, and the power it grants, still valid, when there is no cause for grievance or when equitable terms are rejected?" Edward Koch, editor of *Guildsman*, believed that unions stimulated class antagonism and therefore subverted elimination of class consciousness, a goal of the Popes as Koch interpreted the encyclicals. He went further by arguing that Catholics should reject compromises with the economic system and secular labor associations for Catholic organizations which would promote the vocational group system.[18]

Although *America* looked positively upon industrial unionism and gave limited support to the early CIO, the issues of sit-down strikes and communism changed its emphasis. Jesuit Paul L. Blakely stressed the "essential injustice of the so-called 'sit-down' strike. They are trespassers upon the property of the Corporation's right in law and in justice to demand that they be evicted is undoubted." He followed this with other articles attacking the arguments favoring sit-downs. *America* then attacked Lewis because of his association with communists. In an editorial entitled "Mr. Lewis' Friends," it acknowledged that "We like Mr. Lewis' type of union," but added "we do not like Mr. Lewis' manners, and still less do we like some of Mr. Lewis' close associates," which it classified as "more nearly red than pink." Another editorial declared that when "the C.I.O. welcomes Communists as members, approves many as organizers and advances others to high position in its counsels, mild denunciations of Communism by President Lewis bewilder the public and make it suspicious of the CIO's ulterior purposes." *America* subdued its anticommunist attacks only when it advocated unity between the AFL and the CIO. Thus in January 1938 it not only absolved Lewis but declared that "the C.I.O. is about as Communistic as the American and National baseball leagues." It shortly returned to its original theme. In an editorial entitled "Comrade Lewis?" it asked "Is John L. Lewis Insane?" for appointing Harry Bridges to organize the West Coast. "Mr. Lewis may not be a member of the Communist party," it stated, "but he is assuredly at home in any Communist gathering." After asking whether Lewis is "determined to stamp the C.I.O. as a Communist affiliate," *America* suggested that the federation "will do well to elect another leader. Mr. Lewis is dragging it into the ditch."[19]

The CIO, of course, had many supporters among the Catholic leadership during the 1930s as the role of the Catholic Worker Movement, labor priests, and the Association of Catholic Trade Unionists in defending the CIO against charges of communist domination indicate. Although officially neutral, these groups, along with John Ryan, gave de facto aid to the CIO. CIO support also came from other areas.

The *Christian Front,* one more outgrowth of the Catholic Worker Movement, also claimed to be neutral in the rivalry between the AFL and the CIO. *"The Christian Front* takes sides with no particular party. It neither approves nor condemns the CIO." Yet it depreciated craft unions as having "little success in the United States." It added that the AFL could not really defend its inefficient "organizational technique . . . but rather that certain old-line union leaders are afraid of their position." Curiously unlike most Catholic spokesmen, the *Christian Front* supported the sit-downs: "we must in all honesty recognize the unpleasant truth that the strikers are fighting fire with fire: *their tactic is a defense tactic.*" It vehemently denied the communist charges levied against the CIO. "It is just as dishonest to call the CIO a communistic union because some of its members are Communists as it is to call it a Catholic union because some of its leaders are Catholics." It supported its position by publishing an article on industrial unions by John L. Lewis. *Christian Front* also published excerpts from a Charles Owen Rice radio talk sponsored by the Textile Worker's Organizing Committee as "an example of a simple presentation of the Church's labor doctrine." In it Rice praised John L. Lewis as "the splendid leader of the CIO," who with "other men of good character and high ability . . . has done a difficult job well." The article ended with a plea for the CIO. "What we need is not less CIO and less progressive legislation. We need more of both."[20]

Commonweal obliquely supported the CIO sit-downs by depicting them as a natural outgrowth of dehumanized mass production. It added that "the technique of the CIO exactly meets and neutralizes the technique of modern mass production. There is logic, if not legality, in Mr. Lewis' tactics." The *American Ecclesiastical Review* presented a lengthy study arguing that sit-downs do not represent "moral theft" or "violent trespass." The author, Jerome D. Hanna, presented the Haas argument that sit-down strikers defended a property interest held in their jobs. *Catholic Charities Review* as well continued its subdued support of the CIO after the sit-downs. Although it contended "that there is more than enough room for both types of organization," it attempted to prove that industrial unions are "better adapted to the organization of large scale competitive industries."[21]

The *Catholic Digest* condensed several pro-CIO articles. One from *The Ligourian* supported the CIO by citing *Osservatore Romano*, the semi-official organ of the Vatican. *Osservatore Romano* described the CIO as "more flexible and more practical" than the craft structure. *The Ligourian* quoted the papal source as stating that "American unionism has a great future in store" with the CIO. From this endorsement *The Ligourian* concluded that the "CIO has the correct principle for successful unionization of labor." Condensing an article from *The Cowl, Catholic Digest* presented the view that to call the CIO communist was not simply erroneous but an aid to communism, for "the laborer who benefits by the CIO will begin to credit his improved condition to communist activity." It pointed out that the "number of communist leaders in the CIO is small and Mr. Lewis is not one of them." To claim that "the organization has taken radical adherents," it suggested, "is neither just nor good logic." In addition, members of the hierarchy such as Archbishop Robert E. Lucey, Senior Auxiliary Bishop of Chicago Bernard James Sheil, Cardinal George C. Mundelein, and Archbishop Edward Mooney lent their voices to the CIO cause. Monsignor Reynold Hillenbrand taught and influenced a generation of priests in a pro-union direction. Many of them went on to actively support the CIO. [22]

Catholic concern about the CIO had several thrusts. Hostile churchmen argued that the new federation's "radical" ideology would corrupt Catholics and American society as a whole. Others, however, claimed that the CIO would benefit the largely Catholic industrial work force and, therefore, Catholics should help the federation. Spokesmen in both groups believed that Catholics could affect the intellectual direction of industrial unionism. Some argued that Catholicism should radicalize the CIO while others contended it should channel the CIO in a conservative direction. Thus groups such as the Association of Catholic Trade Unionists, Catholic Radical Alliance, and priests of individual dioceses set up labor schools and became active in union affairs while labor priests became the intimates of union leaders. The Catholicity of CIO members, the commitment of its leaders, and the general, although not unanimous, support of the CIO thrust Catholicism into the labor movement conflicts of the 1930s.

The Association of Catholic Trade Unionists eventually focused its attention primarily on conflict within the labor movement. The organization began, however, as a complex ideological hybrid tying Catholic corporate thought to the industrial scene of depression America.

CHAPTER EIGHT

The Association of Catholic Trade Unionists

Traveling on the New York City subway in 1937, Martin Wersing, an organizer of the Utility Workers Union, read an abandoned copy of the *Catholic Worker.* Impressed by an article written by Catholic convert John Cort, Wersing soon began attending informal gatherings at the New York Catholic Worker house. There he found many Catholic reformers who, like himself, believed the Catholic Worker Movement too utopian and not forceful enough in dealing with communism. Dissatisfied with the Catholic Worker Movement, social reformers John Cort, Edward Squitire, Edward Scully, and George Donahue gathered around Wersing to organize the Association of Catholic Trade Unionists (ACTU). Although a distinct organization after February 27, 1937, the ACTU used the New York Catholic Worker Movement facilities. In fact, it held the initial organizational meeting at a kitchen table in Catholic Worker headquarters. During its first year the ACTU continued to hold meetings at the worker center as the Catholic Worker Movement freely provided space, telephone, and mimeograph. In March of 1938 the ACTU opened its own office above a local Communist party headquarters.[1]

The members chose Wersing as president and labor priest John P. Monaghan as chaplain. Although Father Monaghan had considerable influence among the ACTU leadership, the controlling force remained in the original lay hands. Chaplains served solely as advisors. However, to hold ACTU membership one had to be Catholic and also a union member—chaplains of each chapter and lawyers who operated the ACTU legal department constituted the only exceptions to the latter requirement. The ACTU refused to admit non-Catholics because the organization's "fundamental purpose is to spread the teachings of the Catholic Church, and it could hardly expect persons who do not accept their teachings to aid in spreading them." Although the ACTU wanted the bishop of each diocese to consent to establishment of a local chapter, the association operated with complete autonomy receiving little or no direction from the hierarchy.[2]

The ACTU originally consisted of separate regional chapters comprised of members from local unions of that area. ACTU chapters, although stimulated by the New York group, originated from various labor sources. The Chicago group resulted from a strike by the American Newspaper Guild against the Hearst chain. In San Francisco a department store strike in the fall of 1938 resulted in the establishment of a Catholic ad hoc committee to inform the store's clientele of the church's position on labor. The local ACTU evolved from this committee. A Boston ACTU emerged the same year, devoting itself almost exclusively to education. This chapter grew out of a Catholic Worker study group. Paul Weber of the Newspaper Guild organized one of the largest chapters, that of Detroit. By 1940 the ACTU had eight chapters which sent delegates to a convention establishing a loose national organization presided over by a director. Subsequently a national council representing each chapter met twice a year; however, the organization's local units remained highly autonomous.[3]

The Association of Catholic Trade Unionists was established to bring the social and economic teachings of the Catholic church to average Catholic trade unionists, and in this way into the American labor movement. Official ACTU statements, accepted by most laymen and students of the subject, depicted the association as a unified organization originally guided by a Catholic corporate theory and stimulated by corporate implications of papal encyclicals, particularly Pius XI's *Quadragesimo Anno*.[4]

Catholic corporate theory has had a long history and numerous conflicting interpreters. Generally, the theory promoted societal reform in order to replace capitalism and its presumed by-products, "rugged individualism" and competition. The corporate system would re-create the social unity and sense of community theoretically inherent in the Catholic-dominant Middle Ages. To achieve this millennium a thoroughly planned and noncompetitive economy would be directed by representatives of employee, employer, and professional associations, and guided by the strong arm of the state. While corporate state theory has seldom been mentioned by name in papal encyclicals, allusion has been made to it.

The ACTU, however, did not adopt a standard version of corporate thought or simply respond to the implications of *Quadragesimo Anno.* The chief eastern and midwestern local units of the ACTU, those of New York City and Detroit, each adopted its own ideological emphasis. The Detroit ACTU advocated a clearer corporate position than the New York group, but even the Detroit unit had stronger commitments to immediate pragmatic goals than to corporate theory.

According to the official Detroit viewpoint, a "Christian revolution," the official ultimate aim of its "corporativism" concept, would reinstate Christianity as the essence of economic and social life. The individual would have to reform himself and reorganize societal institutions to meet the needs of all, thus creating an organic society where a sense of community would sublimate individual competition.[5]

The Detroit ACTU interpreted the papal encyclicals as a way of ending capitalism without going to the extremes of socialism. The corporate economic structure should be based, they argued, on employer and worker associations. Each employer association would be made up of the stockholders of each corporation in a given industry. The worker associations would be the traditional unions. Both associations of a given industry would be tied together by a representative "joint board." This board, later called guild in the ACTU newspaper, *Labor Leader,* would be responsible for all economic activity within its specific industry. It would determine the price of products, wages, working conditions, hours, levels of production, and dividends, and, in addition, care for the industry's poor, sick, and aged.[6]

The price of the product should be "the just price," that is, not greatly in excess of production costs. This would include costs of materials, labor, taxes, reserves, depreciation, and other expenses of production; fair return for investors; and reasonable compensation for management. A "living wage" would have to be an annual wage that could support the worker in comfort and security while still providing a surplus for cultural expenditure and savings. The ACTU gave workers' income priority over dividends from capital investment, but did not eliminate "legitimate interest" on investment.[7]

Another task of the joint board would be to select representatives to a national economic council. The council, or congress as the ACTU later called it, would carry out national economic planning and would ensure that the wealth of the country as a whole was more evenly distributed.

" 'Want in the midst of Plenty' would be ended." The national council would safeguard the common good, "all production would be for use and not mere profit."[8]

The Detroit group advocated a transformed economic order. Basic political changes, they believed, were unnecessary. Some federal laws prohibiting restraint of trade would have to be repealed, but the political order would remain untouched. For the most part the state would be divorced from the economic sphere since the individual would not have to be protected from giant corporations. The state itself would no longer be corrupted by involvement in private, regional, or economic interests, although government would, at times, have to intervene in cases of social distress.[9]

This limited role of government differed with traditional Catholic corporate theory, which depicted the economic system as a means of changing the national political power structure and envisioned the state as having a primary responsibility in directing economic life. Traditional corporate thinkers expanded the role of the state while the Detroit ACTU depreciated it.

Although the Detroit ACTU did not give the national government its usual status in corporate theory, the Detroit unit did commit itself, at least theoretically, to major social and economic change. This commitment expressed itself in articles propagandizing corporate theory and tying corporate reform with the intentions of the Detroit ACTU. Issues of its newspaper, the Michigan *Labor Leader* (later the *Wage Earner*), included a long series on the corporate state. Although the Detroit ACTU did not attempt to supplement its corporate plans with action, it expressed definite corporate goals. In contrast the New York *Labor Leader* published only a small number of articles illustrating dissatisfaction with capitalism and desire for change in a corporate direction. None, however, were written by union members of the ACTU but were contributed by clerical free-lance authors. The articles did not connect corporate reform to the New York ACTU; rather they theoretically discussed corporate state potential. The New York group developed a different emphasis, over-whelmingly stressing the pragmatism of immediate nonmillennial goals.

Its pragmatism cannot be seen in official statements of purpose, which did not truly indicate the institution's purposes. Insight into the ACTU's ideological commitment may be derived from unofficial statements of the ACTU leadership and press. In an interview in 1947, Edward Scully, head of the New York ACTU legal department, gave the basic position of the New York ACTU when he said, "We have no illusions of creating a system that will produce the results of the *Quadragesimo Anno.* We are only attempting to get maximum good out of what we can work with." John Cort, one of the ACTU founders and a contemporary Catholic social analyst, considered whether the ACTU should work for goals such as stock sharing, seats on corporation boards of directors, and a portion of the profits. Although he considered these things necessary in creating a truly just, Christian democratic society, he felt the time was not opportune for such goals. If one demanded these things he could be labeled, Cort believed, "a crackpot, and a Communist crackpot at that. . . . In a sense too he is a crackpot. Because he is going too fast." This statement of the major ACTU propagandist is particularly revealing since his articles on the ACTU often listed "rights and duties of a worker" which had a definite corporate leaning, but differed from his unofficial pronouncements.[10]

In the first issue of New York *Labor Leader* an article entitled "Stand of the ACTU" gave the future focus of its ideological commitments. It stressed desirability of union organization and anticommunist activities. It did not mention its corporate theory position. The Michigan *Labor Leader* summed up the ACTU's role in one of its early issues. The ACTU "has no clever, mechanical, unworkable economic solution. . . . Its only solution is day-to-day practice of Christianity." The New York *Labor Leader* stated the ACTU position as "the attitude of men determined to cleanup their own back and front yards and set their houses in order before anything else." Of the impetus of *Quadragesimo Anno,* Cort said, "It would be a pious exaggeration, however, to say that these men were motivated exclusively by a desire to put the Pope's demand into effect in America. It would be more accurate to say that from their own experiences they had seen ... how good and how necessary is the institution of trade unionism." They had seen, Cort pointed out, how racketeers and communists gained control when Christian idealism lagged. This latter fear became an overriding concern of the ACTU.[11]

Of the five founders of the ACTU, two had reacted to communist activities in their union of utility workers; one of these, Martin Wersing, originated the idea for the ACTU. A third member of the founding group, John Cort, advocated establishing the ACTU because the millennialist Catholic Worker Movement, which dominated Catholic social movement, was not as thoroughly anticommunist as he desired. The pragmatic contemporary issue of communist involvement in the labor movement emerged as the major ideological concern of the ACTU within trade unionism. In 1940 at the first national convention of the ACTU, a resolution passed calling for expulsion from the ACTU of any member who supported a communist or fellow traveler for union office. The second convention passed a resolution which advocated barring communists from labor union office. The ACTU took these steps because it believed that the growth and influence of communism was a decisive factor in depression America. "We recognized, of course that there was *in fact* a widespread class war going on," Cort stated in 1939. A speech by Archbishop Edward Mooney to an ACTU May Day rally in Detroit typified the interest of those who supported those views of the ACTU. The Archbishop felt that "a historic contest is being waged in the American Labor Movement today ... [between] Marxian chaos or Christian social order." The Archbishop strongly endorsed the ACTU anti-communist program.[12]

Week after week the *Labor Leader* ran articles and editorials damning the communists in and outside the American labor movement. It scorned Communist party attempts to make light of their differences with the ACTU and objected to union officials concerned with foreign affairs. The latter issue arose because of tenderness of the Franco issue. The *Labor Leader* advocated that actists, as it called ACTU members, bore from within Marxist-dominated unions if chance for success existed. If communists were entrenched too solidly, the ACTU counseled withdrawal from such a union and establishing a rival within the same jurisdiction as the communist-dominated one.

Just as the ACTU leadership's unofficial statements provided insight into the organization ideology, ACTU daily activities also revealed its true commitment—support of industrial unionism and attacks on communism in organized labor. In helping organize industrial unions ACTU leaders believed they promoted a more equitable society by helping workers better themselves, and also provided a bona fide trade unionist image for the ACTU. The ACTU bolstered industrial unionism most effectively during strikes, especially organizational strikes.

The actists sometimes simply argued the striking union's case in the *Labor Leader,* telling its readers that goods produced by a struck employer could not be bought in good conscience by a Catholic. One such statement comprised two columns with a black border and titled in large print: "Don't Aid Injustice." A list of companies currently being struck in the area followed. At other times the ACTU joined workers on picket lines. Like the Catholic Worker Movement, actists demonstrated by using their own distinctive placards aimed at Catholic clientele of the struck establishment. The ACTU debut in physical involvement in the labor movement came about in such a demonstration. Employees of Woolworth Stores struck, and a national columnist indirectly came to the corporation's defense by stating that Barbara Hutton, who had controlling interest in the firm, had given much to charity. ACTU signs read "Babs gave $11,000,000 to charity, but 'the worker is not to receive as alms what is his due in justice'—Pope Pius XI."[13]

In other strikes the ACTU helped organized labor most effectively by participating in rallies and giving speeches. During labor troubles local parish priests often attacked unions because the clerics associated unionism—particularly the CIO—with communism. In such instances the ACTU sent speakers to address union meetings and rallies. Frequently an actist organizer had a priest accompany him to speak on the encyclicals and on the obligation of Catholic workers to join a bona fide union. Sometimes ACTU members spoke on street corners supporting a strike. In a Boston strike against the John Hancock Insurance Company, for example, Cyril O'Brien, head of the local ACTU unit, brought Father Thomas Fay to speak before the union. O'Brien secured a telegram of support from Father John Monaghan, the highly respected New York labor priest and ACTU chaplain. Monaghan's statements urged selection of a legitimate labor union. The workers chose the United Office Workers as their bargaining agent over the opposition company union.[14]

The ACTU also aided industrial unionism by supporting the Amalgamated Utility Workers (CIO) against the company union of Consolidated Edison of New York. The ACTU began by publishing a special newspaper *Power and Light,* defending legitimate unionism. A short time later the New York *Labor Leader* launched a campaign to partially boycott Consolidated Edison by using candles instead of electricity on Friday nights. The campaign, extending several months, was endorsed by the communist *Daily Worker.*[15]

The activities of the local Chicago unit of the ACTU paralleled actions taken by the New York group. The Chicago group's first major contact with industrial and labor relations came in a 1939 strike by the Newspaper Guild against two Hearst Chicago papers, the *Evening American* and the *Herald Examiner.* The New York and Chicago ACTU newspapers repeatedly voiced support for the guild. A lead editorial in the New York *Labor Leader* attacked the Hearst papers as "purveyors of cheap, sexy filth . . . [now] embroiled in private wars on the American workingman." Soon actists showered the Chicago area with 75,000 leaflets calling for Catholic support of the strike. Distinctive ACTU placards appeared within the picket lines and many local Catholic pulpits gave strikers their blessing.

While Father John Hays led actists in a round of addresses to strike meetings, the official Chicago diocesan paper, the *New World,* enthusiastically supported the strikers. ACTU members in many cities "adopted" strikers, paying five dollars a week to support each worker's family. Bob Greenhock, chairman of the strikers' fund-raising committee, expressed his gratitude to Paul Weber, ACTU Detroit president, for "your support and cooperation as we go on battling Dirty Willie." He added that "this adoption helps us no little as we near the end of our eighth month of strike." Catholic support of the strikers apparently alarmed the Hearst publishers, for they bombarded the *New World* with letters and placed a full-page advertisement in the diocesan paper defending their position. The beleagured publishers did not sway the Catholic hierarchy, for a short time later Bishop Sheil, head of the Chicago archdiocese while Cardinal George Mundelein was in Rome, publically backed the strike.[16]

In New York City the Newspaper Guild carried out a similar strike and once again the ACTU fully supported the union. John Cort made numerous speeches for the strikers, and Thomas Converty, a clerical supporter of the ACTU, joined a citizens' committee opposing the corporation. The ACTU along with the Catholic Worker Movement picketed with the strikers. The Catholic Boys Brigade Band led a strike parade for which Barney Mulladey, a prominent ACTU supporter, acted as grand marshal. The ACTU convinced a locally prominent priest, Edward Lodge Curran, to write letters to the Brooklyn diocese organ, the *Tablet,* endorsing the strikers.[17]

In Detroit, the ACTU totally involved itself in the forefront of American industrial unionism, mainly working with the United Auto Workers. The UAW Chrysler Motors strike of 1939 had continued for some time when it appeared that the union would lose. The recently organized ACTU conferred with Archbishop Edward Mooney and members of the Michigan hierarchy. A few days later the diocesan organ, the *Michigan Catholic,* attacked the corporation and supported the CIO organizing committee. The ACTU spread the message through its newspapers and public meetings. While it is not possible to measure the effect of this support among the predominantly Catholic workers, a knowledgeable, contemporary, and impartial observer stated, "The strike was won, and there was little doubt in the minds of most observers that credit for reversing the trend belonged to the Catholic unionists. The stock of the ACTU shot up."[18]

The ACTU tried to counteract the anti-CIO propaganda of Father Charles Coughlin, especially during the Chrysler strike. Several ACTU chapters censored Coughlin; the Pittsburgh ACTU unit asserted that "Father Coughlin misinterpreted the Pope's encyclicals . . . in practically calling for compulsory arbitration he goes contrary to the principles of American and Christian democracy." The chapter notified its members that "they should not attach any authority to the words of Father Coughlin in urging them to oppose the CIO." One week after Coughlin went on the air urging a return to work at Chrysler, the ACTU bought radio time for a reply by Father Raymond S. Clancy, who opposed the back-to-work movement. The ACTU also set up a Polish organizing committee since Coughlin was particularly strong among Polish-American auto workers. Actists visited various pastors and set up a rally at a Polish church. The ACTU published announcements in *Florojwana*, the local Polish-Catholic parish newspaper. In addition to its work during the Chrysler strike, the Detroit ACTU branch participated in later CIO efforts to organize Ford.[19]

To discuss all strikes actists aided would consume considerable space, for they participated in several hundred. Sometimes they played decisive roles in minor labor confrontations, as when the ACTU brought together the CIO, AFL, and employers at New York City Catholic Worker headquarters to successfully settle a strike involving a string of cigar stores. ACTU's intervention at Columbia University gained previously denied severance pay for eleven women workers. Bookbinders of the largest open shop binding firm called on the ACTU to act as their bargaining agent after problems arose with the AFL. Actists helped direct a strike against the bindery, took part in the organizing campaign, convinced the local to accept industrial unionism, and helped negotiate a contract with a closed shop provision. ACTU disclosures that numerous New York Catholic schools and universities used nonunion printers resulted in a public outcry and a reversal of church policy. The ACTU also helped contract negotiations of recently organized workers in a number of New York plants. After working ten months to organize nonunion plumbers, actists successfully convinced the subsequent union to affiliate with the CIO.[20]

The ACTU's support of emerging industrial unions suggests its allegiance to the CIO during the struggle between the labor federations. Although officially neutral during the depression, the ACTU not only defended the CIO against Coughlin, but also against charges of communist domination. The *Labor Leader* castigated verbal attacks on the CIO by conservative AFL vice-president Matthew Woll. The paper found the "CIO has accomplished a remarkable and much needed task. . . . It was *right* that, in order to attain these just ends, a new type of Union was required.

... It was *not right* for the AFL to suspend the nine original unions which created the CIO." An editorial entitled "Anti-AFL?" denied that the ACTU held this posture, but admitted that it appeared hostile to the AFL because "it is quite true that we are opposed to unions and officials that are phoney, that are lazy, that are living and feeding on the sweat and blood of the rank-and-file, that have sold out the membership."[21]

The ACTU engaged in other activities equally pragmatic and non-utopian as activist union support. It operated a bureau which trained public speakers who delivered talks before labor gatherings and Catholic associations such as the Holy Name Society. Traditional crisis-oriented talks before strike meetings continued as well. The speakers' bureau also administered actist discussions on labor topics over New York area radio stations.[22]

The Catholic Labor Defense League (CLDL), an ACTU subsidiary, further indicated the ACTU's pragmatic contemporary approach. The league, officially formed in April 1938, originally consisted of ten Catholic lawyers who volunteered time for worthy labor cases. The cases fell under several categories. The CLDL represented individual workers whom management prevented from union organizing, individuals dismissed for union activity, and new and unaffiliated unions in contract negotiations. The CLDL also served workers in conflict with their union, conflicts which sometimes happened in racket-controlled unions, occasionally in communist-oriented ones, or often in dictatorially administered unions. When union administrations imposed excessive penalties on violators of union rules, the CLDL also intervened. In addition, it gave advice to small unions on pending labor legislation and handled union demands for back pay resulting from anti-union discrimination by employers violating national labor legislation. Each chapter of the ACTU had either a CLDL unit or, if the chapter was too small, a lawyer on the executive board to handle legal problems. In 1940 the national office directed each local to immediately form a CLDL.[23]

Most institutions attempting to grapple with day-to-day labor problems ran schools to prepare workers for union leadership. The ACTU was no exception. ACTU schools set up in New York City were administered by ACTU personnel. Union members, clerical advisors, or unpaid university faculty did the actual teaching. Traditional academic institutions sometimes provided classrooms. In 1937 the ACTU's first New York school began operations with classroom space donated by the Manhattan extension of Fordham University. The following year the ACTU operated additional schools in Harlem and the Bronx, and in 1939 provided faculty for the labor school at the College of New Rochelle in New York's Westchester County.[24]

The New York schools began with weekly classes studying labor encyclicals. In a short time the ACTU added courses in parliamentary procedure, public speaking, and the ethics of labor. This remained the basic curriculum at all ACTU schools, although courses in labor history, labor problems, and industrial relations were added. Each ACTU ran its schools somewhat differently. The Detroit group worked with the archdiocese, jointly establishing an Archdiocese Labor Institute. A major undertaking, the project ran 33 parish schools and enrolled 1400 student-members in 1940. It limited membership to Catholic trade unionists. In New York, however, any unionist could attend ACTU classes, while the Pittsburgh group, considering neither religion nor union standing a factor, opened its school to all.[25]

Minor activities of the ACTU further indicated its contemporary concerns. Actists or their clerical advisors occasionally arbitrated disputes between labor and capital and sometimes between the AFL and CIO. Actists also became engaged in local party politics. For example, the Detroit group supported Governor Murphy in the campaign of 1938. Murphy had been accused of being a communist or at least a tool of the Communist party. The actists announced through the Catholic press that "propaganda designed to identify Governor Murphy with the interest of communism is a sheer and groundless falsehood." The ACTU also became involved in New Jersey politics. The New York *Labor Leader*, like other prolabor Catholic publications, carried out a long campaign condemning suppression of labor organization in Jersey City by Mayor Hague.[26]

Actists also engaged in political persuasion on the national scene, although they did not consider this a primary responsibility. The organization protested WPA layoffs and fought racial discrimination. It adamantly supported the Wagner Act at its inception and fought proposed changes. Father Sebastian Erbacher accepted a CIO invitation to present ACTU's position over the radio. "The Wagner Act is," he argued, "in its essential principles, in close conformity with the teachings of the Popes and the Church."[27]

A major pragmatic concern of the ACTU, abolition of racketeer-dominated unions, remained one of its official goals. In the 1930s it carried out a journalistic campaign against International Longshoremen's Association president Joseph P. Ryan, whom the ACTU accused of being a corrupt leader of a gangster-ridden union. The actists also attacked New York Teamster locals in the later 1930s and 1940s for the same reasons. In response to a reform movement inspired by teamsters who attended ACTU schools, Daniel Tobin, president of the Teamsters, issued a statement forbidding union members to join religious groups paralleling union organizations. Apparently he felt that the ACTU threatened the loyalty of his members.[28] The ACTU believed that union corruption, an evil in itself, produced a greater evil; it had "opened the door to Communism."

As noted earlier, communist influence in the labor movement became a dominant ideological concern of the ACTU. It eventually became involved in numerous intraunion conflicts between anticommunists and communist supporters. A comparison of two specific cases, the Transport Workers Union and the United Electrical Workers, provides a more detailed understanding of the role of the ACTU than would a cursory examination of all the association's political conflicts.

The ACTU took an anticommunist stand with its formation in 1937, but before 1939 did not follow up this political thrust with extensive or successful union activity. Only two incidents stood out. In one, the ACTU protested to CIO president John L. Lewis the federation's involvement with left-wing groups. The action resulted from secretary-treasurer James Carey's speech before the League for Peace and Democracy, a so-called communist-front group that wanted to lift the embargo on arms to Spain. Carey, later to become an ACTU ally, at the time responded in a letter to John Cort, "I am anxious to have a list of the organizations the ACTU considers United Front in order to be guided in accepting or rejecting invitations."[29]

A second episode of early actist anticommunist activity involved Micahel Quill, president of the Transport Workers Union. Until the fall of 1938 the ACTU and the TWU had amicable relations. The ACTU supported both the union's organizing drives and its fight against racial discrimination. Although in the summer of 1839 mild, incidental disagreements arose between the ACTU and the TWU, the actists still found that "no union in this city enjoyed a better record for responsible and peaceful achievements than the Transport Workers Union." The ACTU soon changed its opinion.[30]

The first major actist attack on the TWU resulted from a Catholic Labor Defense League attempt to defend a foe of TWU leaders. The actists claimed that the union harassed their client simply because he publically disagreed with the leadership. A *Labor Leader* editorial appealed to the "rank and file to crush the growing undemocratic control of the union's affairs by the present union officials." "All opposition," the *Labor Leader* stated a month later, "has been ruthlessly crushed by the officers in power. Men who have dared to voice any objection have been brutally beaten in the streets of New York." Quill countered at the TWU annual convention by labeling the ACTU "a bunch of liars, stool pigeons, stooges and spies." Union officials then decided to visit those TWU New York sections (sublocals) having considerable ACTU members to personally denounce well-known actists. When Quill visited such a section, accompanied by Austin Hogan, New York local president, and John Santy, international secretary-treasurer, they were booed and hooted off the platform. The TWU threatened another group of actists with charges before the union review board for distributing the *Labor Leader* at a section meeting. Their section, however, overwhelmingly supported them and the TWU dropped the charges.[31]

With the August 1939 signing of the Molotov-Ribbentrop nonaggression treaty between the Soviet Union and Nazi Germany, anticommunists in the CIO went on the offensive. Until then, excepting the questions of aid to the loyalist government during the Spanish Civil War, little conflict existed in the CIO over its antifascist position. But the nonaggression treaty reopened the issue. As Len DeCaux, editor of the *CIO News,* later put it: "All right wing [CIO] factions now saw a chance to clobber the left on war issues . . . to lump communists and fascists together for common denunciation."[32]

Responding to the anticommunist offensive, the ACTU accelerated its political activity by using the communist accusation in their conflict with the TWU. In November of 1939 an opposition slate entered the TWU election opposing the union leadership. The *Labor Leader* supported the insurgents, and for the first time began attacking the TWU on communist charges.[33] The union leadership, however, overwhelmingly defeated the actist-supported opposition.

From the last six months of 1939 until the end of 1941, the ACTU and other anticommunist CIO elements proceeded in attacking CIO communists and their allies. The ACTU focused much of its activities on the TWU. It continued to harass Quill, appealing "to TWU members to stay with the union and battle to regain control for the rank and file." It claimed that the TWU members "do not want the present Communist leadership of Mike Quill and his gang," and suggested that the workers petition Philip Murray to "supplant the present leadership of the TWU with a representative of his choosing." Quill considered the threat serious enough to vigorouly chastise the ACTU, although he did not answer their charges. At an open air rally, he called the ACTU "a strike breaking agency [which no decent Catholic would belong to]'' and referred to the *Labor Leader* as "the official organ of the scabs." The ACTU newspaper responded to Quill's charges by again accusing Quill of communist affiliations. "Quill constantly denies he is a Communist but so do most Communists—that is party tactics." Another article added, "If Mike Quill is not a Communist, then I am Napoleon."[34]

During World War II the ACTU sublimated its anticommunist thrust. It limited the TWU campaign to urging—at first clandestinely—that transit workers join District 50 of the United Mine Workers. In 1942 Quill brought the plot into the open and it failed. Two years later the United Mine Workers, with actist support, again unsuccessfully tried to encroach on the TWU jurisdiction.[35]

Although the ACTU did not depose Quill, it carried out a similar campaign against the leadership of the United Electrical Workers Union (UE). Early in 1941 the ACTU took an active role in opposing the left leadership of UE. The ACTU promised the Catholic president of the union, James Carey, "enthusiastic support" if he would join them in their opposition. At the same time, Father Charles Owen Rice, the spiritual advisor of the Pittsburgh ACTU, working closely with the president of the large United Electrical Local 601 at Pittsburgh's Westinghouse plant, came into conflict with the local's communist-oriented executive board. The initial issue involved Westinghouse's dismissal of Joseph Baron, described by Father Rice as a "notorious fellow traveler." The management argued that Baron's activities affected "the prestige of the company." When Local 601 prepared to vote on whether to support Baron, Rice mobilized the Catholic community. Priests with UE congregations read a letter directing parishoners to attend the union meeting. Rice succeeded and the UE administration failed to receive support from a majority of those voting on the Baron question.[36]

Julius Emspak, secretary-treasurer of UE and a major figure in the national union, protested Rice's activities to the Bishop of Pittsburgh, Hugh C. Boyle. Emspak accused Rice of "conducting an active campaign of interference and disruption of our ranks, and exploiting to the limit that prestige which our American communities generally have accorded the clergy." He claimed that Rice's outside interference was "retarding and hindering . . . [collective bargaining] and is materially aiding—for reasons unknown to us—the company." After seeing the letter Rice responded to James Carey, still president of UE, that in Local 601 and in UE as a whole "outside interference came in through Communism and it will go out only when Communism goes."[37]

The ACTU paralleled Rice's tactics with a series of articles in September and October of 1941 supporting the anticommunists in UE and implying that this faction had great strength. ACTU also continued to appeal to UE president Carey, expecting his defection to ACTU ranks. Although other factors may have been involved, Carey did break with the communist faction. But as in the case of the TWU, the ACTU campaign in UE did not end in immediate success. UE members chose the left leadership of James Matles and Julius Emspak over James Carey, who was replaced by Thomas Fitzpatrick as president of the union.[38]

The inability of the ACTU to effect significantly these two intraunion conflicts at this time is not surprising. The ACTU did not have a highly developed and disciplined organization. More important the ACTU could find few allies for their anticommunist crusade. The left, although on the defensive from 1939 until 1941, still retained considerable leverage in the CIO. The communists had provided much of the organizing thrust of the recent 1930s, government had not opened an all out war on the left, and the CIO procommunists found protection under the isolationist umbrella of John L. Lewis and in Philip Murray's desire for labor unity. With the German invasion of the USSR, and the eventual Russian-American alliance, CIO communists found security and respectability—at least until the end of World War II.

By 1946, however, American society found itself in another international crisis. Cold war hostility was rapidly replacing World War II unity and postwar prosperity stood in contrast to the economic collapse of the depression decade. Conflict with the USSR combined with domestic security scandals produced the vision of communist subversion in government. Once Americans accepted the myth of massive communist infiltration, suppression of radicalism and dissent followed. Given the political climate and low unemployment trends, Americans rediscovered their faith in capitalism. To attack the system in the 1950s became tantamount to disloyalty.

Although many new clerics in the 1940s and early 1950s completely rejected the turmoil and wars of the secular world by withdrawing to a life of contemplation and prayer, most American Catholic spokesmen again reflected the secular trends. While the 1950s saw the emergence of the liberal Catholic journal *Cross Currents,* Catholic publications that ten years before considered capitalism totally repugnant had some difficulty in adopting a new position. Most eventually lost their distaste for the competitive system. Some journals such as *America* and *Catholic Mind* were ambivalent, either avoiding the subject of capitalism or occasionally supporting it. Still another segment of Catholic publications, such as *Catholic World,* supported by most diocesan publications, completely switched their viewpoint from repugnance to wholehearted support of capitalism.[39]

The depression-oriented interpretations of the social encyclicals and the many Catholic progressive spokesmen who intellectually matured during the 1930s made complete apology for capitalism unlikely. Thus Catholic liberal journalism did not revert to a wholehearted acceptance of capitalism as it had by the mid-1920s. *Commonweal,* for example, moved from condemnation of capitalism to acceptance of reforming the system through "Christian Industrialism" consisting of such reforms as profit-sharing plans, labor participation in management and boards of directors, and rotation of unfavorable jobs. ACTU publications *Labor Leader* and *Wage Earner,* as well as the SAD journal *Catholic Action,* supported this essentially welfare capitalist position. The *Catholic Worker* alone remained consistent with its anticapitalist tenets. It even attacked Christian industrialism as reformist and class collaborationist.[40]

Other Catholic institutions adapted themselves to new societal political norms. The Social Action Department returned to a more cautious position. Coughlin's Social Justice Movement died with the silencing of its leader during the early days of World War II. The Catholic Radical Alliance became part of the more conservative Association of Catholic Trade Unionists. In fact, Father Rice, the champion of the CIO during the depression, became preoccupied with hunting for communists in organized labor. He aided both the House Un-American Activities Committee and the Federal Bureau of Investigation in their attempts to destroy the radical elements in the labor movement.[41]

In Chicago, on the other hand, Catholic liberals, stimulated by Monsignor Reynold Hillenbrand, fostered some reformist groups, particularly from 1940 to 1947. The Christian Family Movement, Young Christian Workers, Young Christian Students, the Cana Movement, Catholic Interracial Council, and Catholic Labor Alliance continued an idealism that focused on practical problems. Hillenbrand's reformist followers, although wedded to the system, remained unable to continue the momentum for their cautious social innovations. By 1950 little remained of Hillenbrand's group.[42]

The anticommunist program of the Association of Catholic Trade Unionists thrived in an increasingly conservative environment stimulated by the cold war. Unlike its activity in the 1930s when it primarily supported CIO organizing, from the mid-1940s through the 1940s the ACTU mainly fought communist influence in the labor movement. Given

American opinion by 1946 and 1947, the ACTU found itself in a much better position to carry out its anticommunist crusade.

Following the war, the ACTU consolidated its support within the TWU. Actists Raymond Wescott, John Brooks, and Mack Rudolph organized rank and file members into a "tight, tough, trained unit." One hundred and twenty-five men were selected to attend the Catholic Xavier Labor School in New York City. During 1947 the ACTU gained complete control of the TWU unit in the Omnibus Company. All of its union officers had graduated from the Xavier School. The ACTU also made significant inroads into two other New York City transit divisions. A clash developed early in 1947 when the *Labor Leader* reported that Quill, in a Boston speech, attacked the ACTU as "a hindrance, a nuisance and a strike-busting outfit." The Third Avenue section of the New York City TWU local rebuked Quill in a unanimous censure vote. Quill responded that the *Labor Leader* "always fought not only the Transport Workers Union but many other democratic CIO unions as well." For the association itself he had stronger words: "*their cliques are shot through with stool pigeons,* and strike-breakers that after years of futile attempts to break up bona fide labor unions in New York City, and elsewhere, they find themselves now totally discredited." (Emphasis in original.) As a result of this and similar statements, all forty councils of the Knights of Columbus in New York City charged Quill with assisting the spread of atheism.[43]

The TWU conflict reached a climax in 1948. The Communist party supported Henry Wallace and the Progressive party in the presidential elections. Those politically left unions that followed suit courted alienation from CIO national leadership, which supported Harry Truman. Actist leaders clearly indicated they would vigorously oppose Quill if the TWU seceded from the CIO—a possibility considered by communist-influenced unions that intended to establish a new federation. Quill faced an added problem. The Communist party committed itself to a continuation of the five-cent fare in the New York City subways. The American Labor party, at this time procommunist, intended to run Vito Marcantonio for mayor of New York City, using their determination to continue the five-cent subway fare as a major point in their platform. The Communist party wanted Quill to forestall demands for a wage increase until after the election, which was not to be held until 1949. Transit employees, Quill argued, had not received a significant pay increase in two years and procrastination on political grounds would result in revolution in his union. For a time Quill fell in line, but a raise in fare coincided with the material interest of TWU members. In a union referendum two-thirds of the transit workers voted for a fare hike, indicating the strength of Quill's opposition.[44]

The five-cent fare and the Progressive party emerged the significant issues of the 1948 TWU convention. In his keynote address Quill immediately reversed his position and broke with the Communist party. He pointed out that at the CIO convention, Murray "made it clear, that if we were to go forward . . . all members of the CIO should conform to CIO policy." He then shouted to the receptive delegates "some of your officers lined up with the Communist Party and Dixiecrats in order to try to elect Tom Dewey . . . You will return . . . proud that we have shaken off the shackles of the Communist Party once and for all." Later in the convention Quill held up a report submitted by the communist faction. He called it "nothing more than a clip sheet from the 'Daily Worker' for the last six months," and he asked permission from the floor to tear it up. "All in favor of publically tearing up this damnable document, signify by raising your hands . . . Here it goes, boys, here it goes." Quill raised his hands over his head and dramatically destroyed the document.[45]

The communist issue crystallized in the election of officers. Party supporters attempted to delay the election and rally their forces. They failed and Quill's anticommunist slate won by a vote of three to one. The Quill board removed communists from office, abolished other positions to effect the same ends, and passed resolutions favoring the Marshall Plan and Political Action Committee of the CIO. The convention, following ACTU policy, passed constitutional amendments barring communists and their "consistent supporters" from union office. Although the change was complete and the ACTU had played a part in creating a clear anti-communist nucleus, it is difficult to say how crucial a role the ACTU did play. In the TWU, the ACTU provided the main anticommunist force until Quill's reversal of position. Although his break with the Communist party directly resulted from internal disagreements within the union's ruling bloc, the ACTU served as a factor whose following had to be reconciled.[46]

With anticommunism a major issue in American society, the ACTU also had some success in its conflict with UE. During the war years the ACTU had slackened its UE campaign, but in 1946 and 1947 it directed a two-pronged attack on the union. Numerous articles appeared in *Labor Leader,* some attacking communist influence in the union and stressing the gains of the actist faction. Others glorified James Carey. In a typical article the *Labor Leader* claimed the United Electrical New York Local 1227 and the Communist party were virtually one and that local president Hal Simo was not an electrical worker, but a Communist party functionary.[47]

Coinciding with its 1946 journalistic attack, the ACTU sponsored an insurgent group within the union. The actist role grew out of a political conflict in Yonkers, New York Local 453. Anticommunists in the local gained numerical control of the executive board but remained ineffective. In February of 1946, the anticommunist leaders of 453 turned for help to the New Rochelle Labor School, and particularly to one of its faculty members, Father Thomas Darby, an ACTU associate. John Page, the leader of the 453 anticommunists, asked Darby to establish an ACTU school in the union hall. A month later several 453 members met with actist officer George Donahue. He outlined an anticommunist program for the insurgents, including a membership drive, contention for union office in future elections, and coordination of anticommunist efforts with allied actists from other locals. Afew weeks later several 453 members met with actist officer George Donahue. He outlined an anticommunist program for the insur-from four other UE locals joined forces. They agreed to meet regularly and to coordinate their anticommunist efforts. Soon representatives from other locals joined the group, many taking ACTU courses.[48]

The group first published a small anticommunist newspaper directed to UE members and established the United Electrical Workers Committee for Rank and File Democracy. In the summer of 1946 the faction expanded nationally. Members contacted other locals and Father Thomas Darby, the group's spiritual advisor, contacted priests who might be helpful. They added fifteen locals to the original nucleus.[49]

On August 10, 1946, anticommunists in UE held a meeting and organized the Electrical Members for Democratic Action (MDA). This coalition of forces drew up a slate of officers for the next United Electrical Workers convention. The ACTU remained independent from the committee but was linked to it through individual memberships in both organizations. Actually ACTU activity lessened considerably as its New York area group threw itself into MDA activity, primarily preparing for the 1946 UE convention. The convention, however, disappointed the insurgents by electing the union's incumbent leftist leadership. Yet the anticommunist forces had some successes that year. They won control of five local unions having a combined membership of 22,000 and managed to recall from office a leftist president of another local while replacing him with one of their own.[50]

In 1947 the United Electrical Members for Democratic Action published *The Real UE;* they continued their struggle for more than a decade. Some of the insurgent ACTU groups created minor secession movements successfully directing several locals out of UE. Although the ACTU was but a part of a coalition, the union countered by attacking the Catholic organization as the major culprit. A forty-page illustrated pamphlet written by James J. Matles, UE organizational director, accused the ACTU of splitting the labor movement along religious lines. The actists countered with their own pamphlets attacking the UE administration; one written by Father Rice included detailed directions for disrupting meetings and for infiltrating and taking over unions.[51]

Rice, along with John Duffy, a UE member from Local 313, organized ACTU chapters in Pittsburgh residential neighborhoods. New members were schooled in parliamentary procedures, tactics to disrupt meetings, propaganda devices, and similar techniques which might be useful in taking over Pittsburgh's Local 610, the largest UE local with over 17,000 members.

ACTU supporter John A. Metcalfe resigned as president of 610, accusing the local of being communist dominated. "At the bottom of the trouble in local 610 are the activities of a small number of Communists whose plans for control and domination of our local are deeply resented by the enormous majority of Catholics, Republicans, Democrats, and all good labor men." The local's remaining left leadership bitterly complained that union meetings had become a shambles, that religious hostility was created, and that only management benefited from the union's divided membership.[52]

UE spokesmen again petitioned Bishop Boyle, stating that that union members "deeply resent the outside interferences in the affairs of our Union by the Association of Catholic Trade Unions and by the priests of your Diocese." After Bishop Boyle sent Rice a copy of the UE correspondence, the priest responded to his superior that Philip Murray supported the ACTU in their undertaking: "Philip Murray and I have often discussed it. Phil admits that the Reds are in control. He hates them but can do little." Rice added that Murray "often says 'Let the rank-and-file get rid of them.' We of the ACTU are educating the Catholic rank-and-file to move against the Reds." Besides approaching Bishop Boyle, Local 610 through business agent Clyde L. Johnson attacked Rice's close ally in the UE conflict, John M. Duffy, at his home base in UE Local 613. Johnson stated in a letter to 613 that the excutive board of 610 "rejects and condemns any action to interference by John M. Duffy of Local 613 . . . in the affairs of Local 610."[53]

The leftist leadership of UE focused on the ACTU as its immediate enemy and declared it a formidable opponent. Yet the ACTU concentrated its UE activity only in the New York City metropolitan area and in Pittsburgh—the latter thrust dominated by Father Rice. Furthermore, the ACTU was not a tight knit anticommunist force within the union but was made up of decentralized and sometimes differing units. Its significance lay in spearheading the fight against the communists. The ACTU had influence beyond the locals, where it engaged in direct confrontation by bringing attention to the political situation. It indirectly drew in Catholic priests such as John Lerhinan, Anthony Spina, and Michael Mechler, who were not themselves ACTU associates but took an active role in the conflict. The ACTU activity paid off when the AFL-CIO sponsored a rival international electrical workers union in late 1949. Actist-oriented locals that had remained in the union immediately withdrew from UE, becoming the nucleus of the new International Union of Electrical Workers. James Carey, whom the ACTU supported, once again headed an international union of electrical workers.

The ACTU repeated its UE and TWU anticommunist campaigns in several major international unions: the American Newspaper Guild, National Maritime Union, United Public Workers, Mine Mill and Smelter Workers, and the United Auto Workers. The association also had influence in those predominantly Catholic unions, such as the United Steel Workers, where communism remained an external issue. Philip Murray, as USW president, surrounded himself with Catholic anticommunists. While most USW leaders were not actists themselves "they found in the ACTU," as Len DeCaux stated, "the doctrinal oil for their steely machines."[54]

The activities of the ACTU indicated its pragmatic day-to-day orientation. Although it officially accepted the Catholic corporate state as its millennial goal for the labor movement, statements and intentions of the New York leadership and activities of the organization as a whole confirm that promotion of trade unionism in the 1930s and anticommunism in the 1940s emerged the primary ACTU concerns.

The theoretical millennialists of the ACTU were in reality committed to pragmatism. While a dualism within the ACTU ideological framework existed during its early years, pragmatism shortly became its actual, though seldom admitted, byword. Its corporate position did not die as a result of a clear intellectual conflict; rather it withered away as the views of the New York lay leadership gradually prevailed. During the depression the ACTU undoubtedly aided many young unions, especially in organizational stages. It helped unions by providing strike aid, by making the pro-union Catholic position known to strike breakers and clientele of struck companies, and, especially, by having its members and priests attack anti-CIO red baiters. Edward Marciniak, Catholic social critic and early ACTU participant, correctly pointed out that the ACTU labor schools trained many union leaders and the association had influence in the Catholic press which gradually affected Catholic as well as union attitudes. Republication of *Labor Leader* articles in numerous Catholic newspapers throughout the country undoubtedly aided the image of the labor movement and particularly the CIO. The ACTU did not develop a mass organization but its influence, as labor economist and historian Philip Taft pointed out, cannot be judged by numbers. Social critic Richard Rovere found that the ACTU "had taken its place as one of the most considerable of labor's pressure groups." Yet ACTU effectiveness came primarily in later years. It achieved much of its political goals as part of various anticommunist coalitions.[55]

In numerous unions the ACTU served as a ready nucleus around which anticommunists gathered once the change in political attitudes made their goals possible. In the TWU and UE conflicts the ACTU spearheaded the thrust of conservative forces. The ACTU helped cleave from the CIO its communist wing and in so doing helped build the path to the merger with the AFL. But without the votes, ideas, and tactical effectiveness of the communist unionists the CIO liberals lost much of their influence within the labor movement.

CHAPTER NINE

Catholic Institutions, Labor, and the Times

Both Catholic social action and social theology reflected the historical current. In the 1920s, church opinion, institutions, and leaders generally echoed the satisfaction with the status quo which permeated the middle-class American viewpoint. Even John Ryan felt compelled to dim his Progressive party beacon to be more in keeping with the conservative sentiments of other church leaders. With the 1929 crash and the subsequent depression, Catholic leaders again reflected new attitudes. Hostility to capitalism became commonplace on the part of church spokesmen and Catholic analysts, not surprisingly, rediscovered such views in past encyclicals. But like the rest of society, Catholic leaders could not agree on a united response to the economic crisis. While Roosevelt's New Deal—which Americans considered innovative and experimental—received significant Catholic support, clergy and laity also advanced other alternatives ranging from Father Coughlin's Christian Front to Dorothy Day's Catholic Worker Movement.

American Catholic leaders and institutions, fitting the historical trend, supported organized labor. But the Catholic leadership's virtual alliance with the traditional union movement preceded the fashions of the day. From the late nineteenth century, a major segment of the American church looked toward organized labor as an aid to the laboring classes. Catholics held working class status in greater proportion than other religious groups. Even the hierarchy usually had working class backgrounds. But during the depression the impetus supporting unionism seemed greater than before. Catholic spokesmen advocated major reform in dealing with the economic crisis, yet the attacks on Catholicism by various state governments in the 1920s and the thorough defeat of Alfred E. Smith in the presidential race of 1928 aroused suspicions of strong government on the part of much of the Catholic leadership. Organized labor, in implying reform through the private sector, thus had an added appeal.

Like the spokesmen for organized labor, concerned Catholic leaders split into AFL and CIO camps, but most Catholic groups active in labor supported the CIO and industrial unionism. Numerous CIO national and local unions acknowledged Catholic aid. CIO leaders, especially, felt that statements by prelates supporting the new federation, and thus in effect damning the red baiters, particularly aided their unions during many key strikes. Although Catholic institutions made some contribution to the rise of the CIO, the federation would have had a similar overall success without this support, even though the path to recognition might have been more difficult to travel. On the other hand, if the church had placed itself in opposition to the CIO (as a small but determined segment desired), American labor history might have been different. The religiously divided labor movements of Belgium, France, Italy, Germany, and Canada indicate the potential problem Catholic leaders could have created if they chose a separatist federation as a course of action. Likewise, to have thrown institutional Catholic power behind the AFL could not but damage the emerging CIO, which needed to organize Catholics in great numbers. But church spokesmen and institutions favored American unions and with some exceptions enthusiastically supported the CIO, working toward its acceptance by Catholic labor.

Several goals of the American prelates were accomplished with the emergence of the CIO. Both union leaders and Catholic spokesmen wanted to uplift the great mass of industrial workers from the depths of poverty. Although social Catholic leaders deplored the division between the AFL and the CIO, they looked upon the CIO's organization of American industrial workers, who were in large part Catholics, as achieving one of their labor goals. In addition some labor-oriented clerics viewed unionism as a first step in the direction of a Catholic-oriented industrial utopia. The CIO, they hoped, could serve as an avenue to a cooperative system. They expected that after the CIO completed its initial organizing, labor's reformist zeal would evolve further. Archbishop Lucey spoke for many within church labor circles when he urged John L. Lewis to demand greater unionist penetration of traditional management domains. Church reformers failed in prodding labor to further reform. Although papal encyclicals influenced individual labor leaders of the Catholic faith, these men could not easily affect the labor movement as a whole.

The concerns of labor-oriented Catholic leaders and Catholic institutions went beyond the labor movement. To some groups, such as the Catholic Worker Movement, the worker himself claimed the main focus of attention. In combining direct personal involvement with the worker, highly utopian ends, and practical aid to organized labor, the Catholic Worker Movement became the focus for radical Catholicism. The movement aided both the worker and organized labor, but its main effect was intellectual and long term. Because it was the first major American Catholic radical institution the movement became a magnet for Catholic youth disgusted with the effects of capitalism during the depression decade. Thus Catholic intellectuals could break with the social and economic system by supporting the Catholic Worker Movement while not divorcing themselves from their Catholic background.

Once involved with the Catholic Worker Movement, some supporters found its ideology too extreme and left the movement. The apprenticeship, however, often had an effect. Dissidents from within the movement organized other worker-oriented groups. Although in the 1950s dialogue between the Catholic Worker Movement and these groups often consisted of mutual recriminations, during the 1930s the Catholic Worker Movement played the role of parent, aiding its offspring in their quest for their individual concerns. Out of the Catholic Worker Movement grew the Association of Catholic Trade Unionists, Catholic Radical Alliance, Catholic Labor Alliance, and Pax, the Catholic association of conscientious objectors. Independent Catholic labor publications such as the *Christian Front* and institutional organs such as *Work, Labor Leader,* and *Wage Earner* were often edited by the Catholic Worker alumni. Over the years, numerous Catholic editors and writers for national liberal Catholic periodicals came out of the Catholic Worker Movement. Thus the movement had major significance for the Catholic left. In acting as a catalyst for the intellectual, the Catholic Worker Movement directly and indirectly served as a primary source of Catholic radical and labor activities during and after the 1930s.

Other major sources of Catholic labor activities were clerical. Father John Ryan stamped his progressive influence on the Social Action Department of the National Catholic Welfare Conference at its origin. The expanded departmental role during the 1930s continually reflected his concerns and, with few exceptions, his point of view. The Social Action Department primarily affected clerics who often treated the department's pronouncements as a declaration of the hierarchy. Ryan's reformism thus aided organized labor, particularly the CIO. The average priest in the 1930s dealt directly with workers, came from a working-class background, and functioned in a depressed economic climate. Thus while his environment encouraged prolabor inclinations, the SAD assured him of the legitimacy of his views.

Some labor priests received impetus from the SAD; others from the Catholic Worker Movement. Labor clerics themselves, whether activists like Charles Owen Rice or administrators like John Boland, provided further clerical bases to Catholic labor activities. Priests joined both government and picket lines in attempting to aid the poor and bring about recovery and reform. Father Rice personified the activist priest. Although Pittsburgh remained his home base, he fought for the CIO cause in several states and helped in numerous organizing conflicts.

When the tide changed in the later 1940s and cold warriors had rediscovered a red menace in organized labor, Rice threw his energies into the witch hunt while liberal Catholic labor leaders such as Murray and Brophy also gave their support to the anticommunist thrust. Many of the labor priests and Catholic labor-oriented institutions, excepting the Catholic Worker Movement, followed the new fashion. The ACTU led the way, appearing to have considerable influence.

The communists assumed that the ACTU had a cohesive, disciplined, and highly effective organization. The *Daily Worker* referred to the association as the "right wing" of the labor movement. It claimed that the ACTU was totally concerned with red baiting, accused it of being a "union splitting group" rebuffed by legitimate unionists, and claimed it supported the Taft-Hartley Act to promote a speed-up program of cooperation with employers. The Communist party's theoretical journal *Political Affairs* further pictured the ACTU as part of a hierarchical conspiracy to infiltrate the labor movement, led by reemergent Coughlinites.[1]

The communists exaggerated and misunderstood the role of their Catholic opposition. The ACTU was often disorganized, sometimes ineffective, and occasionally in conflict with the hierarchy. The association had some important political successes, but these occurred in alliance with other anticommunist elements.

The ACTU appeared successful because it reflected the attitudes of the cold war years. The emergence of effective anticommunism in organized labor even preceded the hysteria led by Joseph McCarthy. The period from 1946 to 1949 is best regarded as the climax of the postwar attack on the left in the labor movement. Communist influence in organized labor suffered considerably. The ACTU faction often emerged as the first outspoken anticommunist group appearing in a CIO union. In some unions, as conservative sentiment grew, active anticommunists closed around this Catholic nucleus. In most cases the ACTU served as one contingent in an anticommunist coalition. Its role, nevertheless, remained important. The ACTU thus bolstered the historical tendency, as emergent conservatism in the United States fostered the achievement of Catholic anticommunist goals in the labor movement.

With the expulsion of the communist unions from the CIO came the weakening of progressive idealism in organized labor. When the CIO merged with the conservative AFL, the remaining liberal industrial unionists were numerically overwhelmed. They have yet to recover. The same conservatism that ended significant communist influence in the CIO buried the American Catholic social and economic goals of the 1930s, for these too seemed radical and therefore un-American. Not until the 1960s, in an atmosphere that generated the chaotic and anarchistic new left, did social Catholicism and Catholic radicalism become revitalized.

Catholic journalistic attitudes from 1920 to 1940 can be seen by examining national Catholic periodicals available at major Catholic universities or by studying diocesan newspapers. The best newspaper collections are at the American Catholic Historical Society Library in Philadelphia and at Notre Dame University. Histories of newspapers and journals seldom mention Catholic sources, although the annual *Catholic Social Year Book* (Oxford: The Catholic Social Guild) contains a useful list.

The attitudes of Catholic labor leaders concerning Catholic labor goals and the Catholic church's influence of labor leaders have been mentioned in several secondary sources. Mark Karson makes this his central theme in the study *American Labor Unions and Politics, 1900–1918* (1956). Historian Aaron Abell, *American Catholicism and Social Action* (1963), and economists Selig Perlmann, *A Theory of the Labor Movement* (1949), and David Saposs, "The Catholic Church and Labor" (*Modern Monthly,* June 1933), suggest Catholic influence, but none of them pursue it further.

In seeking the possibility of a direct relation between church philosophy and the attitudes of Catholic labor leaders, one must concentrate, therefore, on primary sources. Of those Catholics who were on the executive board of the CIO during the 1930s, the papers of Philip Murray and John Brophy are at the Catholic University Archives. Unfortunately, the papers of James Carey were unavailable to the author; and while his

Catholicism has been the subject of several of his speeches, these, as well, are not easily obtained.

In examining Catholic numerical influence in the labor movement, the educated approximations by observers such as Martin P. Mayer, "Catholic Church and the Union Movement" (*Labor and the Nation,* March—April 1947), were quite accurate if judged by sociological studies done shortly thereafter. Wesley Allensmith's *Information Service* (May 1948) is based on data compiled shortly after World War II and is particularly useful because he distinguished between the AFL and CIO. An earlier study by Hadley Cantril, "Educational and Economic Composition of Religious Groups" (*American Journal of Sociology,* March 1943), is also useful. In determining Catholic membership in leadership positions, *Who's Who in Labor* (1946) is a useful source.

In dealing with individual priests involved in the labor movement during the 1930s, the New York ACTU organ *Labor Leader* was most helpful. Barbara Warne Newell, *Chicago and the Labor Movement* (1961), provides insight and factual material concerning the Chicago scene. The Charles Owen Rice papers are at Pennsylvania State University. The University of Pittsburgh Archives also has considerable Rice material. The John P. Boland papers are at the University of Notre Dame. The Francis J. Haas papers are at the Catholic University of America. On Father Haas see also Thomas E. Blantz, "Father Haas and the Minneapolis Truckers' Strike of 1934" (*Minnesota History,* Spring 1970), and Thomas E. Blantz, "Francis J. Haas: Priest in Public Service" (Ph.D. dissertation, Columbia University), 1968). Most of the minor Catholic labor-oriented groups can also be examined through *Wage Earner,* the organ of the Detroit ACTU; *Catholic Worker,* which also provides information on the Catholic Radical Alliance; the ACTU *Labor Leader,* New York edition, which is useful for many groups; and the CIO papers at the Catholic University Archives. National Catholic periodicals, especially *Commonweal,* also provide insight and information concerning the smaller Catholic institutions devoted to the worker.

When dealing with national Catholic labor-oriented groups, significant secondary material is available. Both John Ryan and the Social Action Department which he directed are covered briefly by the Abell work mentioned above and in surveys such as John Tracy Ellis, *American Catholicism* (1955). A more detailed presentation can be found in Sylvia Batdorf, "The Work of the Social Action Department of the NCWC in All Phases from 1920" (Master's thesis, Catholic University, 1933) and in William James Lee, "The Work in Industrial Relations of the Social Action

Department of the NCWC, 1933–1945" (Master's thesis, Catholic University, 1945). Both of these studies are factual with little interpretation. These works can be supplemented by the pamphlets and the SAD journal (under changing title) and by the records of SAD-sponsored industrial conferences.

The thoughts of John Ryan on labor and economic questions are discussed in Broderick, *Right Reverend New Dealer;* Patrick Gearty, *The Economic Thought of John A. Ryan* (Catholic University of America Press, 1953); and an especially thorough chapter in David Joseph O'Brien's excellent work, *American Catholics and Social Reform, The New Deal Years* (1968). There are a considerable number of Ryan's books and articles that could be examined. The more important in dealing with labor are *A Living Wage* (1910); *Distributive Justice* (1916); *The State and the Church* (1922); "Moral Aspects of Labor Unions" (in *Catholic Encyclopedia,* 1910); his autobiography, *Social Doctrine in Action; Declining Liberty and Other Papers* (1927); *Seven Troubled Years* (1936); *A Better Economic Order* (1935); and numerous articles that appeared in Catholic periodicals, especially the SAD journals. The valuable Ryan papers are available at the Catholic University Archives.

The early publications about Father Coughlin were in two categories, those wholeheartedly supporting him and those thoroughly damning him. In the former category are two works by admirer Ruth Mugglebee, *Father Coughlin of the Shrine of the Little Flower* (1933) and *Father Coughlin* (1935). *Father Charles E. Coughlin* by L. B. Ward, written in 1933, has a similar perspective. On the other side are such works as John R. Carlson, *Undercover* (1943); R. G. Swing, *Forerunners of American Fascism* (1935); and John Spivak, *Shrine of the Silver Dollar* (1940).

Reinhard H. Luthin, in *American Demagogues, Twentieth Century* (1954), gives an unsympathetic academic appraisal. In recent years, articles by James Shenton, "The Coughlin Movement and the New Deal" (*Political Science Quarterly,* September 1958) and "Fascism and Father Coughlin" (*Wisconsin Magazine of History,* Fall 1960) argue that Coughlin was inconsistent and confused rather than a fascist. Charles F. Tull, *Father Coughlin and the New Deal* (1964), supports Shenton's analysis.

Primary sources dealing with Father Coughlin include his major sermons. These were published throughout the 1930s in a series of short books. The most relevant for the concerns of this study are *Eight Lectures on Labor, Capital and Justice* (1934); *Eight Discourses on the Gold Standard and Other Kindred Subjects* (1933); and *A Series of Lectures on Social Justice* (1938). Coughlin articles and those of his supporters that appeared in *Social Justice* shed light on his movement. Unfortunately, the Coughlin papers were not available, nor were the Coughlin materials in the U.S. National Archives. The B'nai B'rith Anti-Defamation League has some materials in its archives in New York City, as does the Wayne State University Archives in Detroit. The Wayne Oral History project contains information on Coughlin's labor activities. The *New York Times, Detroit News*, and *Detroit Times* provide pieces of the factual picture.

William D. Miller's *A Harsh and Dreadful Love* (1973), which is superbly written, thoroughly researched Dorothy Day and the Catholic Worker Movement; it constitutes the most complete study of the movement. David O'Brien, mentioned previously, provides an excellent chapter examining Catholic Worker intellectual activities during the 1930s and James Arnquist's "Images of Catholic Utopianism and Radicalism in Industrial America" (Ph.D. dissertation, University of Minnesota, 1968) also has an extensive chapter on the movement. With the exception of a biography of its founder, *Peter Maurin, Gay Believer* (1959) by Arthur Sheehan, one of Maurin's followers, little else has been written on the Catholic Worker Movement. Several dissertations touch on the movement. Vernon Halloway, "Pacifism between Two Wars, 1919–1941" (Ph.D. dissertation, Yale University, 1949); Gordon Zahn, "A Study of the Social Backgrounds of Catholic Conscientious Objectors in Civilian Public Service during World War Two" (Master's thesis, Catholic University of America, 1950) and Frank Sicius, "Catholic Conscientious Objectors during World War Two" (Master's thesis, Florida State University, 1973), discuss its pacifist aspect; Eleanor Carrol, "The Catholic Worker" (Master's thesis, Catholic University, 1935), wrote of the movement from the point of view of social work.

The major primary sources concerning the Catholic Worker Movement consist of Dorothy Day's books, especially *The Long Loneliness, the Autobiography of Dorothy Day* (1939), and *Loaves and Fishes* (1963). Peter Maurin's "Easy Essays" appear frequently in the *Catholic Worker* and were last compiled and dated in *The Green Revolution, Easy Essays on Catholic Radicalism* (1961). This can be supplemented by Day's articles that appeared in national Catholic journals and in the *Catholic Worker*. In addition Ade Bethune, staff artist for the *Catholic Worker*, wrote *Work* (1939), discussing the philosophical position of the Catholic Worker Movement during the 1930s. The movement's papers are housed at Marquette University.

The Association of Catholic Trade Unionists has been given more academic attention. Several dissertations present a factual background of the organization. See Joseph F. Oberle, "The Association of Catholic

Trade Unionists" (Ph.D. dissertation, Catholic University, 1941), and Richard Ward, "The Role of the ACTU in the American Labor Movement" (Ph.D. dissertation, University of Michigan, 1958). Harold L. Wattel's "The Association of Catholic Trade Unionists (Master's thesis, Columbia University, 1947), and Henry Winestine, "The Catholic Church and Labor in the U.S." (Master's thesis, Columbia University, 1949) were helpful for the 1930s. Philip Taft in "The Association of Catholic Trade Unionists" (*Industrial and Labor Relations Review,* January 1949) gives a concise, objective history. Norman McKenna, a frequent writer on Catholic social questions, wrote a useful article in "Catholic Trade Unionists in America" (*Month,* November 1940). Michael Harrington in "Catholics in the Labor Movement: A Case History" (*Labor History,* Fall 1960) argues that the ACTU has been less influential than either its supporters or detractors believed.

ACTU primary sources consist of the various ACTU publications, especially the *New York Labor Leader,* the *Michigan Labor Leader,* and its successor, the *Detroit Wage Earner.* One of the ACTU founders, John Cort, wrote many articles examining the ACTU and kindred questions. His articles appeared regularly in national Catholic periodicals. The proceedings of the early ACTU conventions are available at the New York Public Library; the organization's papers, while not in an orderly state, are available at the ACTU Central Office in New York City.

Chapter One. *Catholicism and American Labor Reform—*
Mid-Nineteenth and Early Twentieth Centuries

1. Dennis T. Lynch, *The Wild Seventies* (New York, 1941), p. 71;
   Samuel Rezneck, "Distress, Relief and Discontent during the Depres-
   sion of 1873–1879," *Journal of Political Economy*, Dec. 1950, p.
   498; Louis Adamic, *The Story of Class Violence in America* (New
   York, 1937), pp. 19, 27; Robert V. Bruce, *1877: Year of Violence*
   (Indianapolis, 1959), p. 56; Philip S. Foner, *History of the Labor
   Movement in the United States* (New York, 1947) 1:442–48.
2. Aaron Abell, "Origins of Catholic Social Reform in the U.S.: Ideological Aspects," *Review of Politics*, July 1949, pp. 296–97; Raymond A.
   Mohl and Neil Betten, "The History of Urban America: An Interpre-
   tive Framework," *History Teacher*, June 1970.
3. Robert D. Cross, *The Emergence of Liberal Catholicism in America*
   (Cambridge, 1958), pp. 22–70.
4. Ralph H. Gabriel, *The Course of American Democratic Thought* (New
   York, 1956), pp. 66–69; also see Isaac Thomas Hecker, *The Church
   and the Age* (1887); Vincent F. Holden, *The Early Years of Thomas
   Hecker* (Washington, 1935); Abell, "Origins of Catholic Social Reform," p. 301.
5. Aaron Abell, *American Catholicism and Social Action* (Notre Dame,
   1963), p. 47; "Wealth and its Obligations," *North American Review*,
   Apr. 1889, pp. 385–94; "Some Defects in our Political and Social

Institutions," ibid., Oct. 1887, pp. 345–54; Marc Karson, *American Labor Unions and Politics, 1900–1918* (Carbondale, 1956), pp. 527, 542; Allen S. Ubil, *Life of Cardinal Gibbons, Archbishop of Baltimore* (New York, 1922), p. 37; Cross, *The Emergence of Liberal Catholicism*, p. 105.

6. Cross, *The Emergence of Liberal Catholicism*, pp. 38–43; Ireland to Gibbons, 21 July 1884, #930104, Archives of the Archdiocese of Baltimore; John Ireland, *Church and Modern Society* (New York, 1903), 2:357; Francis Downing, "Contributions to the Labor Movement," in *Church and Society*, ed. Joseph Moody (New York, 1953), p. 815; *Catholic World*, Dec. 1896, pp. 419–20; ibid., Nov. 1923, pp. 218–22.

7. Aaron Abell, "American Catholic Reaction to Industrial Conflict: The Arbitral Process, 1885–1900," *Catholic Historical Review*, Jan. 1956, pp. 387, 399.

8. James D. Arnquist, "Images of Catholic Utopianism and Radicalism in America" (Ph.D. diss., University of Minnesota, 1968), pp. 205–6, 263–72; F. W. Grafton, S. J., "The Catholic Social Platform," *Catholic World*, Sept. 1911, p. 797; Joseph McSoreley, C.S.P., "The Catholic Laymen and Social Reform," *Catholic World*, Nov. 1910, p. 190; William J. Kerby, "Aims in Socialism," *Catholic World*, July 1907, p. 510.

9. Karson, *American Labor Unions and Politics*, pp. 235–36; Abell, *American Catholicism and Social Action*, pp. 672, 170; Morris Hillquit and John A. Ryan, *Socialism: Promise or Menace* (New York, 1914), pp. 42, 249; John A. Ryan, "A Catholic View of Socialism by a Catholic Priest," *New Century*, 22 Mar. 1902; John A. Ryan, "May a Catholic be a Socialist?" *Catholic Fortnightly Review*, 1 Feb. 1909, pp. 70–71; John Ryan, *Social Doctrine in Action* (New York, 1941), pp. 112–13.

10. "Views on the Labor Movement," *Catholic World*, Mar. 1870, pp. 784–89; Abell, *American Catholicism and Social Action*, pp. 48–49; Robert C. Reinders, "T. Wharton Collens: Catholic and Christian Socialist," *Catholic Historical Review*, 1966, p. 233.

11. Archbishop Corrigan to Bishop McQuaid, cited by Abell, *American Catholicism and Social Action*, p. 62; Abell, *American Catholicism and Social Action*, pp. 64–66, 80.

12. Abell, *American Catholicism and Social Action*, p. 143; Robert E. Doherty, "Thomas J. Haggerty, the Church and Socialism," *Labor History*, Winter 1962, pp. 43–46.

13. Selig Perlman, *A Theory of the Labor Movement* (New York, 1949), p. 169; Peter Dietz, "The AF of L," p. 11, cited in Karson, *American Labor Unions and Politics*, p. 221; Peter Collins, *Central Blatt and*

Social Justice, May 1912, pp. 35—36; David Saposs, "The Catholic Church and the Labor Movement," *Modern Monthly*, June 1933, p. 296.

14. Karson, *American Labor Unions and Politics*, pp. 224, 528.
15. Abell, *American Catholicism and Social Action*, p. 149; Cross, *The Emergence of Liberal Catholicism*, pp. 45, 107.
16. See Conway in "Knights of Labor," *Donahoe's Magazine*, May 1886, pp. 443—44; for details on Catholic church and Knights of Labor conflict, see H. J. Browne, *The Catholic Church and the Knights of Labor* (Washington, 1949); for the role of one outspoken prolabor priest, see William B. Faherty, "Father Cornelius O'Leary and the Knights of Labor," *Labor History*, Spring 1970, pp. 175—89; Cross, *The Emergence of Liberal Catholicism*, pp. 117—18.
17. Abell, *American Catholicism and Social Action*, pp. 47—58; *Catholic World*, Sept. 1888, p. 842.
18. Saposs, "The Catholic Church and the Labor Movement," p. 226; Abell, *American Catholicism and Social Action*, pp. 72—80; John A. Ryan and J. Husslein, *The Church and Labor* (New York, 1924), p. 161; Edward McSweeney, "State Socialism," *Catholic World*, Feb. 1888, p. 690; Jean-Yves Calves and Jacques Perrin, *The Church and Social Justice* (Chicago, 1961), p. 76.
19. Text of encyclical as found in Ryan and Husslein, *The Church and Labor*, pp. 57—70.
20. Ibid., pp. 71—88.
21. Quoted in Richard Purcell, "John A. Ryan: Prophet of Social Justice," *Studies*, June 1946, p. 158; Karson, *American Labor Unions and Politics*, p. 235. The work of individual clerics in supporting organized labor, aiding the worker indirectly through political activity, and helping the poor directly through Catholic institutions, encompasses too vast an area to examine in considerable detail. There were, for example, priests who acted as labor mediators and kept in close contact with union leaders in their localities. See Sister Mary Herrita Fox, "Peter E. Dietz: Pioneer in the Catholic Social Action Movement" (Ph.D. diss., University of Notre Dame, 1950). The Central Verein, a Catholic organization of Americans of German origin, sponsored various workmen's organizations to foster trade union activities (Karson, *American Labor Unions and Politics*, p. 240; Abell, *American Catholicism and Social Action*, pp. 175—77). On the West Coast a labor-oriented priest in 1902 established *The Leader*, a union labor journal; he was active in the organization of unions, particularly in the teamsters' attempt to secure recognition. See Bernard C. Cronin, "Father Yorke and the Labor Movement in San Francisco 1900 to 1910" (Ph.D. diss., Catholic University of America, 1943), pp.

179—80. Urban Catholics supported various aspects of the progressive movement. They were mainly interested in secular political objectives, but many fostered legislation benefiting labor. Improved working conditions for women and children and minimum wage legislation were supported by many Catholics, not only the more well known such as John Ryan. Ryan drafted the Minnesota Statute of Minimum Wage enacted in 1913. While Catholic settlement work among the poorer of the workers did not correspond in size and scope to the Protestant settlement house movement, it made some headway in the early twentieth century. In addition to the traditional settlements, the St. Vincent de Paul Society carried out similar services beginning in the late nineteenth century. Occasional workers and homeless men who were not reached by either Catholic settlement houses or the St. Vincent de Paul Society could find missions and services in Catholic establishments developed for the purpose of rehabilitating this sector of society. See Cronin, pp. 130—87.

22. Sister Joan de Lourdes Leonard, "Catholic Attitudes Toward American Labor, 1884—1919" (Master's thesis, Columbia University, 1955), pp. 45, 75—76; Norman McKenna, "Catholic Trade Unionism in America," *Month*, Nov. 1940, pp. 303—7.
23. D. Owen Carrigan, "Martha Moore Avery; Crusader for Social Justice," *Catholic Historical Review*, 1968, pp. 17—38; on Avery's break with the Socialist Party, see D. Owen Carrigan, "A Forgotten Yankee Marxist," *New England Quarterly*, Mar. 1969, p. 42.
24. Karson, *American Labor Unions and Politics*, pp. 270—74.
25. John M. O'Neill, "Something to Think About," *The Miners' Magazine*, 4 Dec. 1913, p. 7.
26. AF of L, *Proceedings of the National Convention*, 1910, pp. 202—3; similar statements are found in the proceedings of the 1911 and 1912 conventions; Marc Karson, "The Catholic Church and the Political Developments of American Trade Unionism 1900 to 1918," *Industrial Labor Relations Review*, July 1951, p. 533; "The Aftermath of the Indianapolis Convention," *Central Blatt and Social Justice*, Oct. 1909, pp. 8—9; *Central Blatt and Social Justice*, Dec. 1904, cited by Karson, *American Labor Unions and Politics*, p. 264; see also p. 242; Abell, *American Catholicism and Social Action*, p. 174.
27. Abell, *American Catholicism and Social Action*, pp. 179—80, 174; Karson, *American Labor Unions and Politics*, p. 256.
28. "The Catholic Threat and the AF of L," *International Socialist Review*, Jan. 1914, p. 150.

Chapter Two. *Catholic Spokesmen and Capitalism—*
1920 to 1940

1. William E. Leuchtenburg, *The Perils of Prosperity, 1914–32* (Chicago, 1958), pp. 180–93; James T. Adams, *Our Business Civilization* (New York, 1929), p. 35.
2. Leuchtenburg, *Perils of Prosperity*, p. 193; Irving Bernstein, *The Lean Years, A History of the American Worker 1920–1933* (Baltimore, 1966), pp. 34–74; Eli Ginzberg and Hyman Berman, *The American Worker in the Twentieth Century* (New York, 1963), p. 155.
3. Ginzberg and Berman, *American Worker in the Twentieth Century*, p. 158; David A. Shannon, ed., *The Great Depression* (Englewood Cliffs, N.J., 1960), p. 36; "No One Has Starved," *Fortune* 5 (Sept. 1932): 19–28.
4. Ginzberg and Berman, *American Worker in the Twentieth Century*, pp. 157–58.
5. Dixon Wecter, *Age of the Great Depression, 1929–1941* (New York, 1952), p. 40; C. O. Enzler, *Some Social Aspects of the Depression* (Washington, 1939), p. 71; Bernstein, *Lean Years*, p. 332.
6. Bernstein, *Lean Years*, p. 331; Wecter, *Age of the Great Depression*, p. 39; Arthur M. Schlesinger, Jr., *The Crisis of the Old Order* (Boston, 1957), p. 171; Clarence J. Enzler, "Some Social Aspects of the Depression" (Ph.D. diss., Catholic University of America, 1939), pp. 31, 32, 41, 43; James Williams, *Human Aspects of Unemployment and Relief* (Chapel Hill, 1933), p. 10.
7. Wecter, *Age of the Great Depression*, p. 38; Bernstein, *Lean Years*, p. 327.
8. Joseph Rayback, *A History of American Labor* (New York, 1959), p. 355; Leo Wolman, *The Ebb and Flow of Trade Unionism* (New York, 1936), p. 16.
9. Merle Curti, *The Growth of American Thought* (New York, 1951), pp. 731–32.
10. Rayback, *A History of American Labor* p. 317.
11. *NCWC Review,* Jan. 1931, p. 506; Dec. 1931, p. 8; *Catholic Action,* Dec. 1932, p. 3; statement of the administrative board of the NCWC, 15 Nov. 1933; *Catholic Action,* Dec. 1933; *Two Basic Encyclicals* (New York, 1943), pp. 157–63.
12. Statement of the NCWC board, reprinted in *Our Bishops Speak,* (Milwaukee, 1952), p. 315; "Present Crisis," 1933, *Our Bishops Speak,* p. 277; *Catholic Action,* Dec. 1936, p. 103; see also George Cardinal Mundelein, "A Cardinal's Warning," *America,* 29 May 1937, pp. 182–83; Mundelein, "A Cardinal's Address," *Catholic Charities*

Review, Apr. 1938, pp. 122–23; Mundelein, "Catholic Action for Social Justice," *Catholic Mind*, Feb. 1938, p. 47.

13. M. J. Hillenbrand, "The Communists," *Commonweal*, 26 Feb. 1937, p. 433; for the various positions Catholic spokesmen took in advocating remedies for the depression and the economic system see David O'Brien, *American Catholics and Social Reform, The New Deal Years* (New York, 1968), pp. 47–69.

14. *Two Basic Encyclicals*, pp. 113, 145, 149, 151.

15. *Proceedings of the National Catholic Welfare Conference*, Feb. 1922, p. 7.

16. National Catholic Welfare Conference *Bulletin* Feb. 1922, p. 7; ibid., Jan. 1931, p. 5; statement at the annual meeting of the hierarchy, ibid., 1931, p. 8; "Changed Conditions of Labor," *Catholic Mind*, 8 June 1931, p. 3; Arthur Sheehan, *Peter Maurin: Gay Believer* (Garden City, N.Y., 1959), p. 162; *Catholic Action*, Dec. 1933, p. 3; "The Leaven of Charity," *Catholic Charities Review*, Oct. 1933, p. 261; address delivered at meeting of Holy Name Society, 3 Jan. 1938, as printed in *Catholic Mind*, 8 Feb. 1938, p. 48.

17. NCWC News Service, 5 Dec. 1932; *Brooklyn Tablet*, 1 Dec. 1932; *Proceedings of the National Conference of Catholic Charities 1932–34*, 18th Annual Convention (1932), pp. 4–6, cited by George Q. Flynn, *American Catholics and the Roosevelt Presidency 1932–36* (Lexington, 1948), pp. 30, 34; ibid., 1935, p. 298; Donald Gavin, *The National Conference of Catholic Charities, 1910–1916* (Milwaukee, 1962), p. 192.

18. *Commonweal*, 4 Mar. 1925, p. 448; 8 Dec. 1926, p. 117; 19 Jan. 1927, p. 285; 4 Apr. 1928, p. 1250; 14 Jan. 1925, p. 254; 18 Nov. 1925, pp. 31–35.

19. Bishop O'Hara, "Catholic Industrial Principles," *Commonweal*, 13 May 1931, pp. 35–36, 27 May 1931, pp. 85–86, 18 May 1934, p.57, 1 Jan. 1934, p. 114; Henry D. Buchanan, "Let Us Be Radical," 8 Oct. 1937, pp. 543–44; George K. McCabe, "Labor Day 1937," 10 Sept. 1937, p. 451; "Facts about Capitalism," 12 Feb. 1937, pp. 541–42; "What Is Capitalism," 29 Apr. 1938, p. 8; Virgil Michel, "The Labor Movement," 3 June 1938, pp. 146–48; Philip Burnham, "Sniping at Capitalism," 3 June 1938, pp. 144–45.

20. Peter Wiffen, "A Few Communists," *Commonweal*, 29 May 1936, p. 124; June Coyne, "My Communist Friends," 27 Aug. 1937, pp. 415–16; Hillenbrand, "The Communists," 26 Feb. 1937, pp. 493–95; Martin Lynch, "Christian Communism," 26 Nov. 1937, pp. 125–26; "Liberty and Poverty," 21 Aug. 1936, pp. 393–94.

21. "Capitalism," *America*, 23 Apr. 1921, p. 22; J. Husslein, "Distributive Private Ownership," 28 Oct. 1922, pp. 330–31; "Wealth and Per

Capita Income," 20 Aug. 1921, p. 425; "Editorial," 11 Feb. 1922, p. 406; "Capitalism and the Courts," 18 Mar. 1922, p. 518; John Ryan, "Confused Ethics and the Minimum Wage," 23 June 1923, p. 226; D. M. O'Connell, "Continuous Unemployment," 29 Sept. 1923, p. 574; 27 Sept. 1921, pp. 522–523; H. S. Spaulding, 18 Nov. 1922, p. 119.

22. S. Barton, "Looking for a Catholic Carnegie," *America*, 14 Mar. 1925, p. 507; "The Shorter Week," 16 Oct. 1926, p. 6; "Some Follies of Capital," 4 June 1927, pp. 173–74; R. E. Shortall, "Power of the Capitalist System," 21 Feb. 1925, p. 453; "AFL Convention," 1 Dec. 1928, p. 173; "Morals and Business," Feb. 1929, p. 399.

23. P. L. Blakely, "Communism or the Union," *America*, 7 Dec. 1929, pp. 207–8; P. L. Blakely, "The Union or Communism," 23 Jan. 1932, pp. 385–86; 28 Jan. 1933, p. 4; "Modernizing Capitalism," 23 Feb., p. 463; also see 22 Oct. 1922, pp. 63–65; "The Depression and the State," 14 Oct. 1933, p. 25.

24. Elizabeth G. Evans, "The Massachusetts Law," *Catholic World*, May 1923, p. 211; Edwin V. O'Hara, "The Oregon Law," p. 207; James F. Cronin, "The Situation in New York," p. 204; John Ryan, "U.S. Supreme Court," p. 200; James F. Cronin, "The Workman and His Wages," July 1922, p. 453; Felix Kelly, "The Key to Success," Aug. 1922, p. 674.

25. *Catholic World*, Oct. 1933, pp. 1, 7; April 1936, pp. 11, 17; J. H. Schackman, "Are Catholics Committed to Capitalism?" Jan. 1939, p. 429.

26. H. Egan, "The Problem of Unemployment," *Catholic Mind,* 22 June
26. H. Egan, "The Problem of Unemployment," *Catholic Mind*, 22 June 1926, p. 235.

27. F. L. Burke, "The Catholic is Anti-Bourgeois," *Catholic Mind*, 8 July 1935, pp. 259–60. Ignatius W. Cox, "A Living Wage in Our Immoral Economic Order," 22 May 1936, p. 19; "The American Liberty League and Our Immoral Economic Order," 26 Feb. 1936, p. 113; "Wages and Our Immoral Order," p. 130; Ignatius Cox, "Anti-Social Wages and Our Immoral Economic Order," 8 Aug. 1937, p. 113; Charles P. Bruehl, "Capitalistic Trends Condemned," 8 July 1935, pp. 246–52; Joseph F. MacDonald, "The Social Revolution and Justice," 8 June 1937, pp. 243–44.

Chapter Three. *Social Action and the National Catholic Welfare Conference, 1920 to 1940*

1. Aaron Abell, *American Catholicism and Social Action* (Notre Dame, 1963), pp. 192, 209; John Tracy Ellis, *American Catholicism* (New York, 1955), p. 141; Winfred E. Garrison, *Catholicism and the American Mind* (Chicago, 1928), p. 195.
2. Sister Mary Herrita Fox, "Peter E. Dietz," pp. 140–45 (see chap. 1, n. 21); Abell, *American Catholicism and Social Action,* pp. 210–11.
3. Ellis, *American Catholicism*, p. 141; Sylvia Batdorf, "The Work of the Social Action Department of the NCWC in All Phases of Industrial Relations" (Master's thesis, Catholic University of America, 1920), pp. 27–28.
4. Francis Broderick, *Right Reverend New Dealer* (New York, 1963), chap. 1; David O'Brien, "Catholic Social Thought in the 1930s" (Ph.D. diss., University of Rochester, 1965), pp. 87–88.
5. *A Living Wage: Distributive Justice* (New York, 1916); *The State and the Church* (New York, 1922), p. 196; O'Brien, "Catholic Social Thought," pp. 92–94.
6. *A Living Wage,* pp. 3–4.
7. Marc Karson, *American Labor Unions and Politics 1900–1918* (Carbondale, 1956), p. 56; Patrick William Gearty, *The Economic Thought of Monseignor Ryan* (Washington, 1953), pp. 86–89; *A Living Wage*, pp. 291–96; *Catholic Encyclopedia* 13 (1910): 724–28; O'Brien, "Catholic Social Thought," pp. 96–97.
8. *A Living Wage*, pp. 18, 180. O'Brien, "Catholic Social Thought," pp. 97–99.
9. O'Brien, "Catholic Social Thought," pp. 100–101.
10. Ibid., p. 102; *A Living Wage*, pp. 213–30; *Social Reconstruction* (New York, 1920), pp. 59, 161–62; Abell, *American Catholicism and Social Action*, p. 199; Ryan, *Social Doctrine in Action* (New York, 1941), pp. 143–45.
11. "The Bishop's Program of Social Reconstruction," *American Sociological Review*, Mar. 1944, pp. 26–27; Abell, *American Catholicism and Social Action*, p. 205.
12. O'Brien, "Catholic Social Thought," p. 103; "Industrial Conciliation," *NCWC Bulletin,* Jan. 1923, p. 19.
13. "A New Task for Labor Unions," *Declining Liberty and Other Papers* (New York, 1927), pp. 209–38, 258–67; "The Industrial Problems and the Way Out," *NCWC Bulletin,* April 1923, p. 20; "Neglect of Catholic Social Thinking," National Catholic Welfare Conference *Bulletin,* June 1922, p. 21; "Moral Aspects of Labor Unions," *Catholic*

Encyclopedia 13 (1910): 726; "A Weakness in Labor Leadership," National Catholic Welfare Conference *Bulletin*, May 1921, p. 17.

14. "Criticism of the Social Action Department," *NCWC Bulletin*, July 1929, p. 17.

15. "Editorial," *NCWC Bulletin*, Dec. 1922, p. 17; Joseph I. Breen, "Our Immigrants: What They Need and How We Are Helping Them," *NCWC Bulletin*, March 1923, p. 5.

16. "NCWC Immigration Bureau Organized," *NCWC Bulletin*, June 1925, p. 5.

17. John F. Rice, "Montana Americanization School Doing Splendid Work," *NCWC Bulletin*, Aug. 1923, p. 7; "Civic Education In Newark Dioceses," June 1926, p. 27; Nov. 1922, p. 13; "Civic Education Campaign Launched in Gary, Indiana," Sept. 1920, p. 16; Abell, *American Catholicism and Social Action*, p. 213; Breen, "Our Immigrants," p. 3; "Civic Education Campaign Launched in Gary, Indiana," National Catholic Welfare Conference, *Bulletin*, Sept. 1920, p. 16.

18. "Annual Reports of the Episcopal Chairman of the NCWC Departments," *NCWC Bulletin*, Dec. 1929, p. 104, Oct. 1927, p. 14; "Urge Human Relations in Industry," National Catholic Welfare Conference, *Bulletin*, Apr. 1922, p. 12; "Social Action Department Assists in Investigation of Engineers' Strike," *NCWC Bulletin*, Mar. 1927, p. 15.

19. Abell, *American Catholicism and Social Action*, pp. 211–12; R. A. McGowan, "Trends in the Labor Movement," *NCWC Bulletin*, Nov. 1925, pp. 28–29; John Ryan, "Criticism of the SAD," National Catholic Welfare Conference, *Bulletin*, July 1921, pp. 16–17.

20. McGowan, "The CCIP," *NCWC Bulletin*, Aug. 1923, pp. 11–13; "Report of CCIP," *NCWC Bulletin*, July 1924, pp. 5–22, Aug. 1925, p. 25; Linna E. Bresette, "The CCIP Hold Fifth Annual Meeting," *NCWC Bulletin*, Aug. 1924, pp. 11–12.

21. Abell, *American Catholicism and Social Action*, p. 229; Edward Marciniak, "Catholics and Social Reform," in *Catholicism in America, A Series of Articles from Commonweal* (New York, 1953), p. 124.

22. John Ryan to Thomas F. Coakley, 5 May 1931, Ryan Papers 1929–33, A–C, Catholic University Archives; "Unemployment in the Coming Winter," *Catholic Charities Review*, Nov. 1930, pp. 223–25; "President Roosevelt's Economic Program," *Studies*, June 1933, pp. 194–204; "The American Presidential Campaign," Sept. 1936, pp. 379–89.

23. John A. Ryan to Hugo L. Black, 7 Apr. 1933, Ryan Papers 1929–33, A–C.

24, "Monsignor Ryan's Economic Program," *Catholic Action*, June 1936, p. 20; "Unemployment and the Coming Winter," *Catholic Charities*

Review, Nov. 1930, pp. 223–25; "The Responsibility of Congress Toward Unemployment," *Catholic Charities Review,* Dec. 1932, pp. 306–8.

25. Ryan Papers, 1936–37, H–Q.
26. *Seven Troubled Years*, pp. 66–72; Ryan to George E. Flood, 25 Apr. 1938, Ryan Papers 1938, E–R; Ryan to Matthew Phillips, Jan. 1936, Ryan Papers 1936–37, H–Q.
27. Ryan Papers 1929–33, A–C; Ryan to Mary Fox, 24 Jan. 1933, Ryan Papers 1929–33, C–F; Ryan to John W. Herring, 23 Sept. 1932, Ryan Papers 1929–33, G–J.
28. Ryan to John B. Andrews, 30 Sept. 1930, Ryan Papers 1929–33, A–C.
29. "The Sit-Down Strike," *Ecclesiastical Review*, Apr. 1937, pp. 419–20.
30. "The Sit-Down Strike," p. 420.
31. ACTU *Proceedings of National Convention, 1940*, p. 83; McGowan to John M. O'Brien, 17 Aug. 1938, Ryan Papers 1938, S–R; Ryan to Ethel Van Benthutsen, 20 Jan. 1934, Ryan Papers 1934–35, A–C; Ryan to Courtnay Dinwiddie, 3 Nov. 1933, Ryan Papers 1929–33, C–F; Ryan to Maurice F. McAuliffe, 20 Feb. 1937, Ryan Papers 1936–37, H–Q; Ryan to Courtnay Dinwiddie, 5 Nov. 1935, Ryan Papers 1934–35, A–C; Ryan to Gertrude Folks Zimand, 4 Dec. 1935, Ryan Papers 1934–35, A–C; Ryan to Alexander Fleischer, 9 Feb. 1931, Ryan Papers 1929–33, C–F; Ryan To A. Epstein, 14 Apr. 1930, Ryan Papers 1929–33, C–F.
32. Ryan to D. J. Meserole, Ryan Papers 1929–33, M–P; Ryan to Abraham Epstein, 14 Jan. 1936, Ryan Papers 1936–37, C–G; Ryan to Haywood Broun, 2 Apr. 1936, Ryan Papers 1936–37, A–B; Ryan to Joseph Chamberlain, 9 Jan. 1935, Ryan Papers 1934–35, A–C.
33. NCWC staff, *Women Workers in Industry* (New York, 1938); *Catholic Action*, May 1936, pp. 5–11.
34. *Labor Leader*, 31 Jan. 1938, p. 1; "Month by Month with the NCWC," *Catholic Action*, Feb. 1932, p. 16; Linna E. Bresette, "Report of Catholic Conference of Industrial Problems Meeting in New York City, Feb. 6–7," Mar. 1933, p. 20; "Labor Rights Defended at San Francisco," June 1933, p. 19; "Archbishop McNicholas Host to Regional CIP Meeting," Apr. 1935, p. 17. The department held other conferences as well on the problems of women in industry and the industrial plight of the Negro. These were usually sponsored jointly with other Catholic organizations and, like the CCIP, came to no conclusions. R. A. McGowan, "Clergy Hail Schools of Social Action," *Catholic Action*, Aug. 1933, pp. 16–17.
35. "Bishops of NCWC Administrative Board Report to Hierarchy at

Annual Meeting," *Catholic Action*, Dec. 1937, p. 22; "Year's Work of NCWC Reviewed by Bishops of Administrative Committee," Dec. 1935, p. 15; "NCWC Activities During 1936 Reviewed by Bishops of Administrative Board," Dec. 1937, p. 15; "NCWC Activities Reviewed by Bishops of Administrative Committee," Dec. 1936, p. 14; "Year's Work of NCWC Reviewed by Bishops of Administrative Committee," Dec. 1934, p. 18.

Chapter Four. The Catholic Worker Movement

1. Arthur Sheehan, *Peter Maurin, Gay Believer* (Garden City, 1959), pp. 43, 48.
2. Ibid., pp. 50–51. *The Sillon* was also the name of the movement's official journal; William Rauch, Jr., "From the Sillon to the Movement Republicain Populaire: Doctor Robert Cornilleau and a Generation of Christian Democrats in France, 1910–1940," *Catholic Historical Review*, Apr. 1972, p. 26.
3. Sheehan, *Peter Maurin,* p. 59; Andreien Dansette, "The Rejuvenation of French Catholicism: Marc Sangier Sillon," *Review of Politics*, 1953, pp. 34–44.
4. Sheehan, *Peter Maurin,* p. 82; J. A. Brieg, "Apostle on the Bum," *Commonweal,* 29 April 1938; pp. 9–11.
5. Sheehan, *Peter Maurin,* p. 83; Brieg, "Apostle on the Bum," p. 11.
6. Dorothy Day, *From Union Square to Rome* (Silver Spring, Maryland, 1938), pp. 28–36, 40, 42, 68.
7. Dorothy Day, *The Long Loneliness, The Autobiography of Dorothy Day* (New York, 1952), p. 11.
8. Peter Maurin, *The Green Revolution, Easy Essays on Catholic Radicalism* (Fresno, California, 1961), pp. 5, 57, 102; Dorothy Day, *House of Hospitality*, (New York, 1939), p. 72.
9. Peter Maurin, *Easy Essays* (New York, 1936), p. 23; Maurin, *Green Revolution*, pp. 3, 5, 24, 98, 215; Day, *Long Loneliness,* p. 280.
10. Maurin, *Green Revolution*, p. 70.
11. Maurin, *Green Revolution*, pp. 7, 52, 60, 62, 70; Day, *Long Loneliness*, pp. 179, 222; Day, *House of Hospitality*, p. 71.
12. Day, *House of Hospitality*, pp. 255–56.

13. Maurin, *Green Revolution*, p. 38; Dorothy Day, *Loaves and Fishes* (New York, 1963), pp. 45, 48, 67, 78; Dorothy Day, unfinished book manuscript, D–3, Box 3, p.109, Marquette University Archives; William D. Miller, *A Harsh and Dreadful Love, Dorothy Day and the Catholic Worker Movement* (New York, 1973), p. 87.

14. See Vernon Halloway, "Pacifism Between Two Wars 1919–1941" (Ph.D. diss., Yale University, 1949).

15. *Catholic Worker*, Sept. 1933, p. 1; Dec. 1936, p. 2; Day, *Long Loneliness*, p. 272. Different points of view were not unusual in the nonauthoritarian Catholic Worker movement. In fact, in this case, many who were not pacifists were also involved in the movement; for Catholic C.O.'s see Frank Sicius, "Catholic Conscientious Objectors During World War Two" (Master's thesis, Florida State University, 1973), and Gordon Zahn, "A Study in Social Backgrounds of Catholic Conscientious Objectors in Civil Public Service During World War Two" (Master's thesis, Catholic University of America, 1950).

16. Maurin, *Green Revolution*, pp. 105, 58.

17. Leslie Paul, foreword in *Be Not Afraid* by Emmanuel Mournier (London, 1951), p. viii; Maurin, *Green Revolution*, p. 105; Maurin, *Easy Essays*, pp. 31, 36, 37, 65; Day, *Loaves and Fishes*, p. 21. For the role of American personalists Paul Hanley Furfey and Virgil Michel see O'Brien, *American Catholics and Social Reform: The New Deal Years* (New York, 1968), pp. 184–92.

18. Albert C. Knudson, *The Philosophy of Personalism, A Study in the Metaphysics of Religion* (New York, 1927), p. 20; Emmanuel Mounier, *A Personalist Manifesto*, trans. Monks of St. John's Abbey (New York, 1938), p. 1; Emmanuel Mounier, *Personalism*, trans. Phillip Mairet (London, 1950), pp. 30, 31; Day, *Long Loneliness*, p. 245.

19. Day, *Long Loneliness*, p. 227; Etienne Borne and François Henry, *A Philosophy of Work*, trans. Francis Jackson (New York, 1937), p. 124; Ade Bethune, *Work* (Newport, 1939), pp. 1, 7.

20. Day, *Long Loneliness*, pp. 184, 202; Maurin, quoted in Bethune, *Work*, p. 30; Bethune, *Work*, p. 4; Borne and Henry, *A Philosophy of Work*, p. 119; Sheehan, *Peter Maurin*, p. 186; Day, *Long Loneliness*, p. 224.

21. Quoted in Sheehan, *Peter Maurin*, p. 186.

22. Day, *Loneliness*, p. 228; *Catholic Worker*, June 1939, p. 3; Sheehan, *Peter Maurin*, pp. 174, 186–87.

23. Day, *Loaves and Fishes*, p. 43; Sheehan, *Peter Maurin*, pp. 131, 133; *Catholic Worker*, May 1939, p. 2.

24. *Catholic Worker*, February 1936, p. 28; Day, *Long Loneliness*, p. 234.

25. Day, *Loaves and Fishes*, pp. 53–57.

26. Maurin, *Green Revolution*, p. 93.

27. Interview with William Gauchat, 13 Dec. 1968; interview with Joseph Zarella, 13 Dec. 1968. Day, *House of Hospitality*, p. 185. The hospice was part of the program of the Sillon, though it did not originate there. It goes back to medieval Catholicism and has existed as a church institution in Europe until the present time.
28. Maurin, *Green Revolution*, pp. 9, 11, 92, 93, 125.
29. Maurin, *Green Revolution*, pp. 1, 11, 92, 93, 125; O'Brien, "Catholic Social Thought," p. 99.
30. Day, *House of Hospitality*, p. 236; Day, *Long Loneliness*, p. 249.
31. *Catholic Worker*, May 1939, p. 1; 15 Dec. 1933, p. 1; May 1939, p. 1; 15 Dec. 1933, p. 5; May 1939, p. 1.
32. *Catholic Worker*, May 1939, p. 1.
33. "House of Hospitality," *Commonweal*, 15 Apr. 1938, p. 683; "For Christ the Worker," *Time*, 18 Apr. 1936, p. 46; Marieli G. Benziger, "Caitas Christ," *Catholic World*, Feb. 1938, p. 6.
34. Interview with Nina Polcyn, 13 Dec. 1968; interview with William Gauchat, 13 Dec. 1968.
35. *Catholic Worker*, April 1938, p. 2; June 1935, p. 1; Sheehan, *Peter Maurin*, p. 144.
36. Sheehan, *Peter Maurin,* p. 145; *Catholic Worker*, 1 Feb. 1934, p. 1; Day, "Tale of Two Capitals," *Commonweal*, 14 July 1939, pp. 280–83.
37. Day, *House of Hospitality*, p. 271; *Catholic Worker,* May 1938, p. 1; unpublished manuscript by Sister M. Zita, S.C., 20 Jan. 1939, *Catholic Worker* Collection, D–4, Box 1, Marquette University Archives.
38. *Catholic Worker*, Sept. 1938, p. 7; Mar. 1939, p. 4; June 1939, p. 3. To the list of houses in June, the New York house added two additional houses established after the list was compiled.
39. John Gillard Bruni, "Catholic Paper Versus Communism," *Commonweal*, 24 Nov. 1933, p. 97; "For Christ the Worker," *Time*, 18 Apr. 1938, p. 46. Following the Great Depression, circulation decreased considerably; see "Dorothy Day's Diary," *Newsweek*, 21 Jan. 1952, p. 85; "Fools for Christ," *Time*, 24 May 1948, p. 56.
40. *Catholic Worker*, July-Aug. 1933, p. 2; Sheehan, *Peter Maurin*, p. 111.
41. Bruni, "Catholic Paper Versus Communism," p. 97; John Sheery, "The Catholic Worker School," *Commonweal*, 3 Aug. 1934, p. 349; *Catholic Worker*, 1 Feb. 1934, pp. 1, 4; 1 Mar. 1934, p. 1; Brieg, "Apostle on the Bum," *Commonweal*, Apr. 1938, p. 12; Eleanor Carroll, "The Catholic Worker" (Master's thesis, Catholic University, 1935), p. 20.
42. Day, *Long Loneliness*, p. 124.
43. Interview with Nina Polcyn, 13 Dec. 1968; interview with Joseph Zarella, 13 Dec. 1968; Dorothy Day to Richard Deverall, 24 Sept.

1935, *Catholic Worker* Collection, W–3.1, Box 3, Marquette University Archives.

44. Day, *Long Loneliness*, pp. 174, 175; Stanley Vishnewski "The Early Days," unpublished manuscript, *Catholic Worker* Collection, W–3.2, Box 7, Marquette University Archives; Day, *Loaves and Fishes*, p. 18.
45. Maurin, *Easy Essays*, pp. 69, 136; Maurin, *Green Revolution*, pp. 131, 135.
46. Day, *Loaves and Fishes*, p. 18; Day, *Long Loneliness*, p. 181; Day, *House of Hospitality*, p. 142, 148; 1936 pamphlet in *Catholic Worker* Collection, D–4, Box 1, unpaginated, Marquette University Archives.
47. *Catholic Worker*, July–Aug. 1933, pp. 1, 5; editorial, Feb. 1936. For differences between Day, who supported the New Deal, and Maurin, who did not, see Day, *Long Loneliness*, p. 174; *House of Hospitality*, p. 71; Maurin, *Green Revolution*, pp. 57, 70. The *Catholic Worker* followed Day's point of view; see *Catholic Worker*, Sept. 1933, p. 6; Oct. 1933, p. 3; Nov. 1933, p. 2; Feb. 1934, p. 71.
48. Stanley Vishnewski, "The Catholic Worker Story," unpublished manuscript, *Catholic Worker* Collection, W–3.2, Box 7, unpaginated, Marquette University Archives. Day, *Long Loneliness*, pp. 206–8; *Catholic Worker*, Mar. 1935, p. 1; Feb. 1935, p. 1.
49. Day, *Long Loneliness*, p. 208; *Catholic Worker*, June 1936, p. 4.
50. Day, *House of Hospitality*, p. 263.
51. Ibid., pp. 180–81, 188; Vishnewski, "The Catholic Worker Story."
52. *Catholic Worker*, Feb. 1935, p. 3.
53. *Catholic Worker*, July 1937, p. 6; June 1936, p. 1; Apr. 1935, p. 1; May 1935, p. 1; Mar. 1935, p. 1; Apr. 1938, p. 1; June 1936, p. 1; Mar. 1935, p. 1; Apr. 1936, p. 1; Feb. 1936, p. 1; Apr. 1936, p. 1; Day, *Long Loneliness*, pp. 207–9; Vishnewski, "The Catholic Worker Story."
54. "For Christ the Worker," p. 47; Day, *Long Loneliness*, pp. 203, 183; *Catholic Worker*, Nov. 1933, p. 3; Sept. 1933, p. 4.
55. Quoted in Day, *Long Loneliness*, p. 174; Maurin, *Green Revolution*, pp. 57, 70; Day, *House of Hospitality*, p. 71.
56. *Catholic Worker*, Sept. 1933, p. 6; Oct. 1933, pp. 3, 6; Nov. 1933, p. 2; Feb. 1934, p. 7.
57. Vishnewski, "The Early Days," *Labor Leader*, 28 Mar. 1947, p. 1; "Peter Maurin," *Commonweal*, 17 Aug. 1949, p. 165.
58. Day, *House of Hospitality*, p. xxxi; *Catholic Worker*, Oct. 1938, p. 4; Day, *Long Loneliness*, p. 226; Sheehan, *Peter Maurin*, p. 149.

Chapter Five. The Labor Priests: The Contrasting Approaches of Charles Owen Rice and John P. Boland

1. Neil O'Connor, "Priests and Labor," *Christian Front,* 3 Oct. 1938, p. 122.
2. *Labor Leader,* 17 Oct. 1938, p. 3; O'Brien, *American Catholics and Social Reform: The New Deal Years* (New York, 1968), pp. 101, 151; Barbara Warne Newell, *Chicago and the Labor Movement: Metropolitan Unions in the 1930's* (Urbana, 1961), pp. 243–45.
3. Edward Marciniak, "Catholics and Labor-Management Relations," in *The American Apostolate,* ed. Leo Ward (Westminster, Md., 1952), p. 19.
4. *Labor Leader,* 13 Nov. 1939, p. 1; 15 Jan. 1939, p. 5; 31 Oct. 1938, speech by Joseph M. Conlon of the ACTU; Newell, *Chicago and the Labor Movement,* pp. 244–45.
5. Carey E. Haigler to the author, 31 Aug. 1971; Brendan Sexton to the author, 10 July 1971; Irwin L. De Shetler to the author, 5 Sept. 1971.
6. The New York City newspapers, *Evening Post, Times, Herald, Tribune, Sun, and World Telegram,* gave thorough coverage to the details of the march and its aftermath from 7 to 17 January; Cox was involved in several coalition attempts. He joined with "Coin" Harvey of Arkansas and held a convention of the Liberty-Jobless Party, but soon the alliance split apart. Pittsburgh *Post-Gazette,* 20 Mar. 1951, p. 9; Aaron Abell, *American Catholicism and Social Action* (Notre Dame, 1963), p. 235; Pittsburgh *Post-Gazette,* 20 Mar. 1951, pp. 1, 9; Pittsburgh *Post-Gazette,* 14 Jan. 1936, clipping in Cox Papers, Pittsburgh University Archives.
7. Pittsburgh *Post-Gazette,* 20 Mar. 1951, p. 9; Pittsburgh *Sun-Times,* 20 Mar. 1951, p. 9; oral history interview with Rice, 5 Apr. 1958, pp. 1, 9, Rice Papers, Pennsylvania State University Archives.
8. Oral history interview with Rice, 6 Feb. 1958, p. 1, Rice Papers.
9. "Remarks by Rice on Peoples Congress for Peace and Democracy," 26–28 Nov. 1937, Rice Papers; pamphlet, CIO central office papers, 1937–1941, Catholic University Archives; Rice, "Statement Concerning Aluminium Workers of America," 26 Mar. 1938, Rice Papers; biographical sketch of Rice by Hugh M. Poe in Rice Papers.
10. *Labor Leader,* 12 Sept. 1938, p. 1; 9 May 1938, p. 3.
11. Rice, oral history interview, 6 Feb. 1958, pp. 2–3; Rice, *The Catholic Worker,* 6 Feb. 1938, p. 6.
12. *Labor Leader,* 1 Aug. 1938, p. 1.

13. "Statement of Rice Charges in *Osservatore Romano*," Rice Papers, Rice Lenten Course at St. Augustine Church, response to 5 Mar. 1938 talk by Fulton J. Sheen, *The Textile Worker*, Aug. 1937, clipping, Rice Papers; *Labor Leader*, 22 Aug. 1938, p. 1; John Brophy to Charles O. Rice, 24 Aug. 1938, Rice Papers; interview with Rice by Richard Deverall in "The Catholic Radical Alliance," *Christian Front* Oct. 1937, p. 142.
14. Interview with Rice by Deverall, "The Catholic Radical Alliance," p. 142; Rice, oral history, 6 Feb. 1958, p. 3, Pennsylvania State University Archives; interview with Rice by author, 5 Nov. 1969.
15. *Catholic Worker*, May 1937, p. 7; June 1937, p. 1; Day, *House of Hospitality,* p. 263; Rice to author, 26 Nov. 1969; Rice, oral history interview with Rice, 5 Apr. 1958, p. 3; "Aluminium Workers Union Approved by Noted Priest, Statement Concerning Aluminium Workers of America," 26 Mar. 1938, news clipping from the *Ledger*, Oct. 1938, Rice Papers.
16. Victor Pasche to Rice, 2 Dec. 1937, Rice Papers; statement by Rice included with letter to Morris L. Ernst, 14 Dec. 1937; Rice interview with author, 5 Nov. 1969.
17. *Catholic Worker*, Apr. 1938, p. 6; Rice, "Pittsburgh Houses of Hospitality." *Information* (clipping) Rice Papers; letter from Rice to author, 26 Nov. 1969.
18. Debate between Rice and Hathaway, 15 Oct. 1938; statement issued by Rice concerning Peoples Congress for Peace and Democracy, 26 Nov. 1937, Rice Papers; Rice interview with author, 5 Nov. 1969.
19. Statement of Rice at meeting of Soho and Gazzan Home, 1 Feb. 1939, Rice Papers; "Owners and Tennants League Protesting Pittsburgh Housing Authority Action," Poe, biographical sketch.
20. Thomas Edward Blantz, "Francis J. Haas: Priest in Public Service," (Ph.D. diss., Columbia University, 1968), pp. 1–2 in abstract and 133–301 which concentrate on Haas's labor activism.
21. Paul Stroh, "The Catholic Clergy and American Labor Disputes," (Ph.D. diss., Catholic University, 1939), pp. 136, 142, 146, 150; *Catholic Worker*, Sept. 1933, p. 6; *Catholic Daily Tribune*, 2 May 1934; clipping in Boland Papers, Box 17, Notre Dame University Archives; *Brooklyn Tablet*, 4 Aug. 1938, pp. 26–27; clipping in Boland Papers, Box 17. Also see Flynn, *American Catholics and the Roosevelt Presidency*, p. 105; Pittsburgh *Post-Gazette*, 20 Mar. 1951, p. 9.
22. Gerald R. Forton, "History of the Diocesan Labor College of Buffalo, New York, 1939–1959," (Ph.D. diss., Niagara University, 1959), pp. 7–10.
23. *New York Times*, 25 June 1937, p. 7; 13 June 1942, p. 10; *Buffalo Times*, clipping in Boland Papers, Box 36.

24. Forton, "History of Diocesan Labor College," pp. 7–10, 3 in abstract; *New York Times*, 16 Nov. 1939, p. 16; Boland Papers, Box 16. Speech on economic planning, 1938–39, Central Congregational Church, Boland Papers, Box 25; John P. Boland, "Labor Relations and the Encyclicals" *Sign*, Jan. 1938, p. 336; *New York Times*, 11 Oct. 1938, p. 12; clippings in Boland Papers, Jan. 1934 to Jan. 1935, Box 17.

25. Boland, "Labor Relations and the Encyclicals," p. 336.

26. *New York Times*, 21 Aug. 1941, p. 12; talk at Catholic Summer School, 38–39, Boland Papers, Box 25; *New York Times,* 7 Sept. 1937, p. 3.

27. Talk at Catholic Summer School, 17 Aug. 1939, Boland Papers, Box 25; WNYC broadcast, 28 Sept. 1940, Boland Papers, Box 25; Boland speech before Central Trades and Labor Assembly of New York, 28 Sept. 1940, Box 25; *New York Times*, 8 Dec. 1938, p. 31; *New York Times*, 6 Mar. 1939, p. 9; *New York Times*, 5 Sept. 1939, p. 33.

28. *New York Times*, 7 Sept. 1937, p. 3; *New York Times,* 15 May 1939, p. 20; *New York Times,* 29 Jan. 1940, p. 9.

29. *New York Times*, 29 Jan. 1940, p. 9; Boland talk at Labor Law Congress of Fordham University, 28 Jan. 1940, Boland Papers, Box 25; Boland talk at Buffalo Labor College, 29 Apr. 1940, Box 25; Boland talk at convention of New York State Federation of Labor, 20 Aug. 1940, Boland Papers, Box 25; *New York Times*, 23 May 1938, p. 20.

30. Boland talk at Labor Law Congress at Fordham University, 28 Jan. 1940, Boland Papers, Box 25; *New York Times*, 6 Feb 1938, p. 2; *New York Times*, 17 Apr. 1941, p. 46.

31. *New York Times*, 22 Apr. 1939, p. 2; *New York Times*, 26 Mar. 1939, p. 3; *New York Times,* 21 Feb. 1938, p. 8; *New York Times,* 4 July 1940, p. 17.

32. Boland, "Labor Relations and the Encyclicals," p. 336; Boland Papers, clipping from *Buffalo Business*, Box 36; telegram from Herbert Lehman to Charles H. Tattle, 9 Dec. 1942, Box 1; *New York Times*, 23 May 1938, p. 20; *New York Times*, 10 Dec. 1942, p. 22; *Labor Leader*, 27 Nov. 1938, p. 1; Neil O'Connor, "Priests and Labor," p. 122.

33. Max M. Kampelman, *The Communist Party vs. the CIO, A Study in Power Politics* (New York, 1957), p. 153; Neil O'Connor, "Priests and Labor," *Christian Front*, 3 Oct. 1938, pp. 122–23.

Chapter Six. Charles Coughlin and the Labor Movement

1. The works concerning Coughlin done in the 1930s and 1940s took one of two positions. His supporters, such as L. B. Ward, *Father Charles E. Coughlin* (Detroit, 1933), and Ruth Mugglebee, *Father Coughlin* (Garden City, 1935), depicted the priest as a modern savior. His detractors, such as John Roy Carlson, *Undercover* (Philadelphia, 1943), R. G. Swing, *Forerunners of American Fascism* (New York, 1935), and John Spivak, *Shrine of the Silver Dollar* (New York, 1940), considered him a modern fascist threat to American society. The major exception to this polemical trend appeared in Charles and Mary Beard, *America in Midpassage* (New York, 1939), p. 198. The Beards analyzed Coughlin as a populist demagogue, defining a populist as a defender of small property owners and an enemy of high finance and large enterprise. Standard texts from the 1950s and '60s usually referred to Coughlin as a proto-fascist or crypto-fascist, and sometimes simply as a demagogue. Two articles by James Shenton, "The Coughlin Movement and the New Deal," *Political Science Quarterly*, Sept. 1958, pp. 352–73, and "Fascism and Father Coughlin," *Wisconsin Magazine of History*, Autumn 1960, pp. 6–11, posed a new interpretation. He argued that previous writers used the term fascist imprecisely and that Coughlin's inconsistencies made him impossible to classify. Charles J. Tull's *Father Coughlin and the New Deal* (Syracuse, 1965) is the most comprehensive scholarly work on Coughlin; although concentrating on other issues, Tull accepted the Shenton thesis. Most recent works, such as David O'Brien, *American Catholics and Social Reform: The New Deal Years* (New York, 1968), also accepted the Shenton analysis; or in other cases, such as George Q. Flynn, *American Catholics and the Roosevelt Presidency* (Lexington, 1968), they did not take a clear stand on the issue. David H. Bennett, *Demagogues in the Depression* (New Brunswick, 1969), argues that Coughlin was influenced by fascism in his later career.
2. Charles E. Coughlin, *Father Coughlin's Radio Sermons, October 30–April 30, Complete* (Baltimore, 1931), pp. 74, 80–81, 96, 117–18, 121; Charles E. Coughlin, *Eight Lectures on Labor, Capital, and Social Justice* (Royal Oak, 1934), p. 124.
3. Charles E. Coughlin, *A Series of Lectures on Social Justice* (Royal Oak, 1935) pp. 26–28.
4. Coughlin, *Eight Lectures*, pp. 74–76, 131.
5. Ibid., pp. 120, 124, 126.

6. AFL *Proceedings* 53 (1933): 52–53; Tull, *Father Coughlin and the New Deal*, p. 68; N. A. Masters, "Father Coughlin and the Social Justice Movement," (Ph.D. diss., University of Wisconsin, 1955), p. 126; *Detroit News*, 26 July 1934 and *Detroit Times*, 26 Mar. 1934, clippings from Coughlin folder, Brown Collection, Wayne State University Archives.

7. Coughlin, *Eight Lectures,* pp. 121–31.

8. Ibid., p. 125; A. B. Magil, *The Truth about Father Coughlin* (New York, 1935), p. 119.

9. Charles Coughlin, *Eight Discourses on the Gold Standard and Other Kindred Subjects* (Royal Oaks, 1933), p. 37; Coughlin, *Eight Lectures*, pp. 9, 11, 83, 157.

10. Coughlin, *Eight Lectures*, p. 66; William C. Kernan, *The Ghost of Royal Oak* (New York, 1940), p. 92; Coughlin, *A Series of Lectures on Social Justice*, p. 57.

11. *Eight Lectures*, pp. 13, 53–54, 56; Tull, *Father Coughlin and the New Deal*, p. 39.

12. Bennett, *Demagogues in the Depression*, p. 40; Arthur Schlesinger, Jr., *The Politics of Upheaval* (Boston, 1960), p. 23. In 1932 Ryan denied that he had ever written anything critical or appreciative of Coughlin, though the year before he attacked the "Theory of the Depression which stresses the factor of currency and money supply," (see Ryan to Thomas F. Coakley, 5 May 1931, Ryan Papers, 1929–33, A–C, Catholic University Archives). At the end of 1933, Ryan became Coughlin's defender for a time; speaking before the Catholic Conference on Industrial Relations, Ryan suggested that Coughlin was "on the side of the angels." At another time he called him "a messenger of God, donated to the American people for the purpose of rectifying the outrageous mistakes they made in the past." *New York Times*, 5 Dec. 1933, p. 7; 3 Dec. 1933, p. 2. Before 1935, and most emphatically in 1931, *Commonweal* was a Coughlin admirer, and in March of 1935 still defended Coughlin after NRA Director Hugh Johnson had attacked him. See "The Clergy and Politics," *Commonweal*, 22 Mar. 1935, pp. 579–80. For Upton Sinclair's endorsement, see Schlesinger, *Politics of Upheaval*, p. 116.

13. Coughlin, *A Series of Lectures on Social Justice*, p. 22; *Social Justice*, 31 Aug. 1936, p. 14.

14. Italics mine; *New York Times*, 16 Aug. 1936, cited in Myles M. Platt, "Father Charles E. Coughlin and the National Union for Social Justice," (Master's thesis, Wayne State University, 1951), p. 95.

15. Tull, *Father Coughlin and the New Deal*, p. 129. A recent study found Coughlin strongest among manual workers and unemployed after 1936. See Seymour Lipset and Earl Raab, *The Politics of Unreason,*

Right-Wing Extremism in America, 1790–1970 (New York, 1970), pp. 172–75.

16. Coughlin, *A Series of Lectures on Social Justice*, pp. 185–86, 194.
17. "Coughlin vs. AFL," *Business Week*, 13 July 1935, p. 15.
18. Clipping, *Detroit Free Press*, July 1935; *Detroit News*, 1 July 1935; *Detroit Times*, 1 July 1935; clippings in AIWA folder of Brown Collection; complete speech in Coughlin folder, Brown Collection.
19. Oral history interview of Richard Frankensteen, 10, 23 Oct. 1959; 6 Nov. 1959; 7 Dec. 1961, p. 15, Wayne State University Archives; interview of Richard Harris, 16 Nov. 1969, p. 13, Wayne State University Archives.
20. Harris interviews, 1 Aug., 29 Sept., 6 Oct. 1961, pp. 13–14; *First Year Book and History of the AIWA*, 14 Dec. 1935, AIWA Folder, Brown Collection; Frankensteen, oral history interview, p. 13; Zarembra, oral history interview, p. 15.
21. Frankensteen, oral history interview, p. 2.
22. R. G. Swing, *Forerunners of American Fascism*, p. 55; Zarembra, oral history interview, p. 15.
23. "Round-up" was later called "Labor Highlights"; Tull, *Father Coughlin and the New Deal*, p. 174.
24. A month after this statement Coughlin found no hope for democracy (see Coughlin, *A Series of Lectures*, pp. 98–99), but was inconsistent on the issue.
25. Charles Coughlin, *Sixteen Radio Lectures* (Royal Oak, 1938), pp. 63–64, 85, 89, 95; George A. Dondero, *Social Justice*, 17 June 1939, p. 14; Coughlin, *Sixteen Radio Lectures*, p. 150.
26. *Social Justice*, 20 Feb. 1939, p. 17; Coughlin to Mussolini, 6 Sept. 1938, National Archives, Captured Italian Documents, Section 23, Document 009613. Telegram, 6 Oct. 1938, National Archives, Captured Italian Documents, Section 23, Document 00916. Telegram, 14 Jan. 1941, National Archives, Captured Italian Documents, Section 23, Document 00923.
27. Quoted in Aaron J. Smith, "Father Coughlin's Platoons," *New Republic*, 30 Aug. 1939, p. 96; Tull, *Father Coughlin and the New Deal*, p. 189; *Social Justice*, 25 July 1938, p. 9; 13 June 1938, 31 July 1935; Tull, *Father Coughlin and the New Deal*, pp. 189, 212. George Britt, "Coughlin's Christian Front," *New Republic*, 29 Jan. 1940, p. 143.
28. LaGuardia Papers, 2539, Box 84, City Affairs Committee #16, Christian Front; C, part 2, Folder A–106–A, New York Municipal Archives and Records Center; James Wechsler, in the *Nation* ("The Coughlin Terror"), accused the New York Police of favoring the Christian Front in its street conflicts. Complaints to the mayor buttressed this charge. In addition, Coughlin exaggerated membership by

New York police in the Christian Front. LaGuardia denied Coughlin's charges and ordered a poll of 16,909 police officers on duty. Of 16,903 who replied, 407 admitted to membership in the Christian Front or to having sought it; all but 27 claimed to have dropped out. La Guardia papers, 728, part 2, Folder A—106—A; Rev. Charles Owen Rice to John Ryan, 10 Feb. 1938, Ryan Correspondence, 1938—R, Catholic University Archives; interview with William Gauchat, 13 Dec. 1968; interview with Joseph Zarrella, 13 Dec. 1968.

29. *Sixteen Radio Lectures*, pp. 94—98.
30. *Social Justice*, 4 Apr. 1938, p. 4.
31. For criticisms of NRA, see *A Series of Lectures on Social Justice*, p. 194; Coughlin, *Sixteen Radio Lectures*, pp. 8, 15; *Social Justice*, 14 Dec. 1936; Kernan, *The Ghost of Royal Oak*, p. 86.
32. *Social Justice*, 24 June 1937, p. 2; ibid., 3 June 1937, p. 2; ibid., 10 June 1937, p. 2; *New York Times*, 6 June 1937, p. 9.
33. In the early 1930s Coughlin attacked Henry Ford for indirectly aiding communism by harsh labor policies and directly aiding communism through business deals with the U.S.S.R.; Tull, *Father Coughlin and the New Deal*, pp. 177—78.
34. Tull, *Father Coughlin and the New Deal*, p. 77; *Detroit Evening Times*, 15 June 1937, p. 3.
35. John L. Spivak, *Shrine of the Silver Dollar*, pp. 120—24; Coughlin from Homer Martin, 19 Jan. 1935, 5 July 1935, 16 Feb. 1935, 25 Apr. 1935, Homer Martin Collection, Correspondence folder, Jan. 1935, Wayne State University Archives.
36. Coughlin, *Am I an Anti-Semite?—Nine Addresses on Various Issues* (Detroit, 1939), p. 25; *Social Justice,* 5 Sept. 1938, p. 5; 19 June 1939, p. 9; Coughlin, *Am I an Anti-Semite?*, p. 25.
37. *Michigan Labor Leader*, 17 Nov. 1939, pp. 1, 2, 4; Kernan, *The Ghost of Royal Oak*, pp. 89, 102; *New York Times*, 3 Aug. 1940, p. 28. For the position of the UAW on Coughlin see *United Automobile Worker*, 26 Nov. 1938, p. 5; *United Automobile Worker,* 24 Jan. 1940, p. 4.
38. Coughlin's followers harassed Jewish transit employees by leaving the priest's anti-Semitic publications conspicuously at those work places that would be most frequented by Jewish personnel. *New York World-Telegram* clipping in Coughlin folder of B'nai B'rith Anti-Defamation League Archives; *New York Times*, 2 June 1939, p. 4.
39. Harold Lavine, *Fifth Column in America* (New York, 1940), p. 89.
40. *Social Justice* 3 July 1939, p. 9; 19 June 1939, p. 7; 2 Aug. 1939, p. 1; *New York Times*, 14 Aug. 1939, p. 2.
41. *Social Justice*, 3 Dec. 1939, p. 3; 19 Jan. 1942, p. 12; *The National Lawyers Guild Presents the Case for the Prosecution of Social Justice*

and Charles E. Coughlin under the Espionage Act of 1917, unpaginated pamphlet.

Chapter Seven. Catholicism and the CIO

1. For origins of the Transport Workers Union see L. H. Whittemore, *The Man Who Ran the Subways, The Story of Mike Quill* (New York, 1968). Some unions, such as the ILGWU, had foreign language locals which provided an indigenous leadership for ethnic workers: ILGWU Local 89 served Italian workers in New York City's dress industry. The Amalgamated Clothing Workers formalized ethnic representation in a different manner. They had a board governed jointly by Italian and Jewish co-managers; Jack Barbash, "Ethnic Factors in the Development of the American Labor Movement," in *Interpreting the Labor Movement* (Madison, 1952), p. 75.
2. For Slavic miners before 1903 see Victor R. Green, *The Slavic Community on Strike, Immigrant Labor in Pennsylvania Anthracite* (Notre Dame, 1968); Wayne State University oral history interview in John Zarembra, p. 15; Len De Caux, *Labor Radical, From the Wobblies to the CIO, A Personal History* (Boston, 1970), p. 332; brief discussions with Patterson, Sargent, and author, 32 Mar. 1970 at St. Joseph's College Labor History Forum; see "Personal Histories of the Early CIO," ed. Staughton Lynd, *Radical America,* May–June 1971, pp. 49–76.
3. Philip Murray, Murray Papers, Box 137, Catholic University Archives; Aaron Abell, *American Catholicism and Social Action*, p. 257; Marc Karson, *American Labor Unions and Politics, 1900–1918*, p. 301; Martin P. Mayer, "Catholic Church and the Union Movement," *Labor and the Nation*, Mar.–Apr. 1947, p. 27.
4. Wesley Allensmith, *Information Service*, 15 May 1948.
5. Using the *Who's Who* resulted in a numerical bias favoring lower levels of leadership. The questionnaire was sent to local officials as well as to presidents of internationals and a greater number of office holders existed at the lower ranks. (There was also a larger number of AFL respondents than of the CIO since craft jurisdictions resulted in a larger number of unions than the industrially based CIO.)
6. Charles Madison, *American Labor Leaders, Personalities and Forces in the Labor Movement* (New York, 1950), p. 311; Philip Murray, "Moral Responsibility of Labor," Murray Papers, Box "1946" Catholic University Archives; the article was mailed to a correspondent by Harry Read, executive assistant to the secretary-treasurer, with the

statement that "You will find everything in the statement is completely in accord with the reasoning in the Papal Social Encyclicals."

7. Philip Murray, "Address at ACTU Breakfast," Murray folder, Detroit ACTU Papers, Box 26, Wayne State University; oral history interview, Charles Owen Rice, 2/6/68, Rice Papers, p. 26; news release from *Michigan Labor Leader,* 29 Dec. 1940, Murray folder, Box 28, Detroit ACTU Papers, Wayne State University; Paul Weber to the Rev. Paul Bussard, 4 May 1946, Detroit ACTU Papers, Murray folder, Box 28; Murray to the *Wage Earner,* Sept. 1946, Detroit ACTU Papers, Murray folder, Box 28; Murray to the Rev. George C. Higgins, 27 Dec. 1948, Murray Papers, Box 59, C– , Catholic University Archives; *Who's Who in Labor* (1946), p. 257; Linna E. Bresette to Murray, 29 July 1949, Murray Papers, 1949–1952, C–F; Box 131; 1951, N–J; Murray to James Elroy, 5/26/52, Murray Papers, Box 134, 1952, C–J.

8. John Brophy, *A Miner's Life,* ed. John O. P. Hall (Madison, 1946), p. 65; Brophy to the editor, *Pittsburgh Catholic,* 27 Aug. 1938, Brophy Papers, 1936–1938, Box 6, Catholic University Archives; Brophy to the editor, *America,* 21 Sept. 1938, Brophy Papers, Box 6, 1937–1938; *Labor Leader,* 2 July 1938; Richard Deverall, "John Brophy Speaks," *Christian Front,* 2 Sept. 1937, p. 126; Richard Deverall, "The Catholic Radical Alliance," *Christian Front,* Oct. 1937, p. 142.

9. Speech by John Brophy, "A New Social Order," 3 Jan. 1938, Brophy Papers, Box 6, 1935–1938, Catholic University Archives; for Lucey statements on CIO, see "The Church Speaks Out for Labor," CIO pamphlet which contains the Bishop's endorsement; Deverall, "John Brophy Speaks," p. 126.

10. "The Common Task of Religion and Labor," *Religious News Service,* Sept. 1943; Walter Romig, ed., *American Catholic Who's Who* (Grosse Pointe, Mich., 1966), p. 5; *Who's Who in Labor* (New York, 1946), p. 51.

11. *Labor Leader,* 25 May 1938, p. 2; 26 Apr. 1938, p. 1.

12. *America,* 30 Sept. 1933, p. 603.

13. Virgil Michel, "The Labor Movement," *Commonweal,* 3 June 1939, p. 148; Edward Mooney, "Duty of Catholic Worker to Join Organized Labor," *Catholic Mind,* 8 Mar. 1939, p. 569; Robert E. Lucey, "Apathy–Our Scourge," *Homiletic and Pastoral Review,* Feb. 1936, pp. 472–74.

14. Flynn, *American Catholics and the Roosevelt Presidency,* pp. 105–7.

15. Ibid.; Joseph G. Rayback, *A History of American Labor* (New York, 1961), pp. 341–43.

16. Rayback, p. 355; Leo Wolman, *The Ebb and Flow of Trade Unionism* (New York, 1936), p. 16.

17. "The A.F. of L. and Changing Times," *Catholic Charities Review,*

Nov. 1933, p. 288; G. Hershfeld, "Organized Labor: An Indictment," *Commonweal,* 23 Mar. 1932, pp. 567–68; "Labor Needs Leaders," *America,* 15 Nov. 1930, pp. 126–27; "Mr. Green Takes His Teathings," 20 Aug. 1932, p. 465; "Labor Union Progress," 11 Feb. 1933, p. 446; "Revolt in the A.F.L.," 18 Aug. 1934, p. 434; "The New Labor Union," *America,* 7 Dec. 1935, p. 158.

18. Joseph N. Fichter, "What's Wrong with the Sit-down Strikes," *Catholic World,* Aug. 1937, pp. 565–68; Eugene Huber, "Socialism: Communism: C.I.O.," Dec. 1938, p. 339; *Tablet,* 16 Jan. and 27 Feb. 1937, cited by O'Brien, *Catholic Historical Review,* pp. 330, 337; "Catholics and the C.I.O.," *Sign,* Nov. 1938, p. 196; "Labor's Right to Organize Today," *Guildsman,* Feb. 1938, pp. 6–7.

19. Paul L. Blakely, "Labor Wages a Losing Battle," *America,* 6 Feb. 1937, p. 417; Blakely, "The Sit-down Strike Harmful to the Union," 13 Mar. 1937, p. 532; Blakely, "Property Rights in the Worker's Job," 10 Apr. 1937, p. 7; "Mr. Lewis and His Friends," 19 Sept. 1936, p. 158; "C.I.O. Communism," 9 Oct. 1937, p. 13; Blakely, "Let There Be Peace Twixt the C.I.O. and the A.F.L." 29 Jan. 1938, p. 388; "Comrade Lewis?" 24 Sept. 1938, pp. 589–90; "The March of Labor," *Christian Front,* Sept. 1937, p. 123.

20. Richard Deverall, "Steel Masters and Slaves," Mar. 1937, p. 43; "Labor on the March," Apr. 1937, pp. 51–52; "The March of Labor," Sept. 1937, p. 123; "John L. Lewis, Industrial Unionism . . . C.I.O.," Apr. 1937, pp. 52–54; Charles Rice, "Priest on Labor," Sept. 1938, pp. 105–6.

21. W. F. Kernan, " 'Rerum Novarum' and Labor," *Commonweal,* 6 Aug. 1937, p. 358; Jerome B. Hannan, "The Moral Right to Sit-down," *America Ecclesiastical Review,* July 1937, pp. 31–39; George L. McCabe, "The American Labor Movement," *Catholic Charities Review,* Feb. 1937, p. 46.

22. L. M. Merill, "The C.I.O. Again," *Catholic Digest,* Sept. 1937, pp. 90–91; "The C.I.O.," *Catholic Digest,* Sept. 1937, p. 89.

Chapter Eight. The Association of Catholic Trade Unionists

1. Joseph F. Oberle, "The Association of Catholic Trade Unionists" (Ph.D. diss., Catholic University, 1941), p. 10; Richard Ward, "The Role of the ACTU in the American Labor Movement" (Ph.D. diss., University of Michigan, 1958), p. 56; Norman McKenna, "Catholic

Trade Unionists in America," *Month,* Nov. 1940, p. 305; John Cort, "Nine Years of ACTU," *America,* 6 Apr. 1940, p. 4; *Labor Leader,* 8 Mar. 1947, p. 4; George Donahue, *Proceedings of Sixth ACTU Convention,* 30 June–1 July 1951, p. 5.

2. ACTU Detroit, *The ACTU,* not dated, p. 8; Harold Wattel, "The Association of Catholic Trade Unionists" (Master's thesis, Columbia University, 1947), p. 25; Ward, "The Role of the ACTU in the American Labor Movement," p. 73; Oberle, "The Association of Catholic Trade Unionists," p. 10; Philip Taft, "The Association of Catholic Trade Unionists," *Industrial Labor Relations Review,* Jan. 1949, pp. 210–18; lay autonomy is reluctantly admitted by critic M. P. Mayer in "The Catholic Church and the Union Movement," *Labor and Nation,* 1949, p. 29; also see talk by Monoghan, *ACTU Proceedings of National Convention,* 1940, p. 11.

3. Oberle, "The Association of Catholic Trade Unionists," pp. 9–11; *Labor Leader,* 14 Nov. 1930, p. 1; Mar. 1938, p. 3; 1 June 1938, p. 4.

4. Oberle, "The Association of Catholic Trade Unionists," p. 41; Ward, "The Role of the ACTU," p. 99; Taft, "The Association of Catholic Trade Unionists," pp. 214–15.

5. *Michigan Labor Leader,* 3 Nov. 1939, p. 2; 17 Nov. 1939, p. 2.

6. Ibid., 29 May 1940, p. 2.

7. Ibid., 7 June 1940, p. 2; 24 May 1940, p. 2.

8. Ibid., 1 Dec. 1939, p. 2.

9. Ibid., 29 Dec. 1939, p. 4; 12 Jan. 1940, p. 2.

10. Edward Scully, 27 Mar. 1947, cited in Wattel, "The Association of Catholic Trade Unionists," p. 86; Workers were supposed to cooperate with employers by setting up vocational groups and industrial councils and through producer cooperation share "as a partner in ownership, management and profits of the industry in which he works." See Cort, "Nine Years of the ACTU," p. 4; Cort, "Catholics in Trade Unions," *Commonweal,* 5 May 1939, pp. 34–36.

11. *Labor Leader,* 3 Jan. 1938, p. 3. (This is the New York City ACTU publication.) *Michigan Labor Leader,* 8 Sept. 1939, p. 2; *Labor Leader,* 3 Jan. 1938, p. 3; Cort, "Nine Years of ACTU," pp. 4–5.

12. Joseph F. Oberle, "The Association of Catholic Trade Unionists," p. 10; Ward, "The Role of the Association of Catholic Trade Unionists," p. 56; Norman McKenna, "Catholic Trade Unionists in America," *Month,* Nov. 1940, p. 305; John Cort, "Nine Years of ACTU," p. 4; *Labor Leader,* 28 Mar. 1947, p. 5; ACTU, *Proceedings of the National Convention,* 1940; ACTU, *Proceedings of the National Convention,* 1941, Appendix D; Cort, "Catholics in Trade Unionism," *Commonweal,* 5 May 1939, p. 34; McCabe, C. J., "Archbishop Mooney Explains ACTU," *Catholic Action,* June 1940, p. 12.

13. *Labor Leader,* 1 Aug. 1938, p. 4; Cort, "Nine Years of ACTU," p. 4.

14. Cort, "Nine Years of ACTU," pp. 4—5; *Michigan Labor Leader*, 2 Oct. 1939, p. 3; *Labor Leader*, 3 Jan. 1938, p. 4; 3 Aug. 1938, p. 3; 17 Oct. 1938, p. 1; 3 Jan. 1939, p. 12.

15. Ward, "The Role of the ACTU," p. 108; *Labor Leader*, 14 Feb. 1938, pp. 1, 4.

16. *Labor Leader*, 6 Mar. 1939, p. 2; 18 Sept. 1939, p. 3; 9 Jan. 1939, p. 1; 6 Mar. 1939, p. 1; ACTU, *Proceedings of the National Convention*, 1940; Bob Greenock to Paul Weber, 26 July 1936, ACTU Papers, Box 8, American Newspaper Guild folder, Wayne State University Archives.

17. *Labor Leader*, 3 Jan. 1938, p. 4.

18. Rovere, "Labor's Catholic Bloc," *Nation*, Jan. 1941, p. 13. Laurence Sullivan to Detroit ACTU, 20 Nov. 1939, ACTU Papers, Box 2, Wayne State University Archives; ACTU Executive Board, 17 Aug. 1939, ACTU Papers, Box 16, Wayne State University Archives; for Coughlin's strength among Polish workers in the auto industry see oral history interview of John A. Zarembra, 11 Aug., 29 Sept., and 6 Oct. 1961, Wayne State University Archives; *Michigan Labor Leader*, 22 Sept. 1939, p. 4; Norman McKenna, "The Story of the ACTU," *Catholic World*, Mar. 1949, p. 453; Richard Deverall to several actists, 24 Aug. 1939, ACTU Papers, Box 30, Wayne State University Archives; Taft, "The ACTU," p. 215.

19. *Michigan Labor Leader*, 22 Sept. 1939, p. 4; Norman McKenna, "The Story of the ACTU," *Catholic World*, Mar. 1949, p. 453; Taft, "The ACTU," p. 215.

20. *Labor Leader*, 3 Jan. 1938, p. 2; 6 Mar. 1939, p. 3; 15 June 1936, p. 1; Taft, "The ACTU," p. 215; interview with Edward Mills by Ward, "The Role of the ACTU," p. 116; interview with John Sheehan in Ward, p. 129.

21. *Labor Leader*, 3 Oct. 1948, pp. 1, 4; *Labor Leader*, 11 April 1938, pp. 1, 2.

22. ACTU, *Proceedings of the National Convention*, 1940, p. 69.

23. Wattell, "The Association of Catholic Trade Unionists," pp. 75, 78; ACTU, *Proceedings of the National Convention*, 1940, p. 39; *Labor Leader*, 8 Aug. 1938, p. 1; Ward, "The Role of ACTU," p. 92.

24. ACTU, *Proceedings of the National Convention*, 1940, p. 9; *Labor Leader*, 17 Oct. 1938, p. 1; 23 Jan. 1938, p. 4.

25. Wattell, "The ACTU," pp. 74, 77; Oberle, "The ACTU," pp. 39—41; ACTU, *Proceedings of the National Convention*, 1940, pp. 9—10, 30.

26. *Labor Leader*, 9 May 1938, p. 1; 12 Dec. 1938, p. 3; 7 Nov. 1938, p. 1.

27. Ibid., 27 May 1939, p. 2.

28. *Labor Leader*, Jan. and Feb. issues, 1938. Norman McKenna, "The Story of ACTU," pp. 453—59; *Labor Leader*, 12 Dec. 1938, p. 1.

29. Taft, "The ACTU," p. 216; George R. Donahue (ACTU executive secretary) to John L. Lewis, 1 Feb. 1939, in Catholic University Archives; CIO central office folder, 1937–1941, A–GOUL. James Carey to John Cort, 3 April 1939, ACTU Archives, New York City.
30. *Labor Leader,* 2 July 1938, p. 2.
31. Ibid., 18 Sept. 1938, pp. 1, 2; 2 Oct. 1939, p. 1; *Michigan Labor Leader* 20 Oct. 1939, p. 1; *Labor Leader,* 16 Oct. 1939, p. 1; 13 Nov. 1939, p. 4.
32. De Caux, *Labor Radical: From the Wobblies to CIO,* p. 327.
33. *Labor Leader,* 25 Mar. 1940, p. 4; 13 Nov. 1939, p. 1.
34. *Labor Leader,* 29 July 1940, p. 2; 9 Sept. 1940, p. 2; Apr. 1941, p. 1; 5 May 1941, pp. 1–2.
35. *Transport Bulletin,* May 1942, p. 1; Aug. 1944, pp. 2–3.
36. Michael Harrington, "Catholics in the Labor Movement: A Case History," *Labor History,* Fall 1960, p. 241; Hugh Cleland, "The Political History of Social Union: Local 601 of the CIO Electrical Workers Union" (Ph.D. diss., Western Reserve University, 1957), p. 156.
37. *Labor Leader,* 21 Apr. 1941, p. 3; Julius Emspak to The Most Rev. Hugh C. Boyle, 13 Mar. 1941; Rev. Charles Owen Rice to James P. Carey, 1 Apr. 1941, United Electrical Workers Papers, University of Pittsburgh.
38. *Labor Leader,* 31 Oct. 1941, p. 1; for the UE–Communist Party Conflict see Max M. Kampelman, *The Communist Party vs The CIO, A Study in Power Politics* (New York, 1957), pp. 121–40.
39. For *Catholic Mind,* see Douglass Woodruff, "Church and Capitalism," 20 Jan. 1950, p. 417; editorial, Oct. 1949, pp. 625–29; Francis J. Corley, "Graduated Family Wage," Nov. 1947, pp. 691–931; Joseph P. Fitspatric, "Catholic Attitudes Toward Labor," Dec. 1949, pp. 724–31; John Cronin, "The Social Problem Today," Nov. 1949, pp. 652–57; Jervis J. Babb, "The Business Rebutte," Oct. 1953, pp. 603–9; D. F. Miller, "Pattern for Economic Justice," Mar. 1950, pp. 140–45; "Pattern for Economic Justice," Feb. 1947, pp. 102–5; George H. Dunne, "Power and Responsibility of Business," Feb. 1952, pp. 79–93; G. M. Cameron, "Socialism and the Church," Apr. 1954, pp. 225–29; Hensler, "Does the Church Approve of the American Economic System," May 1948, pp. 304–13; Francis J. Haas, "Labor, Management and Government," Jan. 1949, p. 2; John C. Cort, "Capitalism: Debate and Definition," 26 Nov. 1954, pp. 221–22. For *Catholic World,* see editorial comment, Dec. 1947, pp. 191–201; John A. Dimnion, "Communism and Capitalism," Jan. 1955, p. 293; editorial, May 1948, p. 106. For *America,* see editorial, "The Economic Man that Matters," 11 Oct. 1947, p. 36; Benjamin L. Masse, "Another Chance for Private Enterprise," 8 Nov. 1947, p. 151.

40. For *Commonweal*, see Edward T. Montalna, "The Views on Capitalism," 26 May 1939, p. 171; Philip Burn, "The Romance of Christian Industrialism," 10 Dec. 1948, p. 221. For *Catholic Action* see McGowan, "Labor Day Statement of NCWC Social Action Department," Sept. 1952, p. 3; Bartholomew J. Eustace, "Charity, Industry and Welfare State," April 1950, p. 401; George G. Higgin, "Cooperation Rather than Conflict," Feb. 1949, p. 406; John Cronin, "Some Approaches to an Industry Council Plan," Apr. 1949, pp. 4–6; also the "Religion and Life" series by McGowan and others, 1948–9.

41. Harrington, "Catholics in the Labor Movement"; Rice's activities during this period have not been examined in depth. The Rice Papers at Pennsylvania State University provide considerable information and should be supplemented by the Union of Electrical Workers Papers at Pittsburgh University.

42. Daniel Callahan, *The Mind of the Catholic Layman* (New York, 1963), p. 88; Andrew M. Greeley, *The Catholic Experience* (Garden City, New York, 1969), pp. 254–59.

43. Wattel, "The ACTU," p. 35; Julius Weinberg, "Priests, Workers, and Communists," *Harpers Magazine*, Nov. 1948, p. 53; *Labor Leader*, 17 Jan. 1947, p. 4; 14 Feb. 1947, p. 4; Michael J. Quill, "As I Was Saying," *TWU Bulletin*, p. 16; L. H. Whittemore, *The Man Who Ran the Subways, The Story of Mike Quill* (New York, 1968), p. 127.

44. William Z. Foster, chairman of the party, informed Quill of the decision to form a third labor federation. Whittemore, *The Man Who Ran the Subways*, pp. 137, 140; Weinberg, "Priests, Workers and Communists," *Harpers Magazine*, Nov. 1948, p. 50; Jack Barbash, *The Practice of Unionism* (New York, 1956), pp. 360–61.

45. *TWU Convention Proceedings, 1948–1952*, pp. 5, 17.

46. *TWU Express*, Dec. 1948, pp. 3, 6.

47. *Labor Leader*, 20 Apr. 1946, p. 4; the UE administration considered Carey and the ACTU as a single faction. Actually these two elements had disagreements and the ACTU *Labor Leader* sometimes attacked Carey.

48. Wattel, "The ACTU," primarily based on interview with Rev. Thomas Darby in 1947, pp. 87–98; Harrington, "Catholics in the Labor Movement," p. 245.

49. Wattel, pp. 94–98.

50. *New York Times*, 23 July 1946, p. 23; *Time*, 23 Sept. 1946, p. 24; *Labor Leader*, 27 Dec. 1946, p. 1; Wattel, "The ACTU," p. 96.

51. The UE pamphlet, "The Members Run Their Union," (New York, 1947), is in the possession of the New York Public Library; a copy of the Rice pamphlet is included in the UE papers at the University of Pittsburgh. The MDA and the ACTU opposed secession from UE;

nevertheless, elements in the coalition directed secession movements. Several actists led such movements although opposed by the ACTU; see Harrington, "Catholics in the Labor Movement," p. 251.

52. Kampelman, *The Communist Party vs the CIO*, p. 129.
53. William Harper to Right Rev. Hugh C. Boyle, 22 May 1947; Charles Owen Rice to Right Rev. Hugh C. Boyle, 7 June 1947; Clyde L. Johnson to Joseph A. Shoteff, secretary, 613, 25 June 1947; UE papers at the University of Pittsburgh.
54. De Caux, *Labor Radical*, p. 487.
55. Edward Marciniak, "Catholic and Labor-Management Relations," *The American Apostolate*, ed. Leo Ward (Westminster, 1952), p. 76; *Labor Leader*, 29 Aug. 1938, p. 1; Taft, "The ACTU," p. 21; Rovere, "Labor's Catholic Bloc," p. 11.

Chapter Nine. Catholic Institutions, Labor, and the Times

1. George Morris "Spotlight on the ACTU," *Political Affairs*, Mar. 1947, pp. 252–60; *Daily Worker*, 12 Sept. 1947; 25 Sept. 1947; 28 July 1947.

INDEX

America, 28-29, 138

American Association for Labor Legislation, 44

American Association for Social Security, 44

American Federation of Labor (AFL), 13, 75, 108-9, 106, 118-9, 122, 134, 145, 147, 150; ACTU's relationship with, 132-3; Catholic membership in, 9, 110; Coughlin's relationship with, 92-3, 105, 107; organization of skilled workers, 2-3; Ryan's relationship with, 38, 44; Social Action Department, 40, 45,

American Newspaper Guild, 144

Americanization. *See* Social Action Department; Immigrants

American Socialist Party, 14

Anti-capitalism: in Catholic leadership, 25-31; and Coughlin, 93-4;

and Maurin, 51-2; and Ryan, 42

Anti-Communism: in ACTU, 128-9, 135-40; in Catholic leadership, 22-4; in TWU, 140-1; in UE, 142-5

Anti-Conscription League, 50

Anti-Semitism: and Charles Coughlin, 99, 102, 106

Anti-Socialism, 13-16

Archdiocese Labor Institute, 134

Assisi, Saint Francis of, 53. *See also* Poverty

Association of Catholic Conscientious Objectors, 72. *See also* Pax

Association of Catholic Trade Unionists (ACTU), 44, 72, 74, 75, 81, 105, 123, 124-45, 148, 149

Automotive Industrial Workers Association (AIWA), 96-8

Avery, Martha Moore, 14